W9-BTG-746

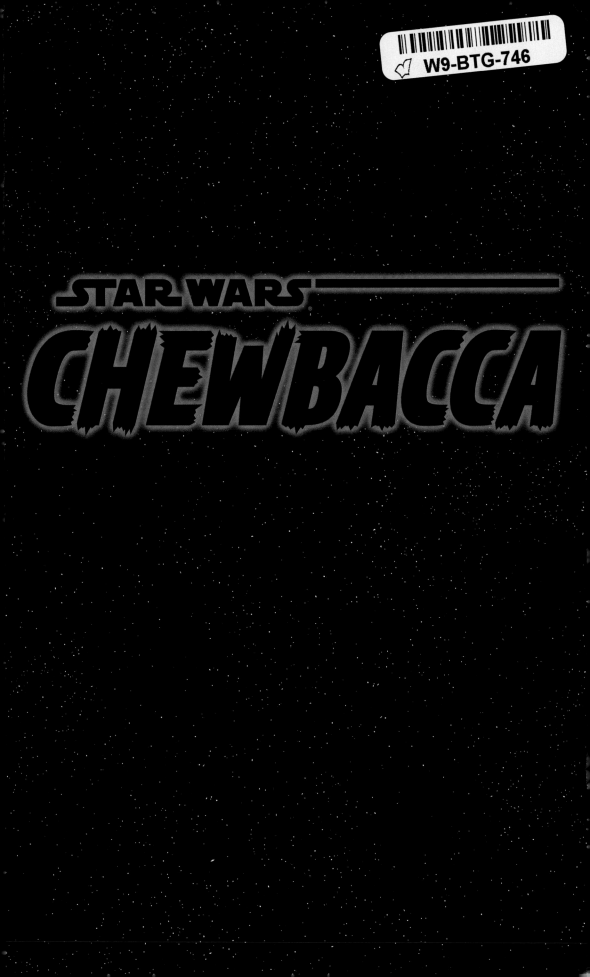

STAR WARS®

CHEWBACCA

CHEWBACCA

Writer	**GERRY DUGGAN**
Artist	**PHIL NOTO**
Letterer	**VC's JOE CARAMAGNA**
Cover Art	**PHIL NOTO**
Assistant Editor	**HEATHER ANTOS**
Editor	**JORDAN D. WHITE**
Executive Editor	**C.B. CEBULSKI**

Editor in Chief	**AXEL ALONSO**
Chief Creative Officer	**JOE QUESADA**
Publisher	**DAN BUCKLEY**

For Lucasfilm:

Creative Director	**MICHAEL SIGLAIN**
Senior Editor	**FRANK PARISI**
Lucasfilm Story Group	**RAYNE ROBERTS, PABLO HIDALGO, LELAND CHEE**

Collection Editor	JENNIFER GRÜNWALD
Assistant Editor	SARAH BRUNSTAD
Associate Managing Editor	ALEX STARBUCK
Editor, Special Projects	MARK D. BEAZLEY
Senior Editor, Special Projects	JEFF YOUNGQUIST
SVP Print, Sales & Marketing	DAVID GABRIEL
Book Designer	ADAM DEL RE

DISNEY   LUCASFILM

STAR WARS: CHEWBACCA. Contains material originally published in magazine form as CHEWBACCA #1-5. First printing 2016. ISBN# 978-0-7851-9320-3. Published by MARVEL WORLDWIDE, INC., a subsidiary of MARVEL ENTERTAINMENT, LLC. OFFICE OF PUBLICATION: 135 West 50th Street, New York, NY 10020. STAR WARS and related text and illustrations are trademarks and/or copyrights, in the United States and other countries, of Lucasfilm Ltd. and/or its affiliates. © & TM Lucasfilm Ltd. No similarity between any of the names, characters, persons, and/or institutions in this magazine with those of any living or dead person or institution is intended, and any such similarity which may exist is purely coincidental. Marvel and its logos are TM Marvel Characters, Inc. **Printed in Canada.** ALAN FINE, President, Marvel Entertainment; DAN BUCKLEY, President, TV, Publishing and Brand Management; JOE QUESADA, Chief Creative Officer; TOM BREVOORT, SVP of Publishing; DAVID BOGART, SVP of Operations & Procurement, Publishing; C.B. CEBULSKI, VP of International Development & Brand Management; DAVID GABRIEL, SVP Print, Sales & Marketing; JIM O'KEEFE, VP of Operations & Logistics; DAN CARR, Executive Director of Publishing Technology; SUSAN CRESPI, Editorial Operations Manager; ALEX MORALES, Publishing Operations Manager; STAN LEE, Chairman Emeritus. For information regarding advertising in Marvel Comics or on Marvel.com, please contact Jonathan Rheingold, VP of Custom Solutions & Ad Sales, at jrheingold@marvel.com. For Marvel subscription inquiries, please call 800-217-9158. Manufactured between 12/18/2015 and 1/25/2016 by SOLISCO PRINTERS, SCOTT, QC, CANADA.

10 9 8 7 6 5 4 3 2 1

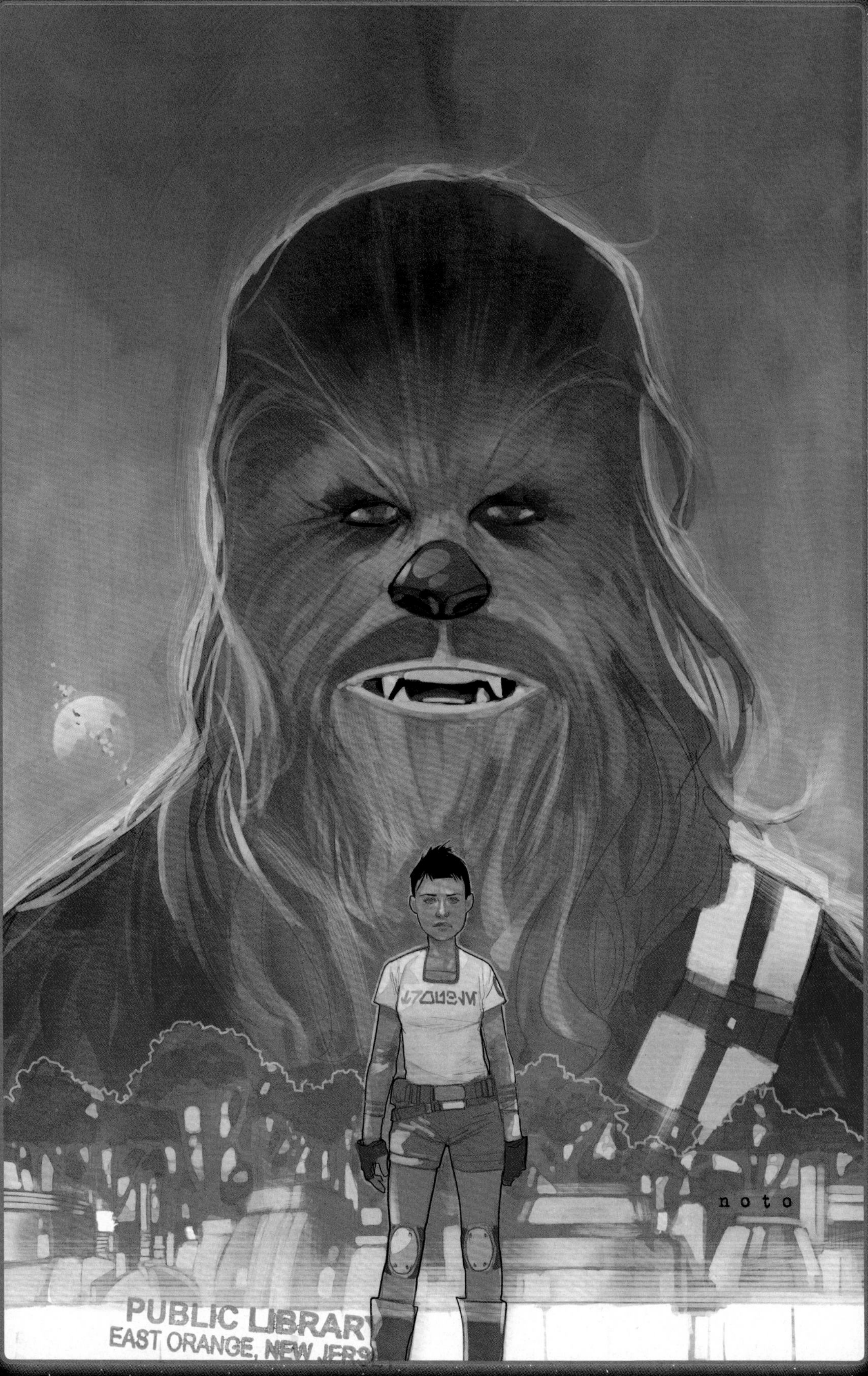
PUBLIC LIBRARY
EAST ORANGE, NEW JERS
noto

CHEWBACCA

It is a period of renewed hope for the rebellion.

The evil galactic Empire's greatest weapon, the Death Star, has been destroyed by CHEWBACCA, warrior son of the planet KASHYYYK...with some help from his trusty sidekick Han and his friends Luke and Leia. But Chewie is not one to grandstand. There is still much to accomplish.

The Battle of Yavin reverberates through the galaxy as our WOOKIEE hero embarks on a very important and personal secret mission. Unfortunately for Chewbacca, his loaner spacecraft proves to be what they refer to in the Outer Rim as a "hunk of junk"....

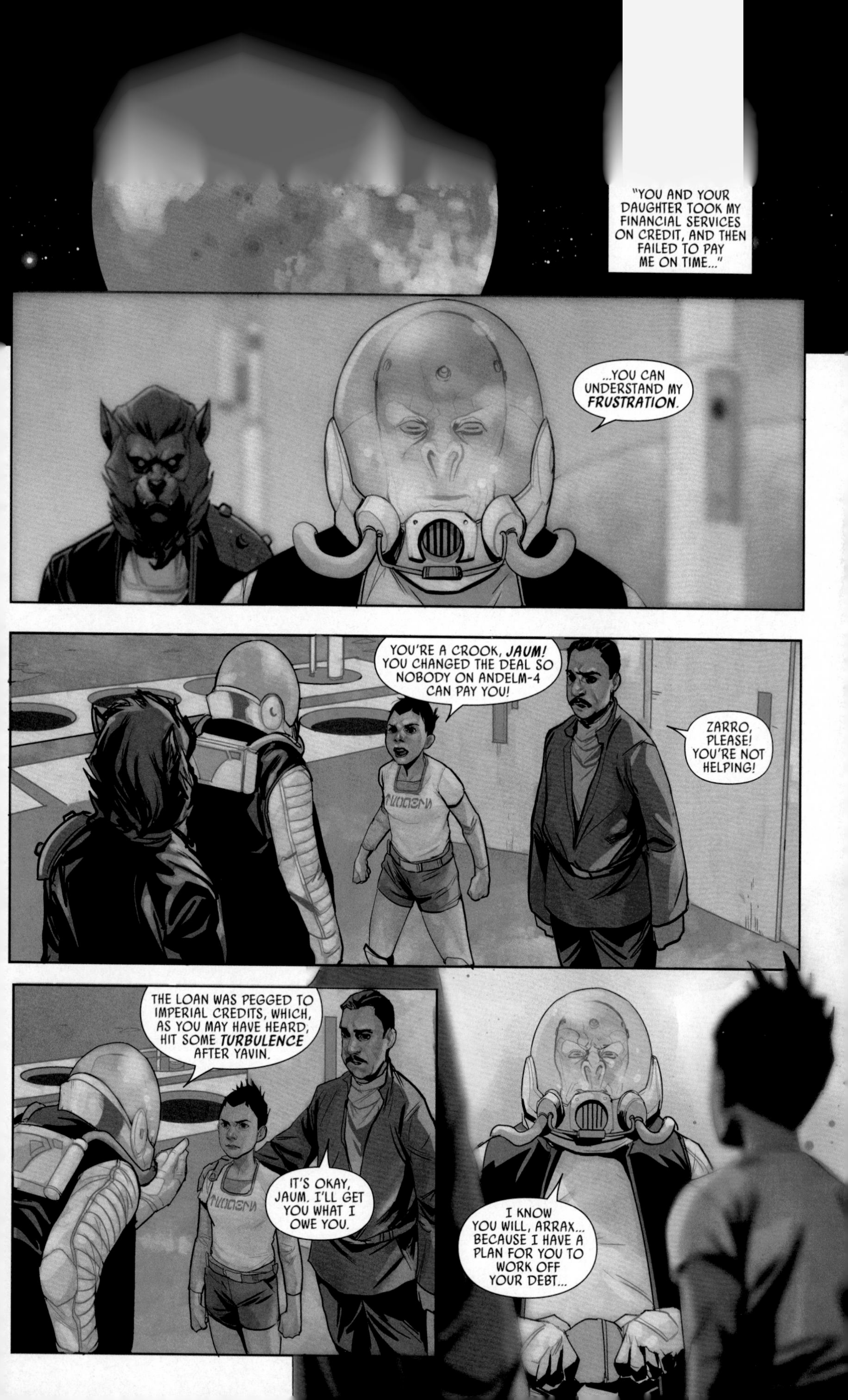
"YOU AND YOUR DAUGHTER TOOK MY FINANCIAL SERVICES ON CREDIT, AND THEN FAILED TO PAY ME ON TIME..."
...YOU CAN UNDERSTAND MY FRUSTRATION.
YOU'RE A CROOK, JAUM! YOU CHANGED THE DEAL SO NOBODY ON ANDELM-4 CAN PAY YOU!
ZARRO, PLEASE! YOU'RE NOT HELPING!
THE LOAN WAS PEGGED TO IMPERIAL CREDITS, WHICH, AS YOU MAY HAVE HEARD, HIT SOME TURBULENCE AFTER YAVIN.
IT'S OKAY, JAUM. I'LL GET YOU WHAT I OWE YOU.
I KNOW YOU WILL, ARRAX... BECAUSE I HAVE A PLAN FOR YOU TO WORK OFF YOUR DEBT...

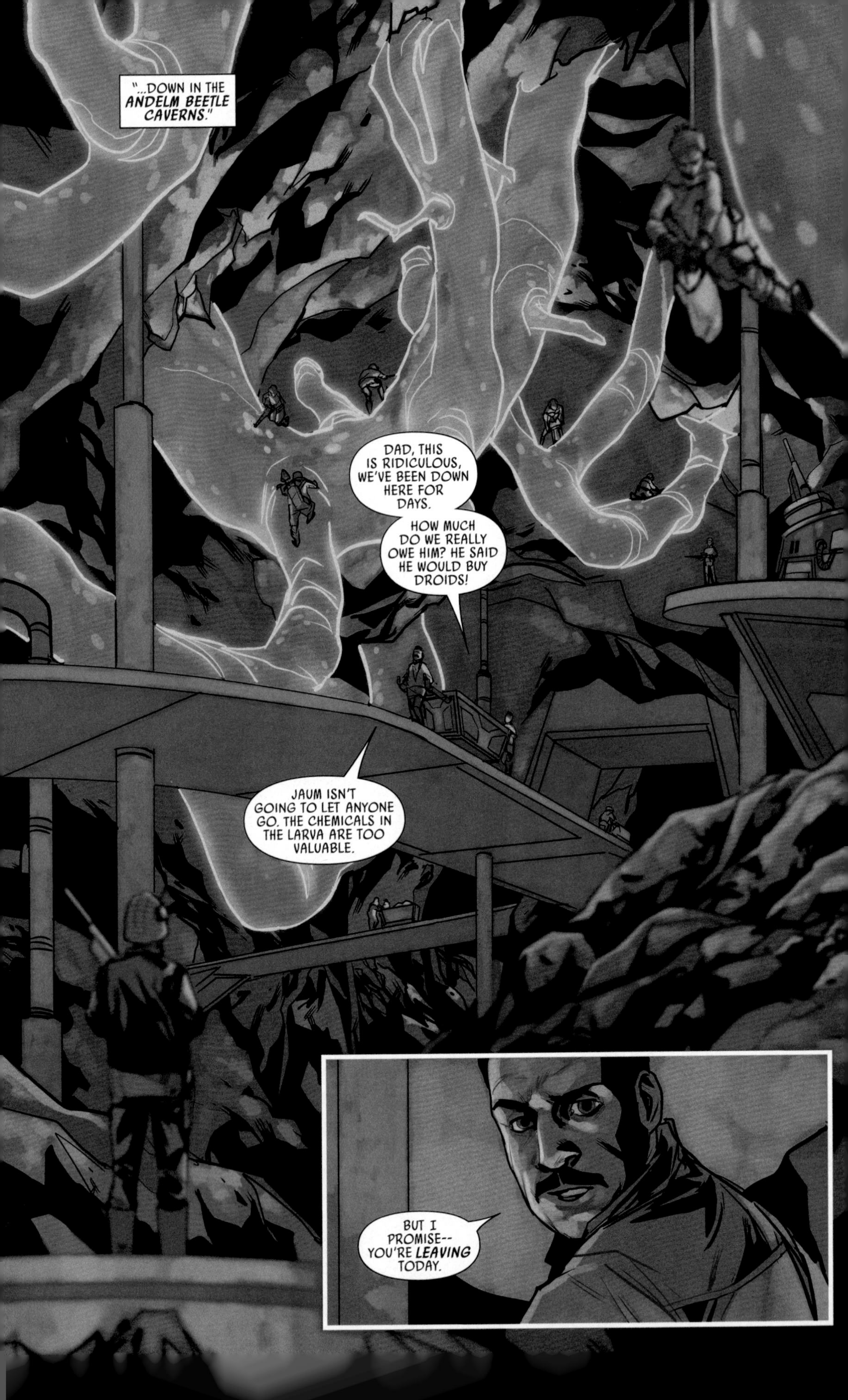
"...DOWN IN THE ANDELM BEETLE CAVERNS."
DAD, THIS IS RIDICULOUS, WE'VE BEEN DOWN HERE FOR DAYS.
HOW MUCH DO WE REALLY OWE HIM? HE SAID HE WOULD BUY DROIDS!
JAUM ISN'T GOING TO LET ANYONE GO. THE CHEMICALS IN THE LARVA ARE TOO VALUABLE.
BUT I PROMISE-- YOU'RE *LEAVING* TODAY.

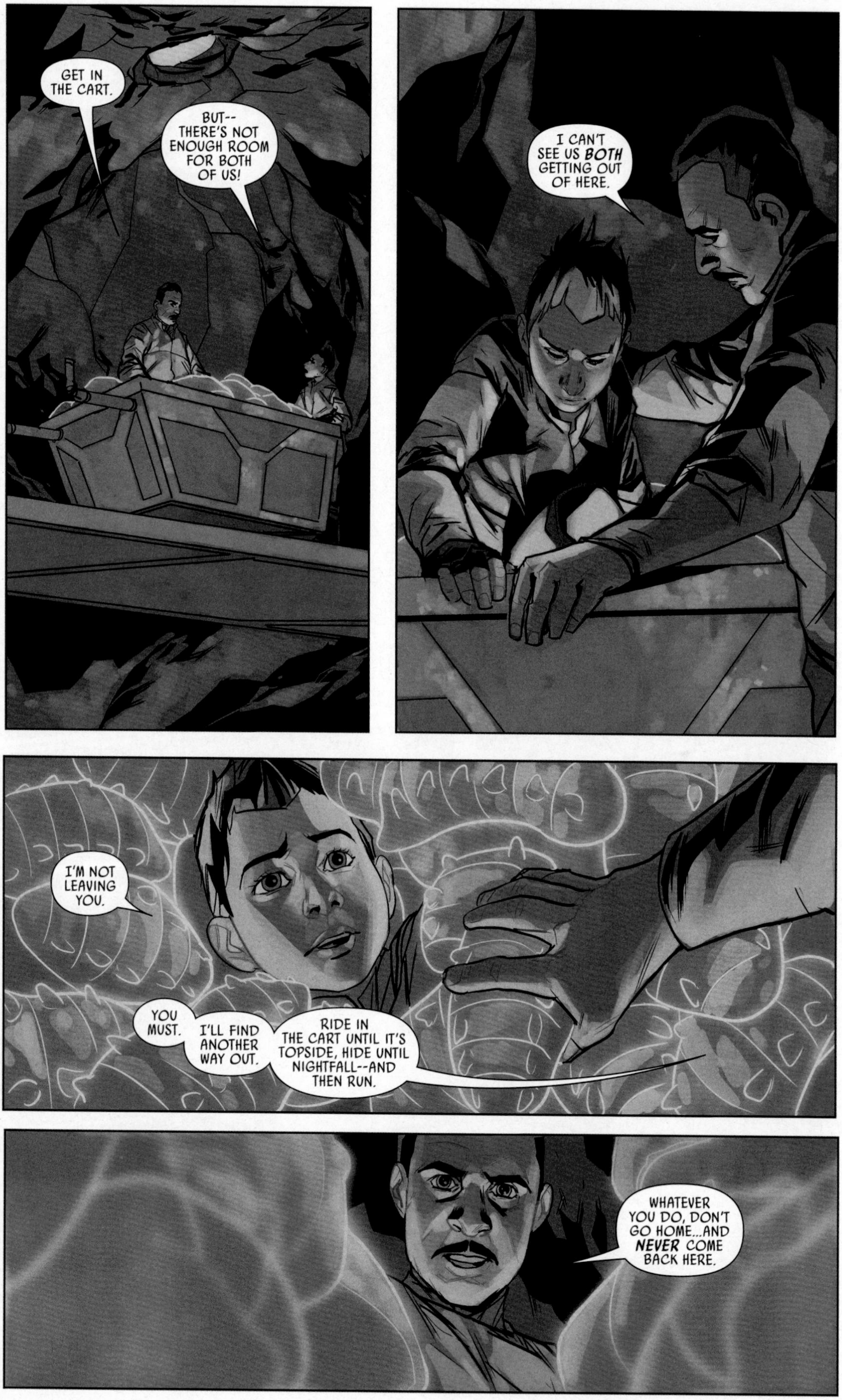
GET IN THE CART.
BUT-- THERE'S NOT ENOUGH ROOM FOR BOTH OF US!
I CAN'T SEE US **BOTH** GETTING OUT OF HERE.
I'M NOT LEAVING YOU.
YOU MUST.
I'LL FIND ANOTHER WAY OUT.
RIDE IN THE CART UNTIL IT'S TOPSIDE, HIDE UNTIL NIGHTFALL--AND THEN RUN.
WHATEVER YOU DO, DON'T GO HOME...AND **NEVER** COME BACK HERE.

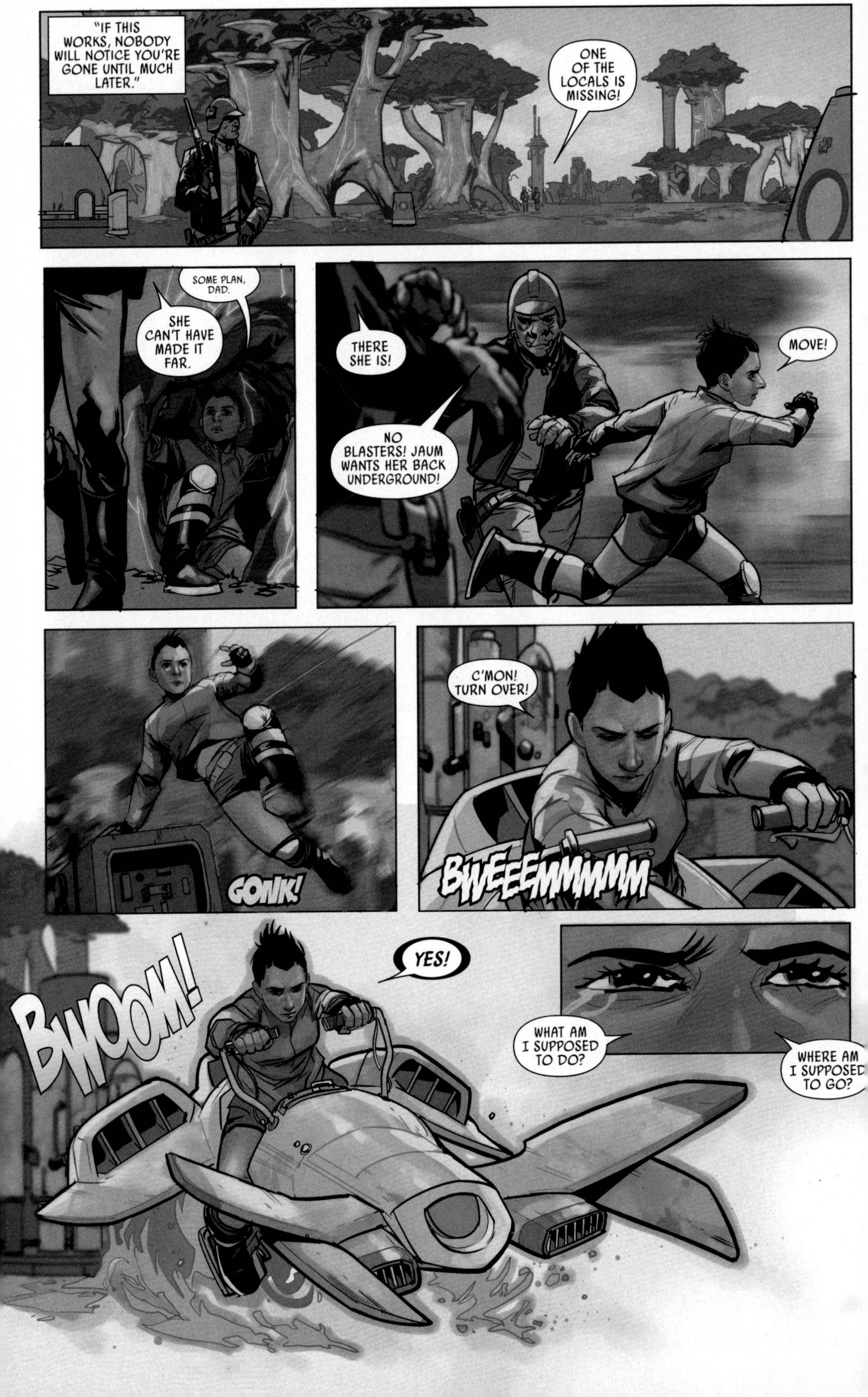
"IF THIS WORKS, NOBODY WILL NOTICE YOU'RE GONE UNTIL MUCH LATER."
ONE OF THE LOCALS IS MISSING!
SHE CAN'T HAVE MADE IT FAR.
SOME PLAN, DAD.
THERE SHE IS!
NO BLASTERS! JAUM WANTS HER BACK UNDERGROUND!
MOVE!
GONK!
C'MON! TURN OVER!
BWEEEMMMMM
BWOOM!
YES!
WHAT AM I SUPPOSED TO DO?
WHERE AM I SUPPOSED TO GO?

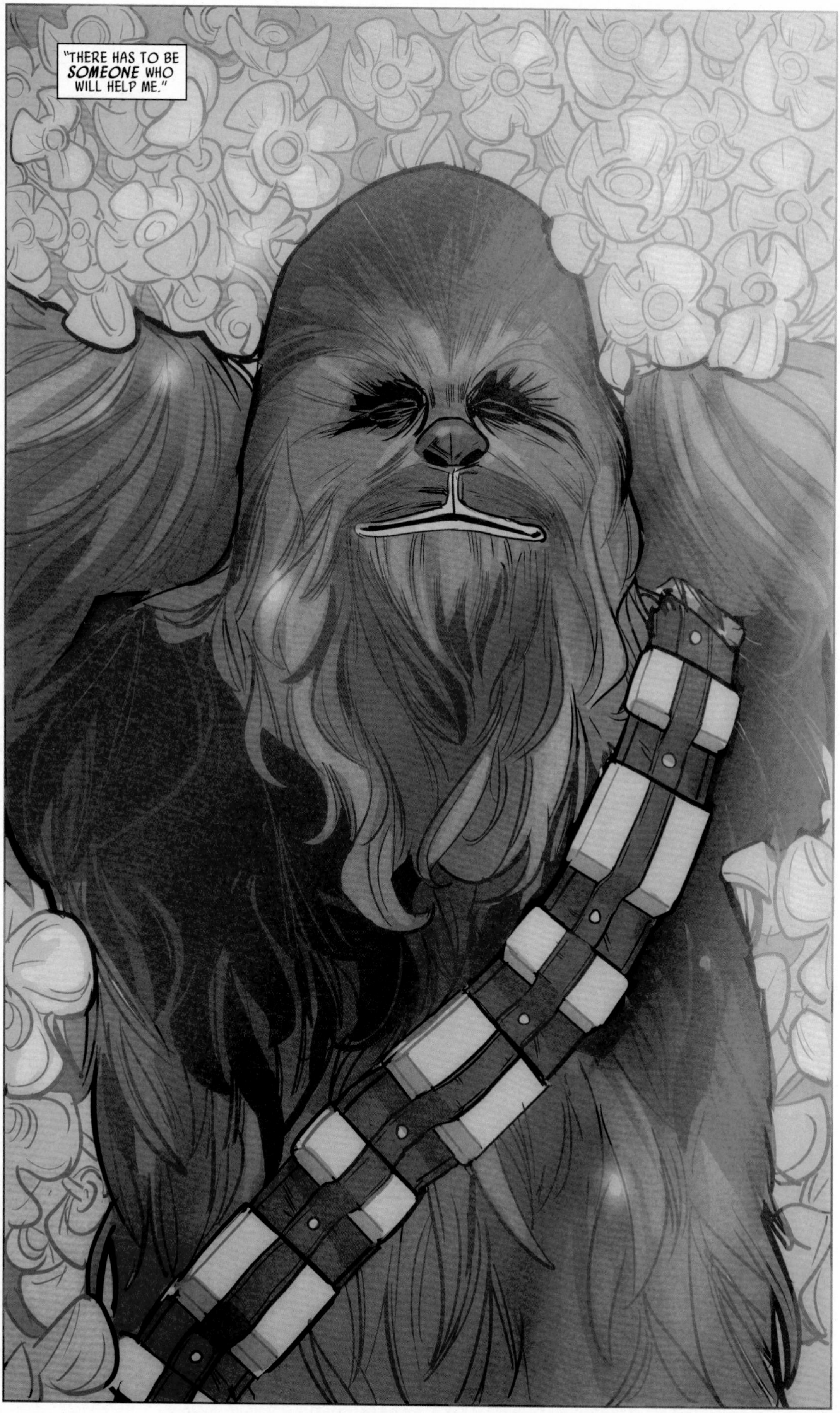
"THERE HAS TO BE SOMEONE WHO WILL HELP ME."

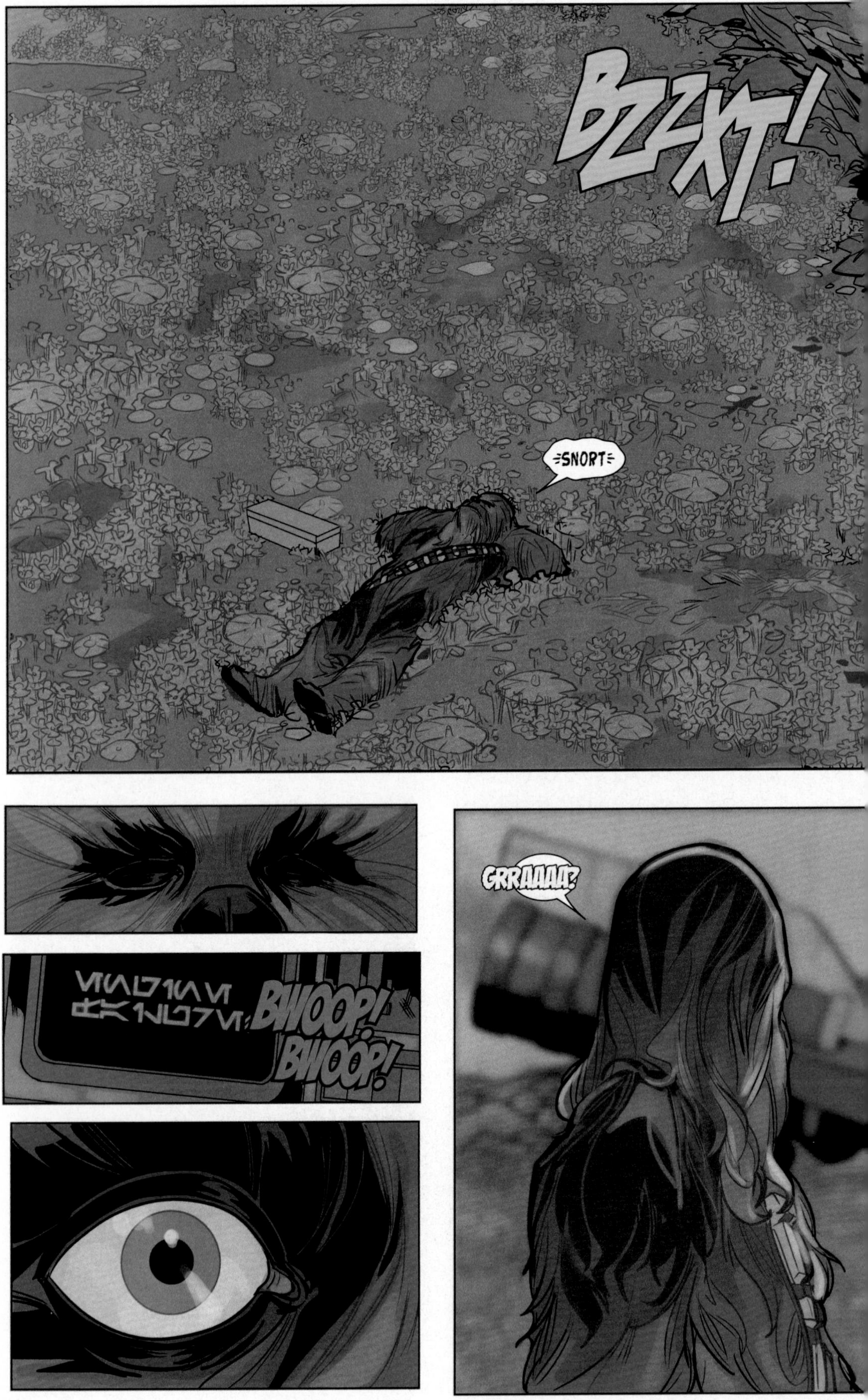
BZZXT!
SNORT
BWOOP!
BWOOP!
GRRAAAA?

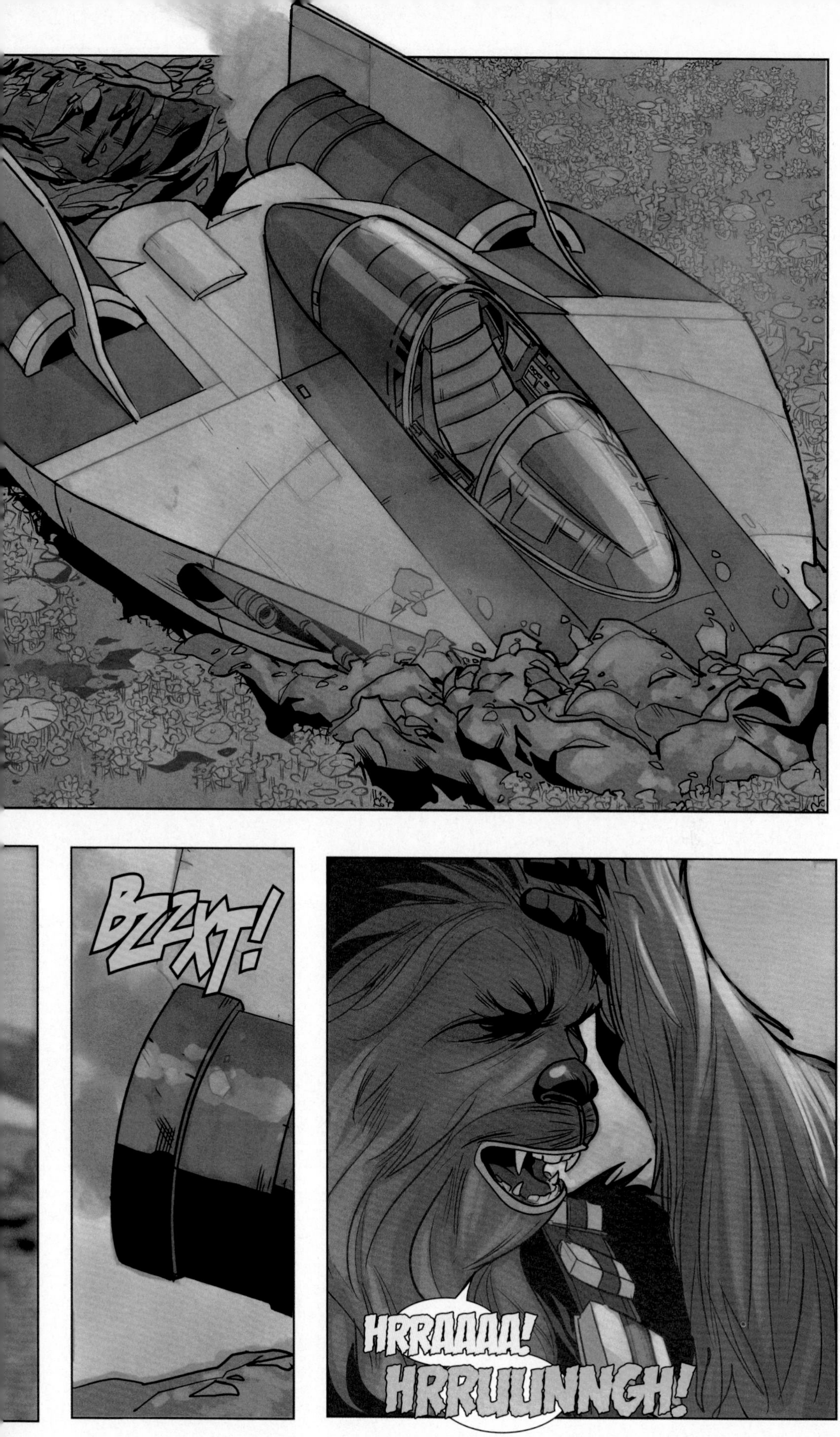
BZZXT!
HRRAAAA!
HRRUUNNGH!

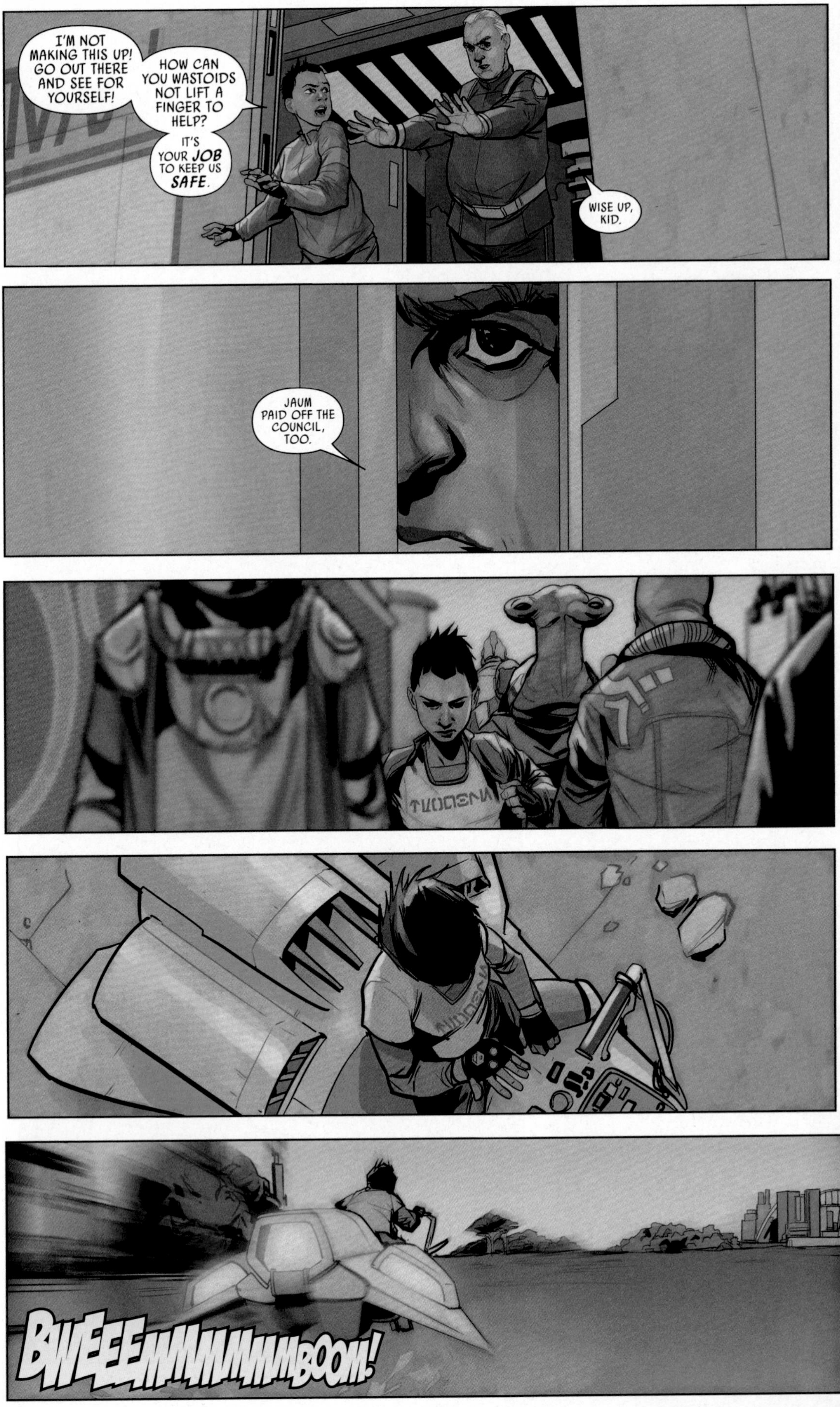
I'M NOT MAKING THIS UP! GO OUT THERE AND SEE FOR YOURSELF!
HOW CAN YOU WASTOIDS NOT LIFT A FINGER TO HELP?
IT'S YOUR **JOB** TO KEEP US **SAFE**.
WISE UP, KID.
JAUM PAID OFF THE COUNCIL, TOO.
BWEEEMMMMMMMBOOM!

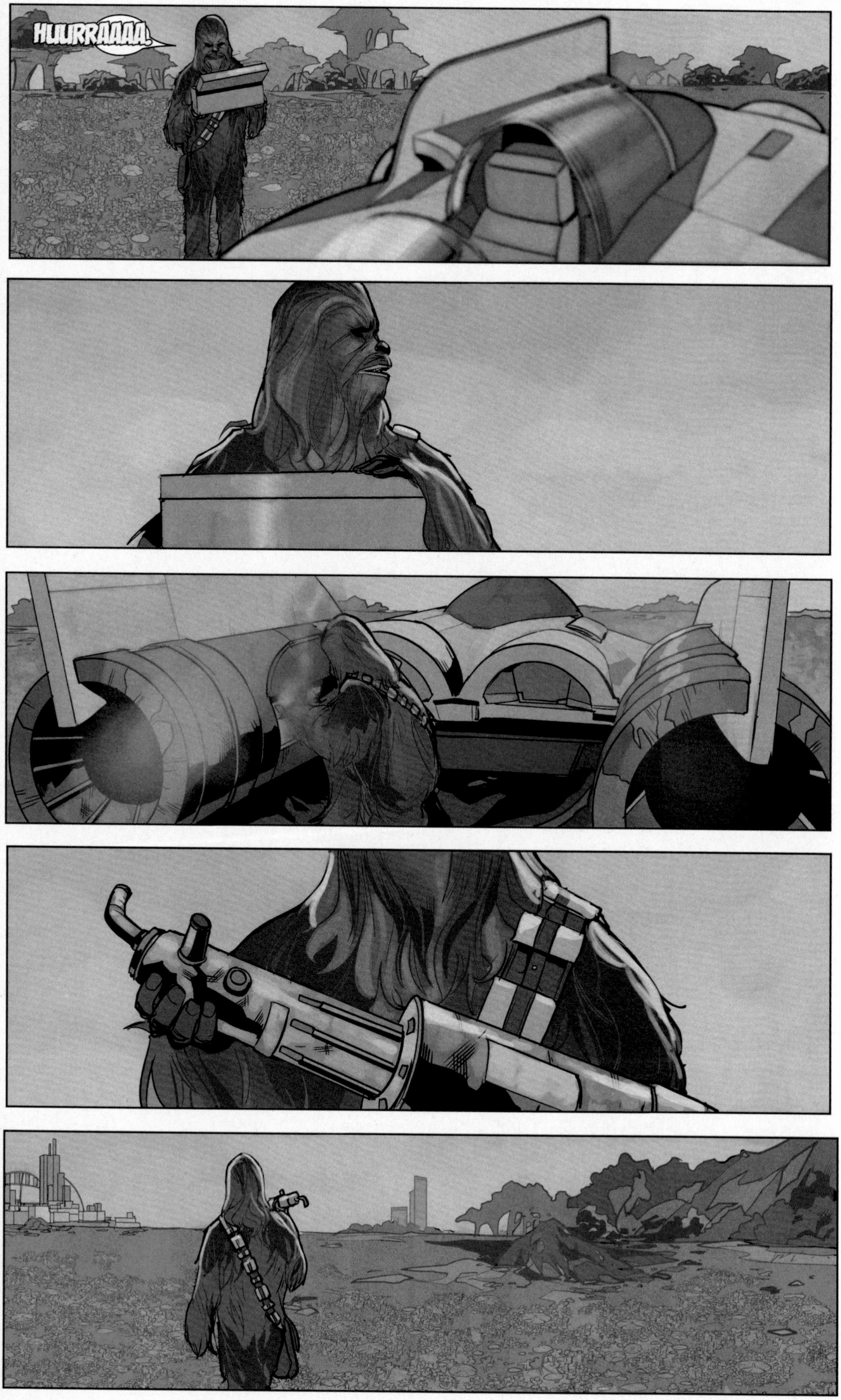
HUURRAAAA!

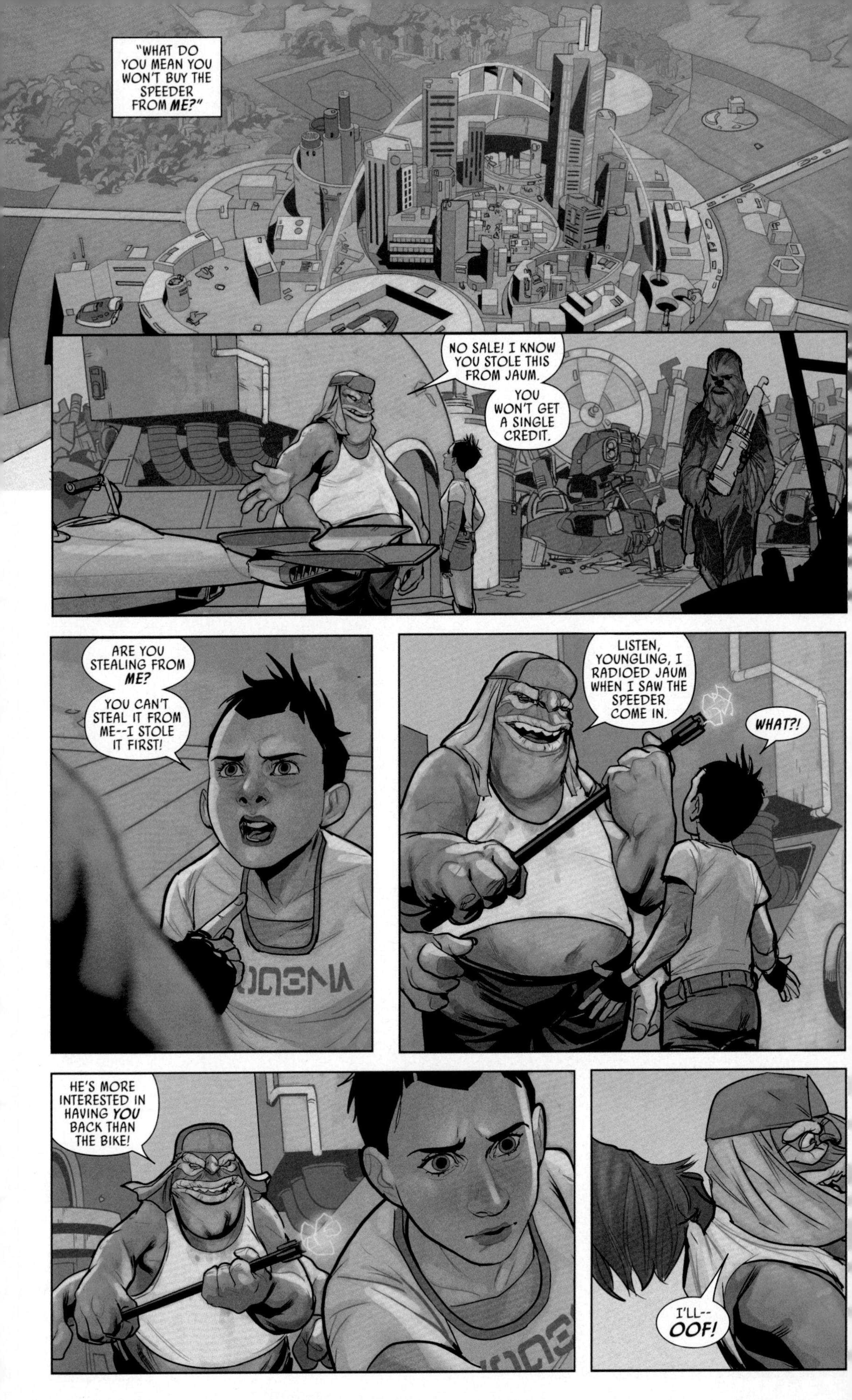
"WHAT DO YOU MEAN YOU WON'T BUY THE SPEEDER FROM *ME?*"
NO SALE! I KNOW YOU STOLE THIS FROM JAUM.
YOU WON'T GET A SINGLE CREDIT.
ARE YOU STEALING FROM *ME?*
YOU CAN'T STEAL IT FROM ME--I STOLE IT FIRST!
LISTEN, YOUNGLING, I RADIOED JAUM WHEN I SAW THE SPEEDER COME IN.
WHAT?!
HE'S MORE INTERESTED IN HAVING *YOU* BACK THAN THE BIKE!
I'LL--
OOF!

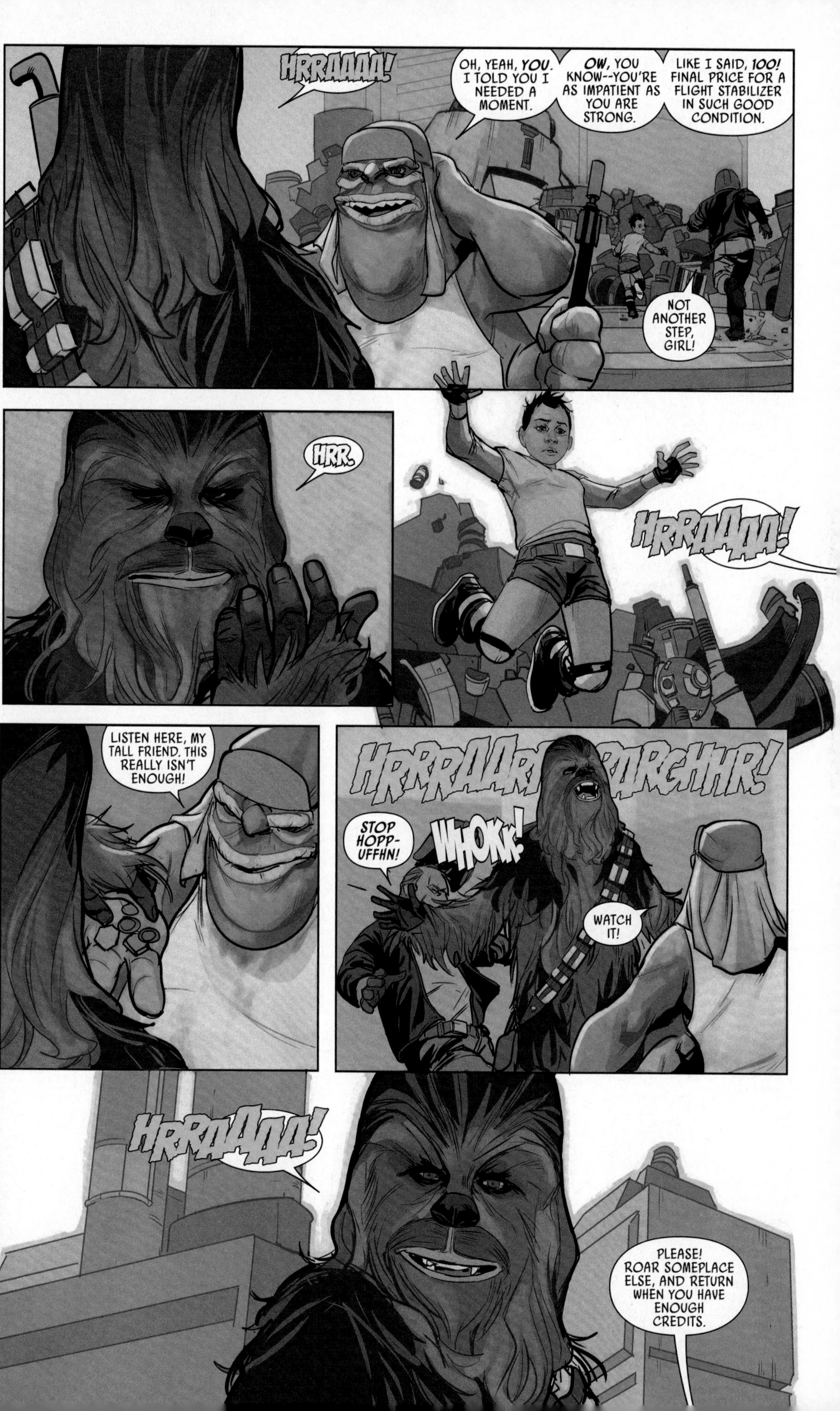
HRRAAAA!
OH, YEAH, *YOU*. I TOLD YOU I NEEDED A MOMENT.
OW, YOU KNOW--YOU'RE AS IMPATIENT AS YOU ARE STRONG.
LIKE I SAID, *100!* FINAL PRICE FOR A FLIGHT STABILIZER IN SUCH GOOD CONDITION.
NOT ANOTHER STEP, GIRL!
HRR.
HRRAAAA!
LISTEN HERE, MY TALL FRIEND. THIS REALLY ISN'T ENOUGH!
HRRRAAR RORGHHR!
STOP HOPP-UFFHN!
WHOKK!
WATCH IT!
HRRAAAA!
PLEASE! ROAR SOMEPLACE ELSE, AND RETURN WHEN YOU HAVE ENOUGH CREDITS.

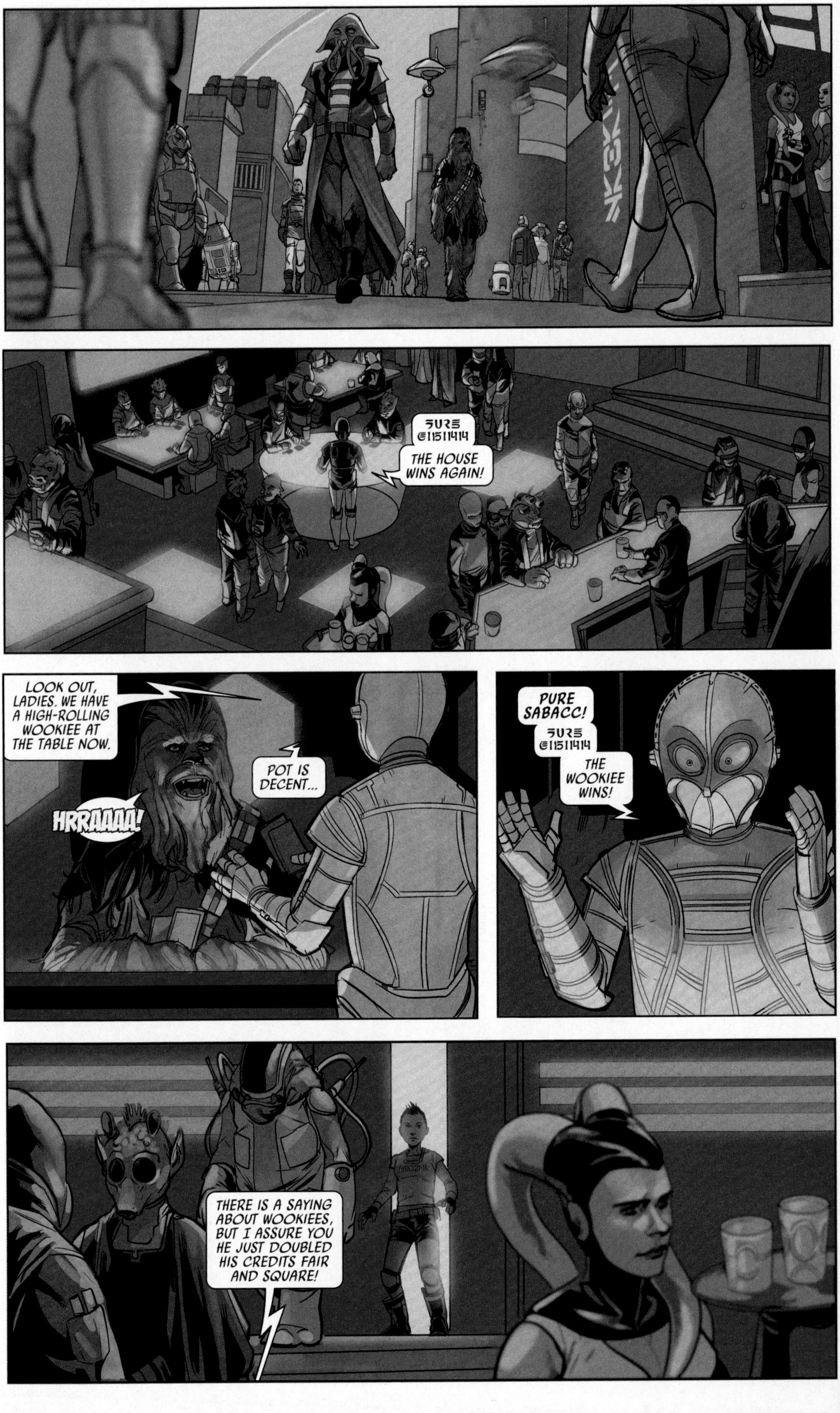
THE HOUSE WINS AGAIN!
LOOK OUT, LADIES. WE HAVE A HIGH-ROLLING WOOKIEE AT THE TABLE NOW.
HRRAAAA!
POT IS DECENT...
PURE SABACC!
THE WOOKIEE WINS!
THERE IS A SAYING ABOUT WOOKIEES, BUT I ASSURE YOU HE JUST DOUBLED HIS CREDITS FAIR AND SQUARE!

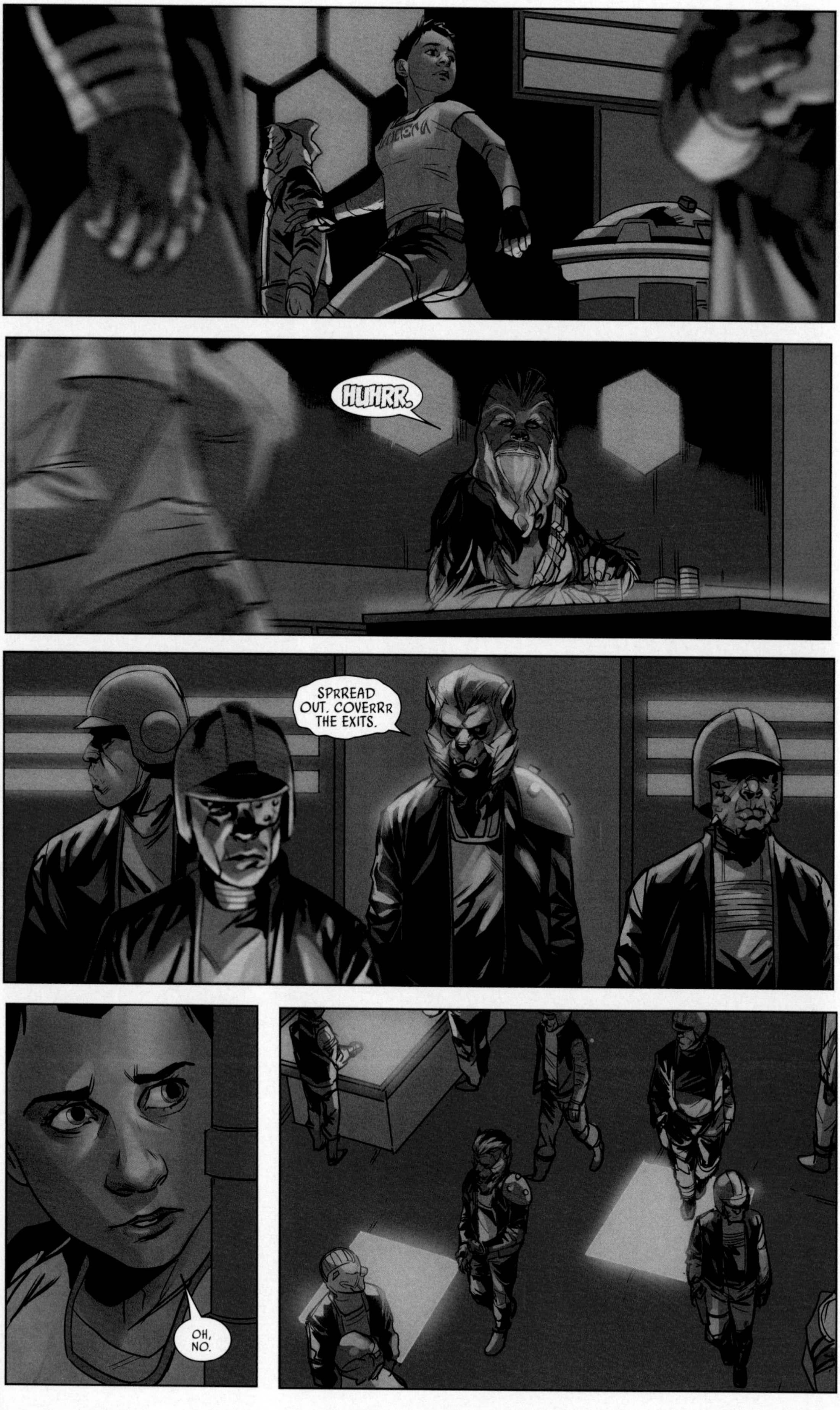
HUHRR.
SPRREAD OUT. COVERRR THE EXITS.
OH, NO.

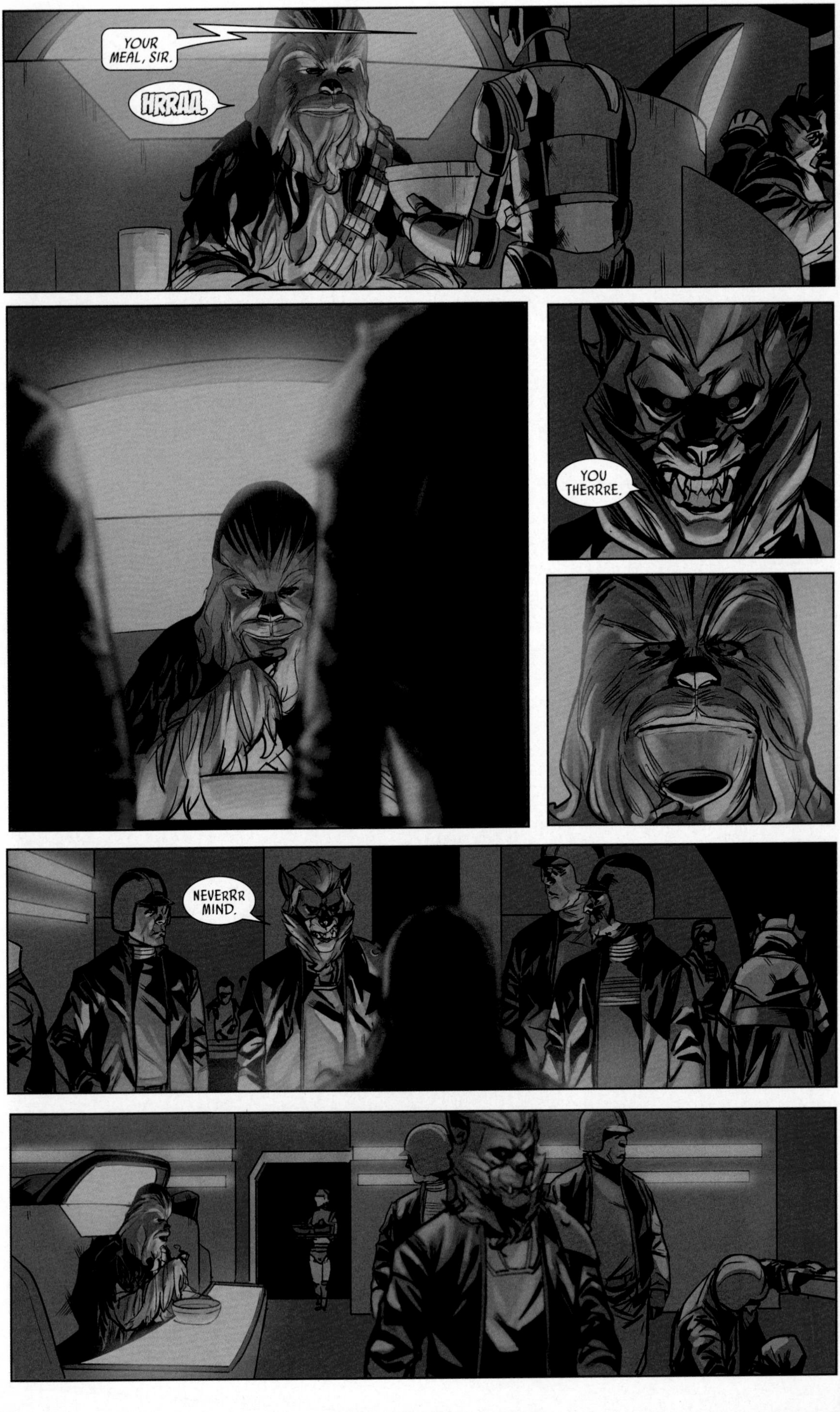
YOUR MEAL, SIR.
HRRAA.
YOU THERRRE.
NEVERRR MIND.

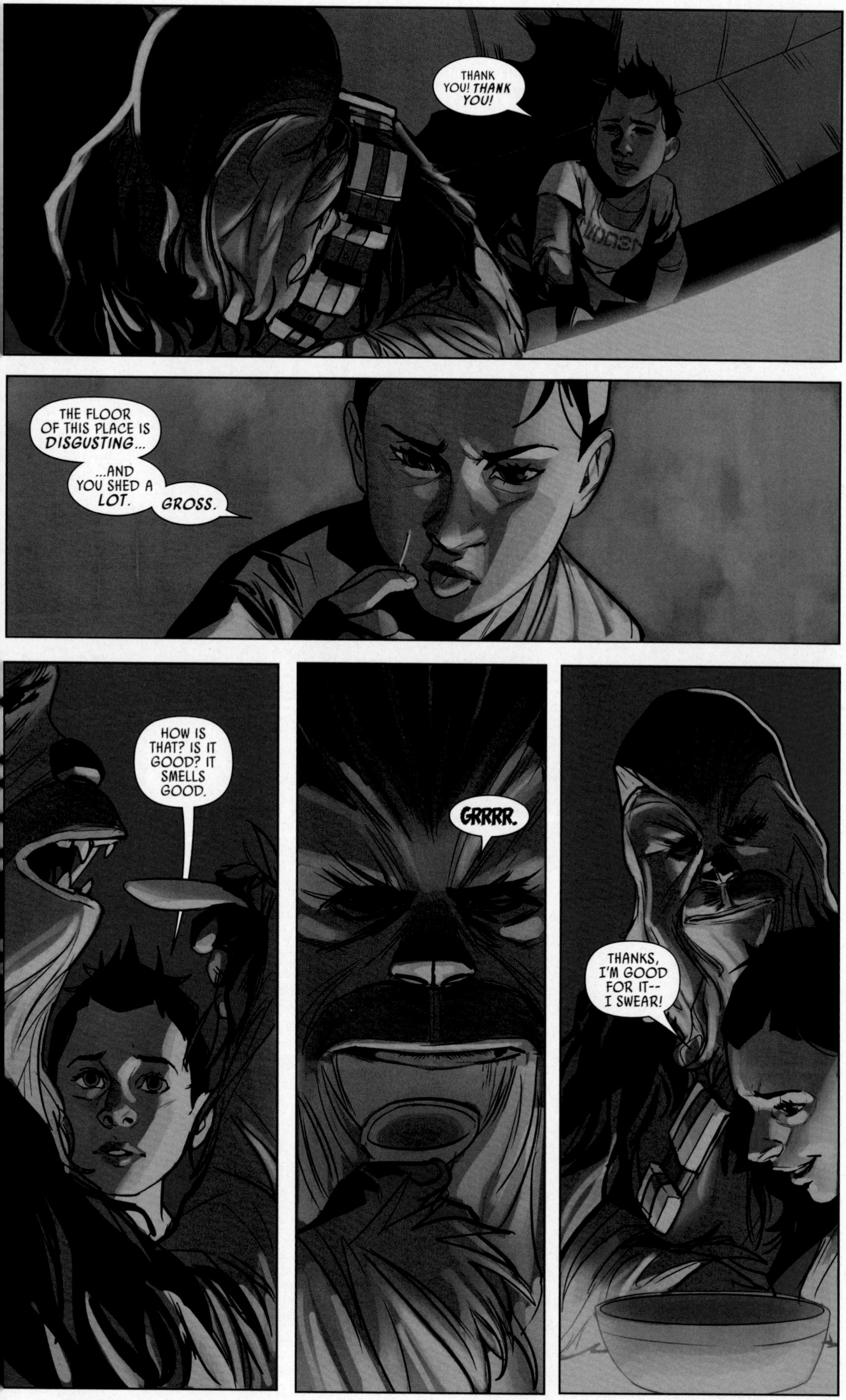
THANK YOU! THANK YOU!
THE FLOOR OF THIS PLACE IS DISGUSTING...
...AND YOU SHED A LOT.
GROSS.
HOW IS THAT? IS IT GOOD? IT SMELLS GOOD.
GRRRR.
THANKS, I'M GOOD FOR IT-- I SWEAR!

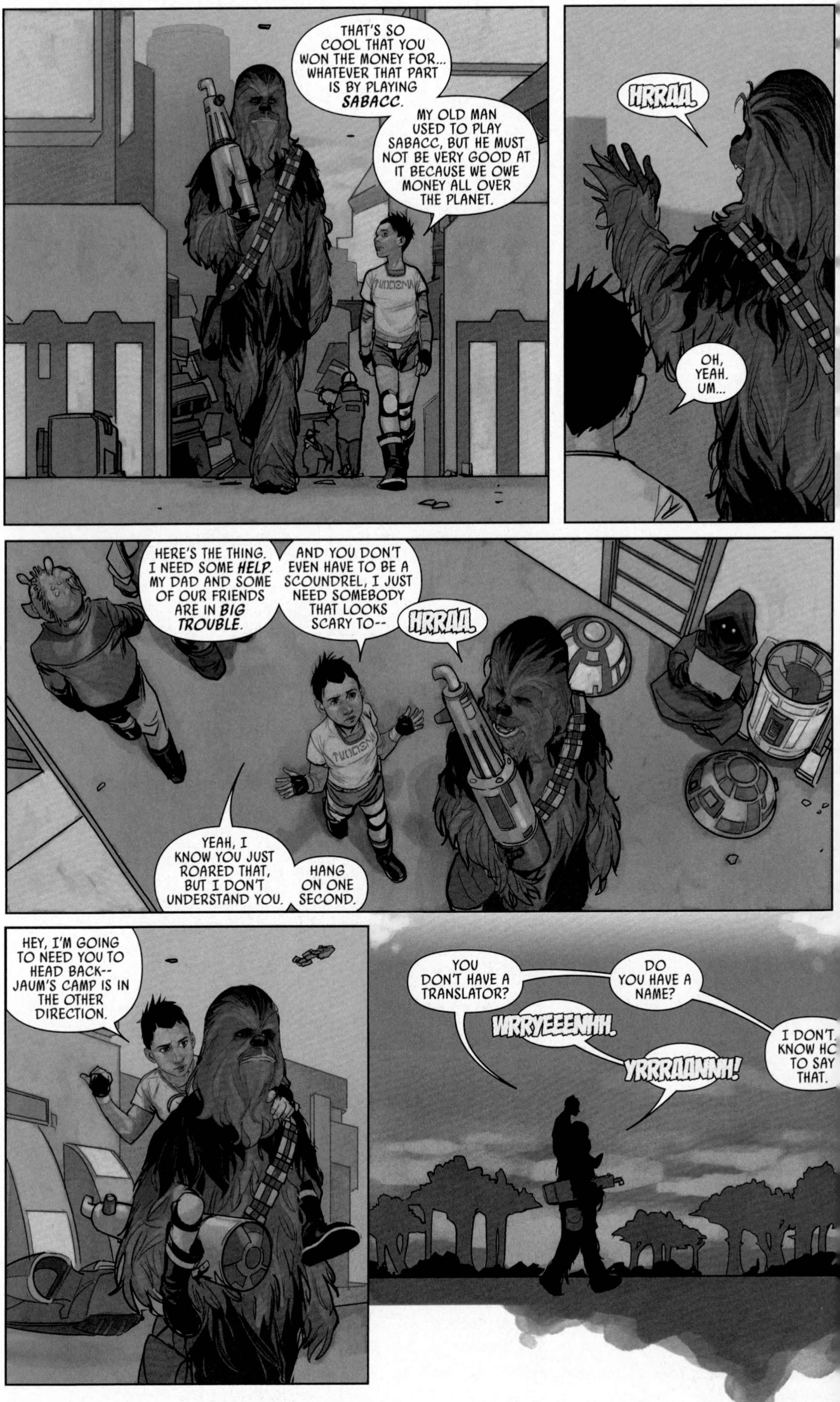
THAT'S SO COOL THAT YOU WON THE MONEY FOR... WHATEVER THAT PART IS BY PLAYING SABACC.
MY OLD MAN USED TO PLAY SABACC, BUT HE MUST NOT BE VERY GOOD AT IT BECAUSE WE OWE MONEY ALL OVER THE PLANET.
HRRAA.
OH, YEAH. UM...
HERE'S THE THING. I NEED SOME HELP. MY DAD AND SOME OF OUR FRIENDS ARE IN BIG TROUBLE.
AND YOU DON'T EVEN HAVE TO BE A SCOUNDREL, I JUST NEED SOMEBODY THAT LOOKS SCARY TO--
HRRAA.
YEAH, I KNOW YOU JUST ROARED THAT, BUT I DON'T UNDERSTAND YOU.
HANG ON ONE SECOND.
HEY, I'M GOING TO NEED YOU TO HEAD BACK-- JAUM'S CAMP IS IN THE OTHER DIRECTION.
YOU DON'T HAVE A TRANSLATOR?
WRRYEEENHH.
DO YOU HAVE A NAME?
YRRRAANNH!

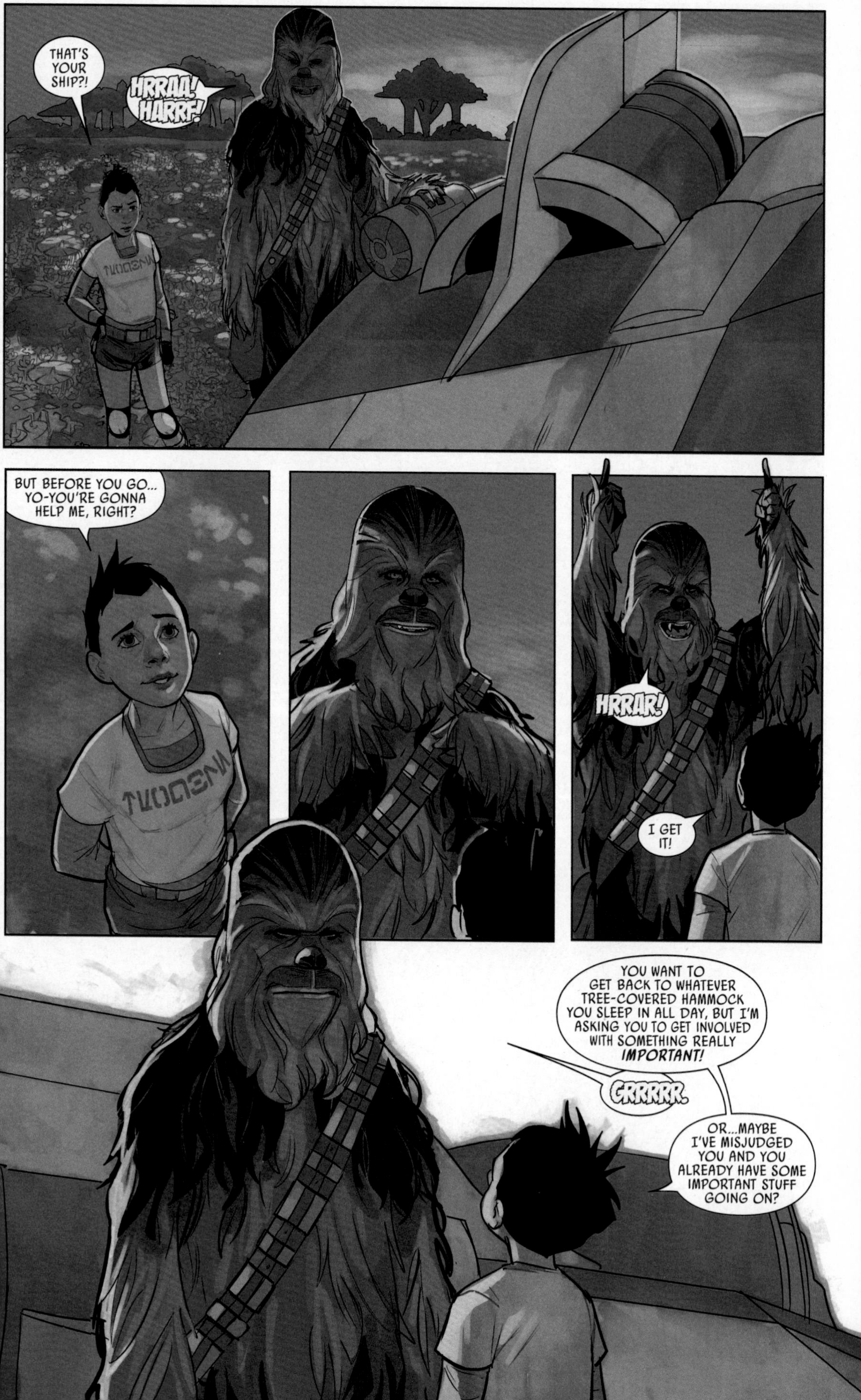
THAT'S YOUR SHIP?!
HRRAA! HARRF!
BUT BEFORE YOU GO... YO-YOU'RE GONNA HELP ME, RIGHT?
HRRAR!
I GET IT!
YOU WANT TO GET BACK TO WHATEVER TREE-COVERED HAMMOCK YOU SLEEP IN ALL DAY, BUT I'M ASKING YOU TO GET INVOLVED WITH SOMETHING REALLY IMPORTANT!
GRRRRR.
OR...MAYBE I'VE MISJUDGED YOU AND YOU ALREADY HAVE SOME IMPORTANT STUFF GOING ON?

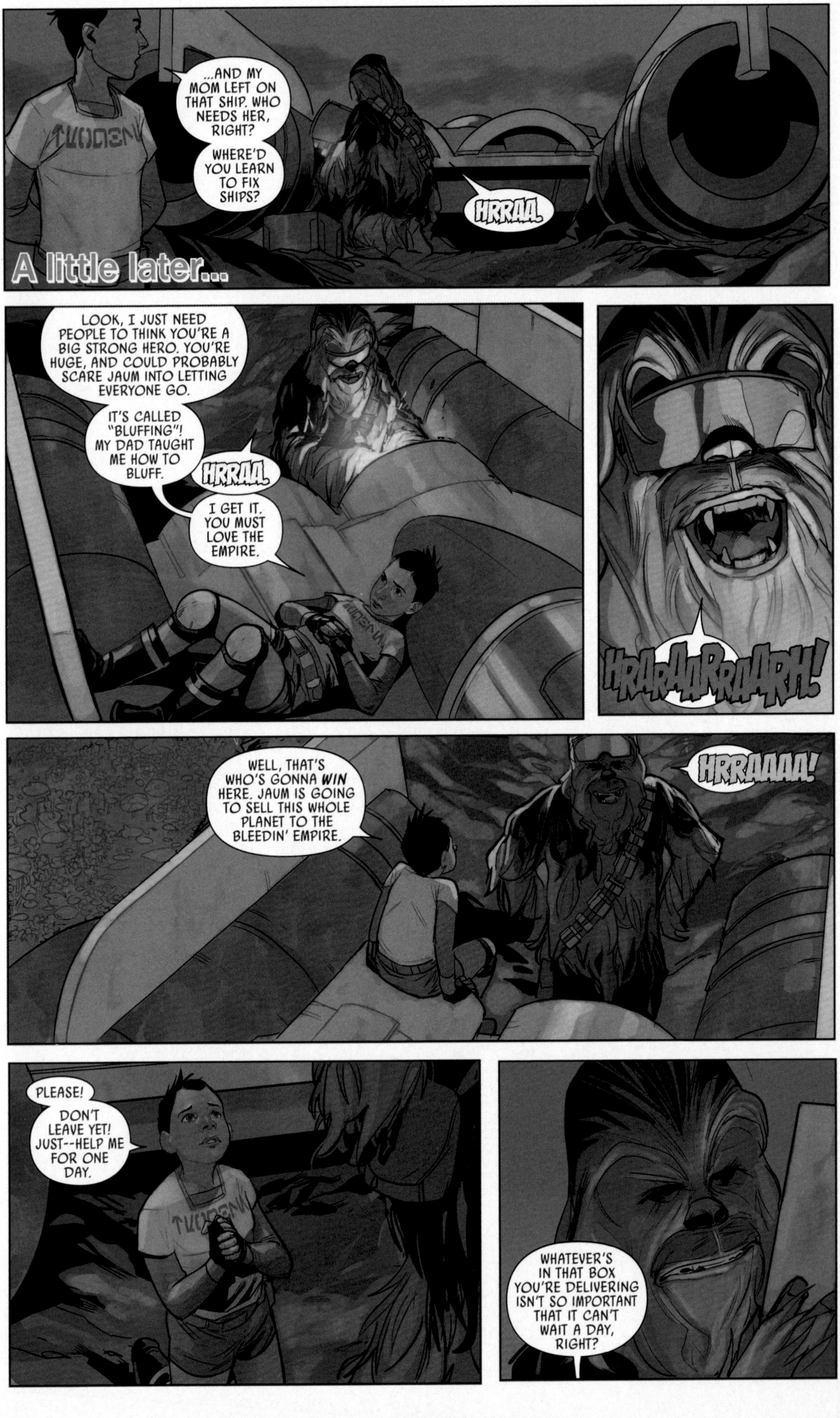
...AND MY MOM LEFT ON THAT SHIP. WHO NEEDS HER, RIGHT?
WHERE'D YOU LEARN TO FIX SHIPS?
HRRAA
A little later...
LOOK, I JUST NEED PEOPLE TO THINK YOU'RE A BIG STRONG HERO. YOU'RE HUGE, AND COULD PROBABLY SCARE JAUM INTO LETTING EVERYONE GO.
IT'S CALLED "BLUFFING"! MY DAD TAUGHT ME HOW TO BLUFF.
HRRAA
I GET IT. YOU MUST LOVE THE EMPIRE.
HRARAARRAARH!
WELL, THAT'S WHO'S GONNA WIN HERE. JAUM IS GOING TO SELL THIS WHOLE PLANET TO THE BLEEDIN' EMPIRE.
HRRAAAA!
PLEASE!
DON'T LEAVE YET! JUST--HELP ME FOR ONE DAY.
WHATEVER'S IN THAT BOX YOU'RE DELIVERING ISN'T SO IMPORTANT THAT IT CAN'T WAIT A DAY, RIGHT?

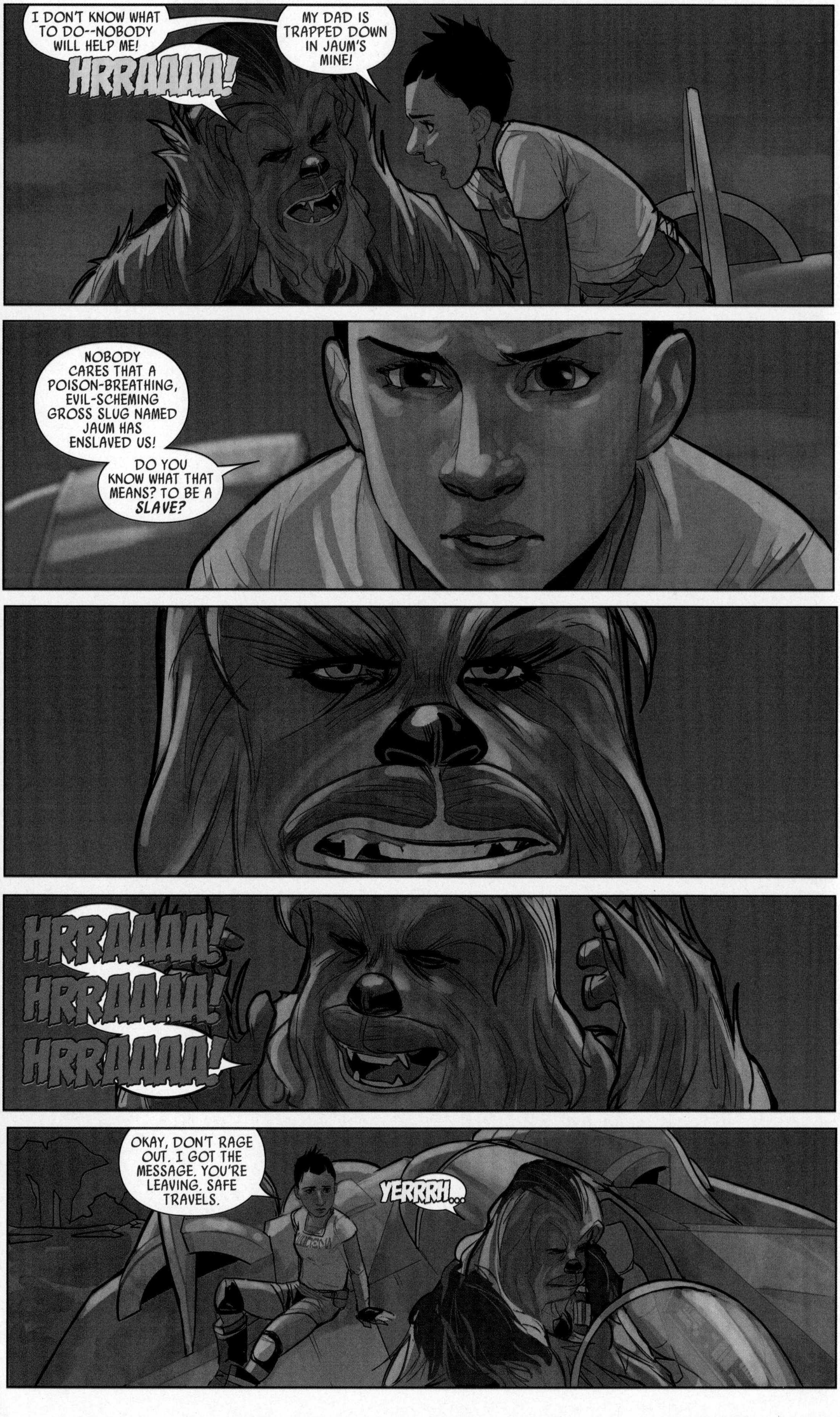
I DON'T KNOW WHAT TO DO--NOBODY WILL HELP ME!
MY DAD IS TRAPPED DOWN IN JAUM'S MINE!
HRRAAAA!
NOBODY CARES THAT A POISON-BREATHING, EVIL-SCHEMING GROSS SLUG NAMED JAUM HAS ENSLAVED US!
DO YOU KNOW WHAT THAT MEANS? TO BE A *SLAVE?*
HRRAAAA!
HRRAAAA!
HRRAAAA!
OKAY, DON'T RAGE OUT. I GOT THE MESSAGE. YOU'RE LEAVING. SAFE TRAVELS.
YERRRH...

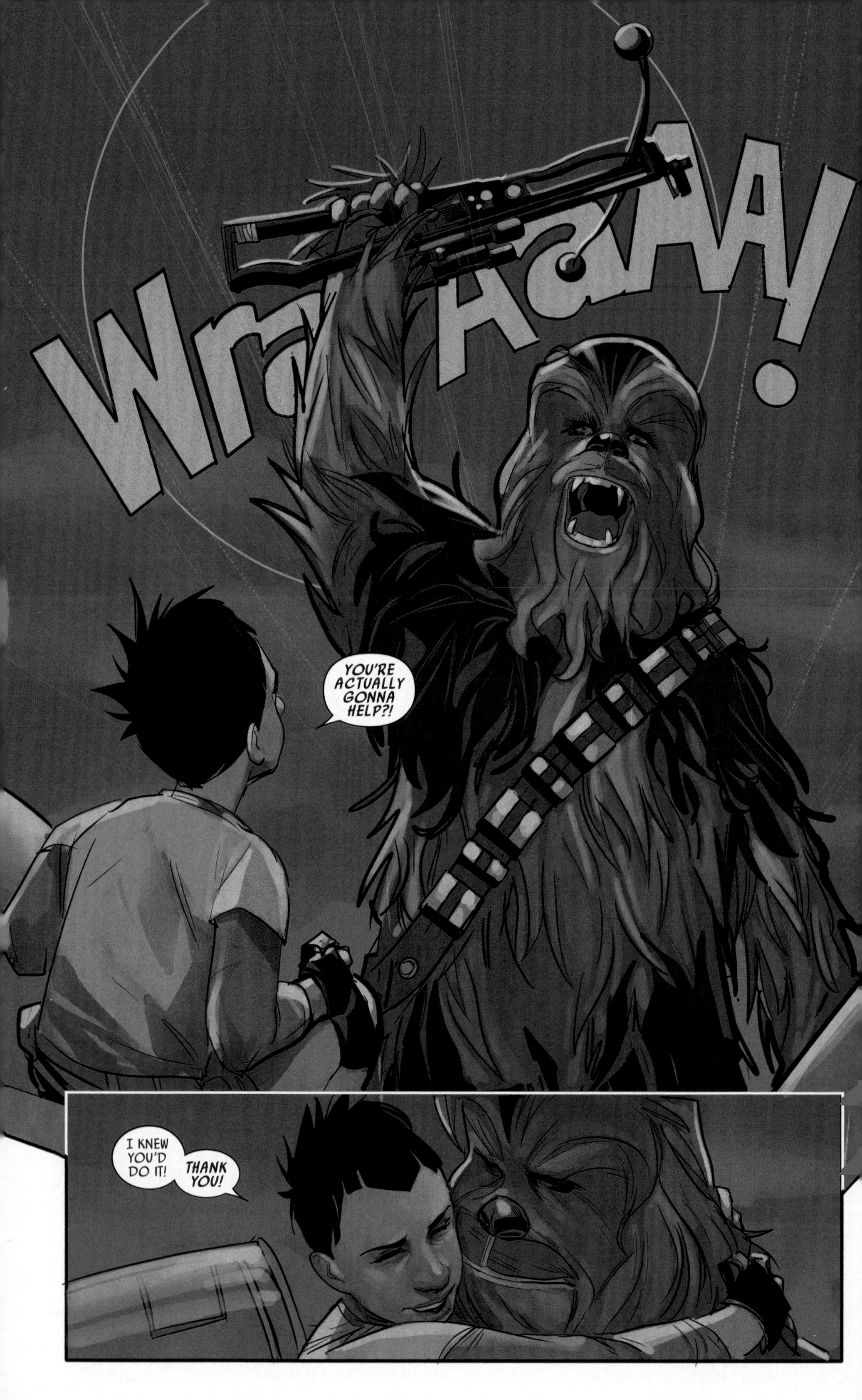
WRAAAAA!
YOU'RE ACTUALLY GONNA HELP?!
I KNEW YOU'D DO IT!
THANK YOU!

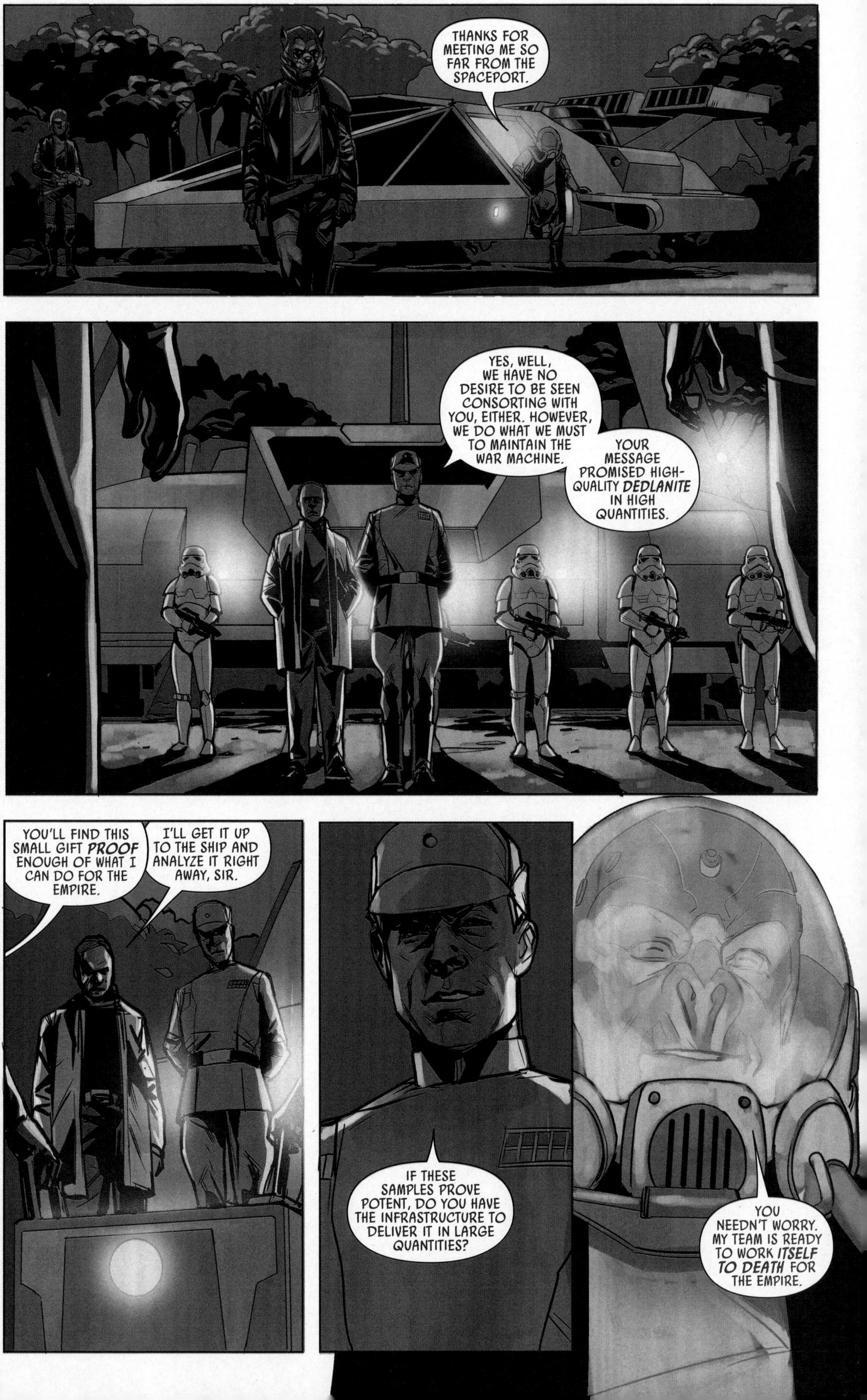
THANKS FOR MEETING ME SO FAR FROM THE SPACEPORT.
YES, WELL, WE HAVE NO DESIRE TO BE SEEN CONSORTING WITH YOU, EITHER. HOWEVER, WE DO WHAT WE MUST TO MAINTAIN THE WAR MACHINE.
YOUR MESSAGE PROMISED HIGH-QUALITY DEDLANITE IN HIGH QUANTITIES.
YOU'LL FIND THIS SMALL GIFT PROOF ENOUGH OF WHAT I CAN DO FOR THE EMPIRE.
I'LL GET IT UP TO THE SHIP AND ANALYZE IT RIGHT AWAY, SIR.
IF THESE SAMPLES PROVE POTENT, DO YOU HAVE THE INFRASTRUCTURE TO DELIVER IT IN LARGE QUANTITIES?
YOU NEEDN'T WORRY. MY TEAM IS READY TO WORK ITSELF TO DEATH FOR THE EMPIRE.

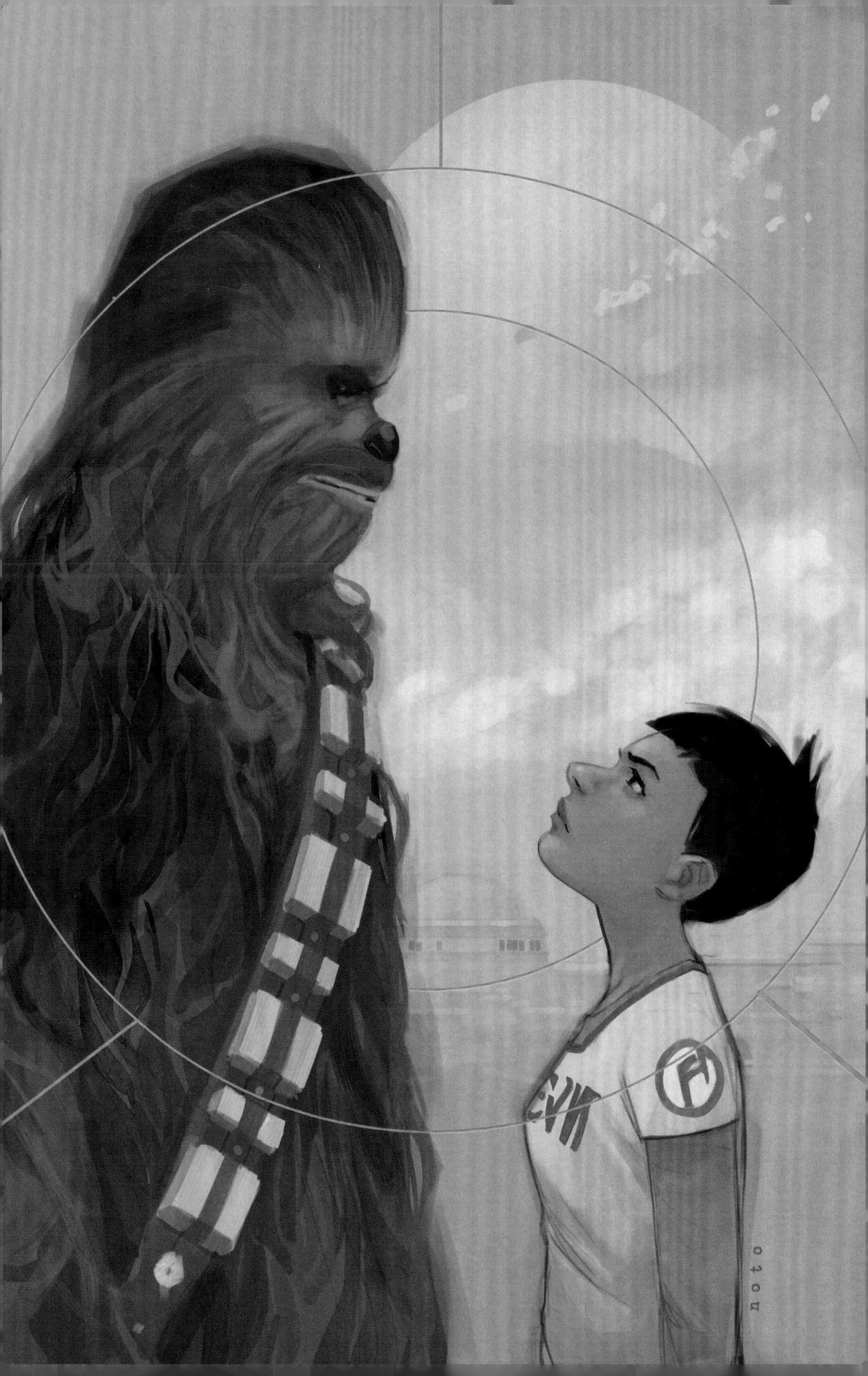

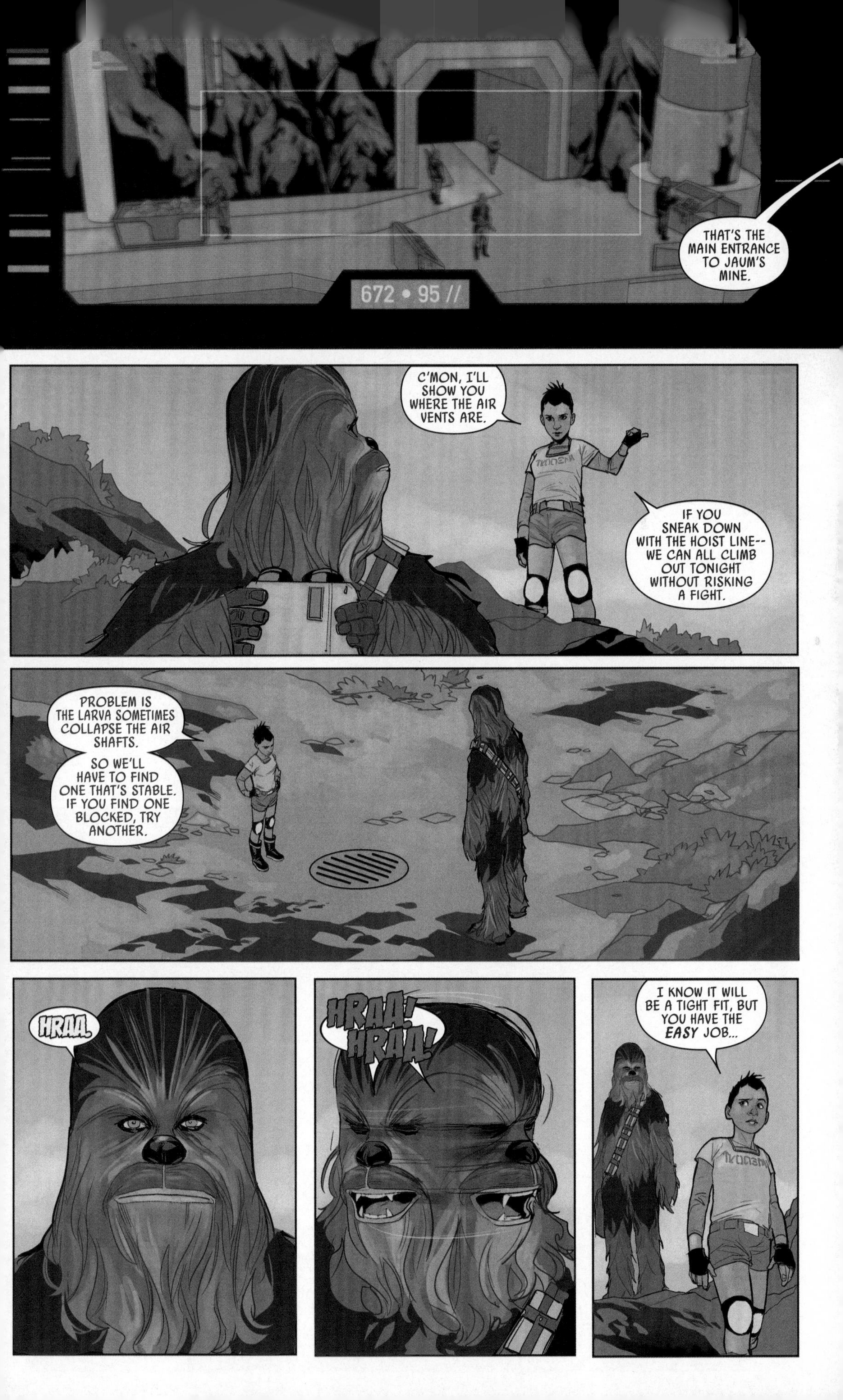
672 • 95 //
THAT'S THE MAIN ENTRANCE TO JAUM'S MINE.
C'MON, I'LL SHOW YOU WHERE THE AIR VENTS ARE.
IF YOU SNEAK DOWN WITH THE HOIST LINE-- WE CAN ALL CLIMB OUT TONIGHT WITHOUT RISKING A FIGHT.
PROBLEM IS THE LARVA SOMETIMES COLLAPSE THE AIR SHAFTS.
SO WE'LL HAVE TO FIND ONE THAT'S STABLE. IF YOU FIND ONE BLOCKED, TRY ANOTHER.
HRAA.
HRAA! HRAA!
I KNOW IT WILL BE A TIGHT FIT, BUT YOU HAVE THE *EASY* JOB...

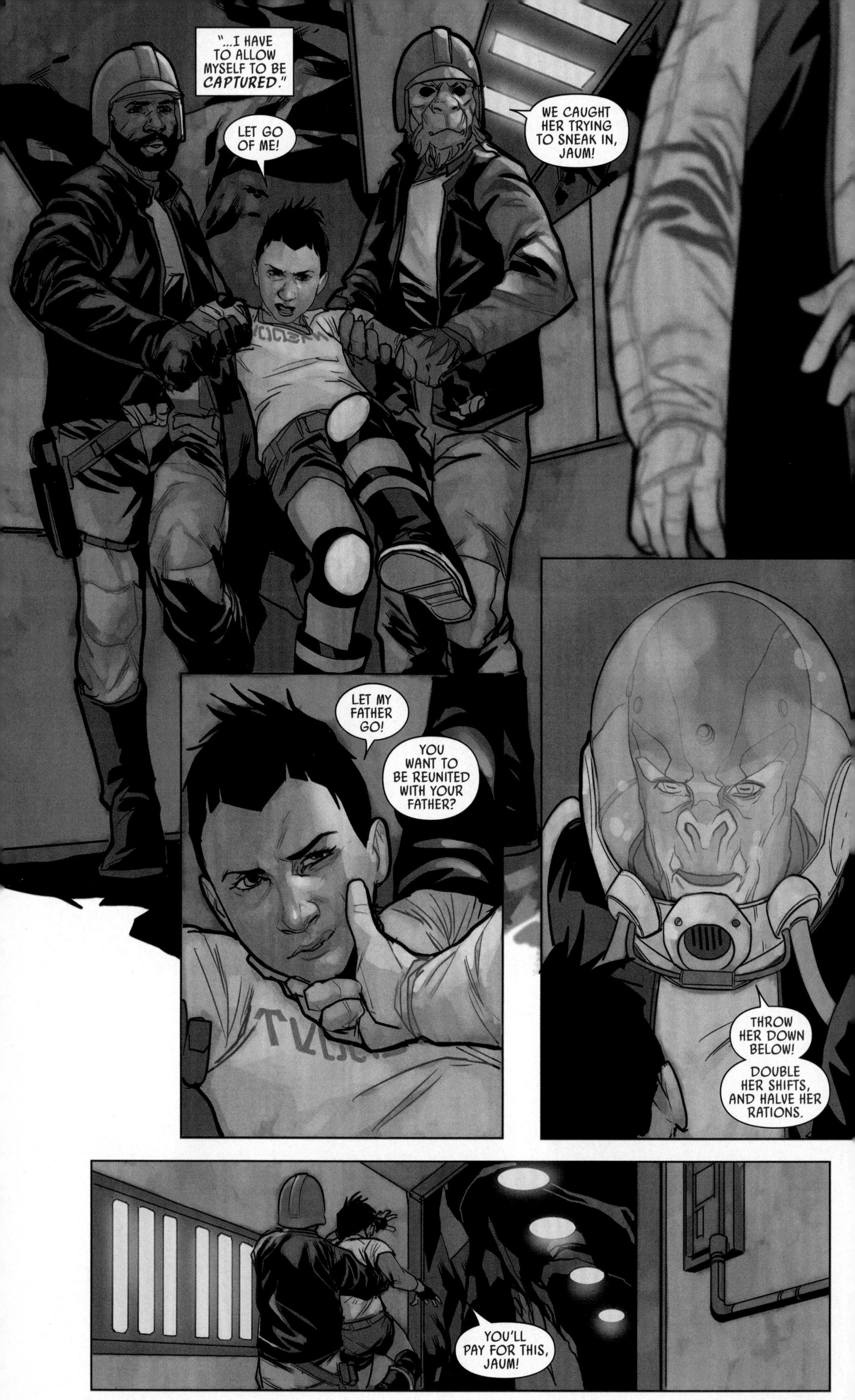
"...I HAVE TO ALLOW MYSELF TO BE CAPTURED."
LET GO OF ME!
WE CAUGHT HER TRYING TO SNEAK IN, JAUM!
LET MY FATHER GO!
YOU WANT TO BE REUNITED WITH YOUR FATHER?
THROW HER DOWN BELOW!
DOUBLE HER SHIFTS, AND HALVE HER RATIONS.
YOU'LL PAY FOR THIS, JAUM!

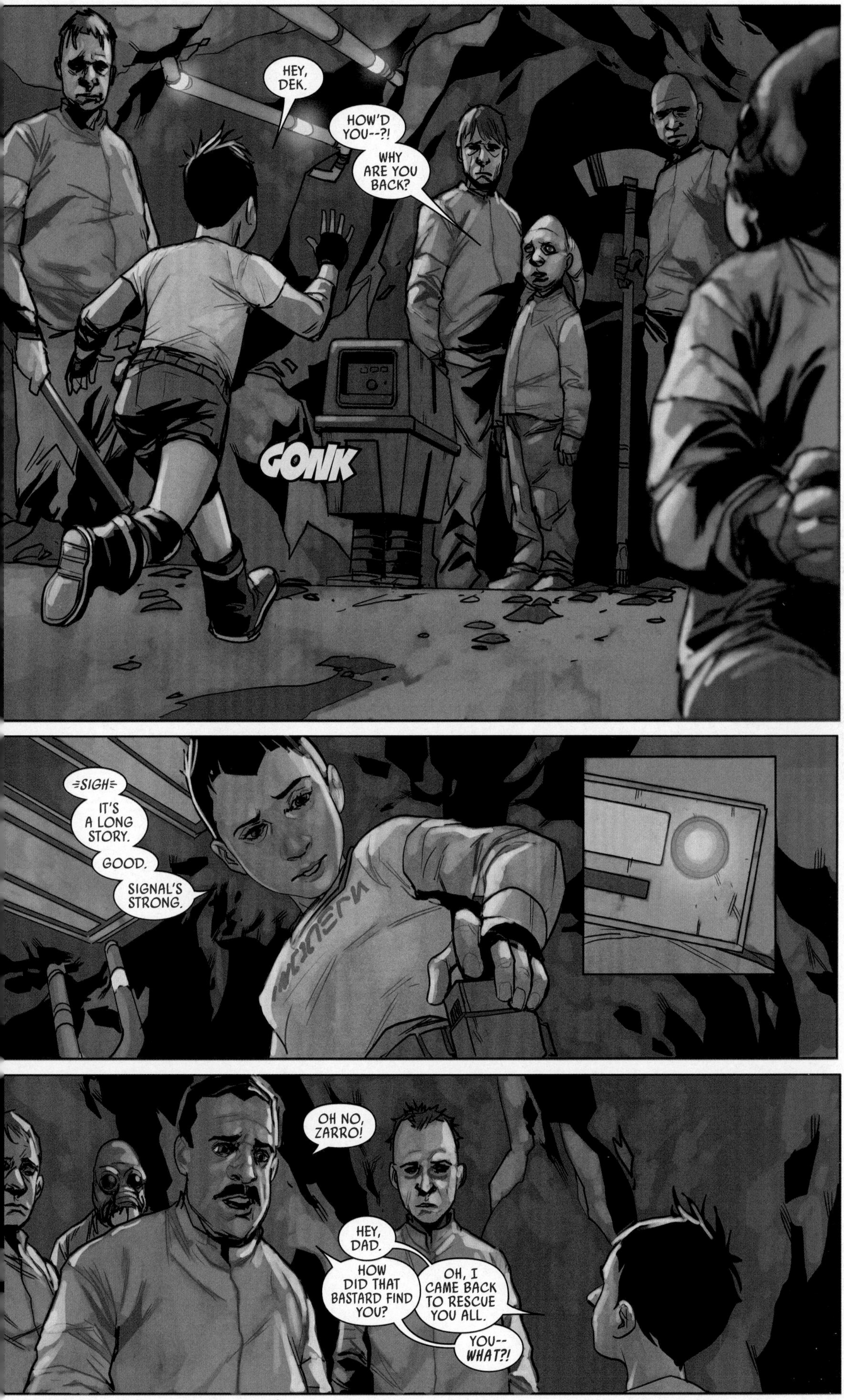
HEY, DEK.
HOW'D YOU--?!
WHY ARE YOU BACK?
GONK
=SIGH=
IT'S A LONG STORY.
GOOD.
SIGNAL'S STRONG.
OH NO, ZARRO!
HEY, DAD.
HOW DID THAT BASTARD FIND YOU?
OH, I CAME BACK TO RESCUE YOU ALL.
YOU-- WHAT?!

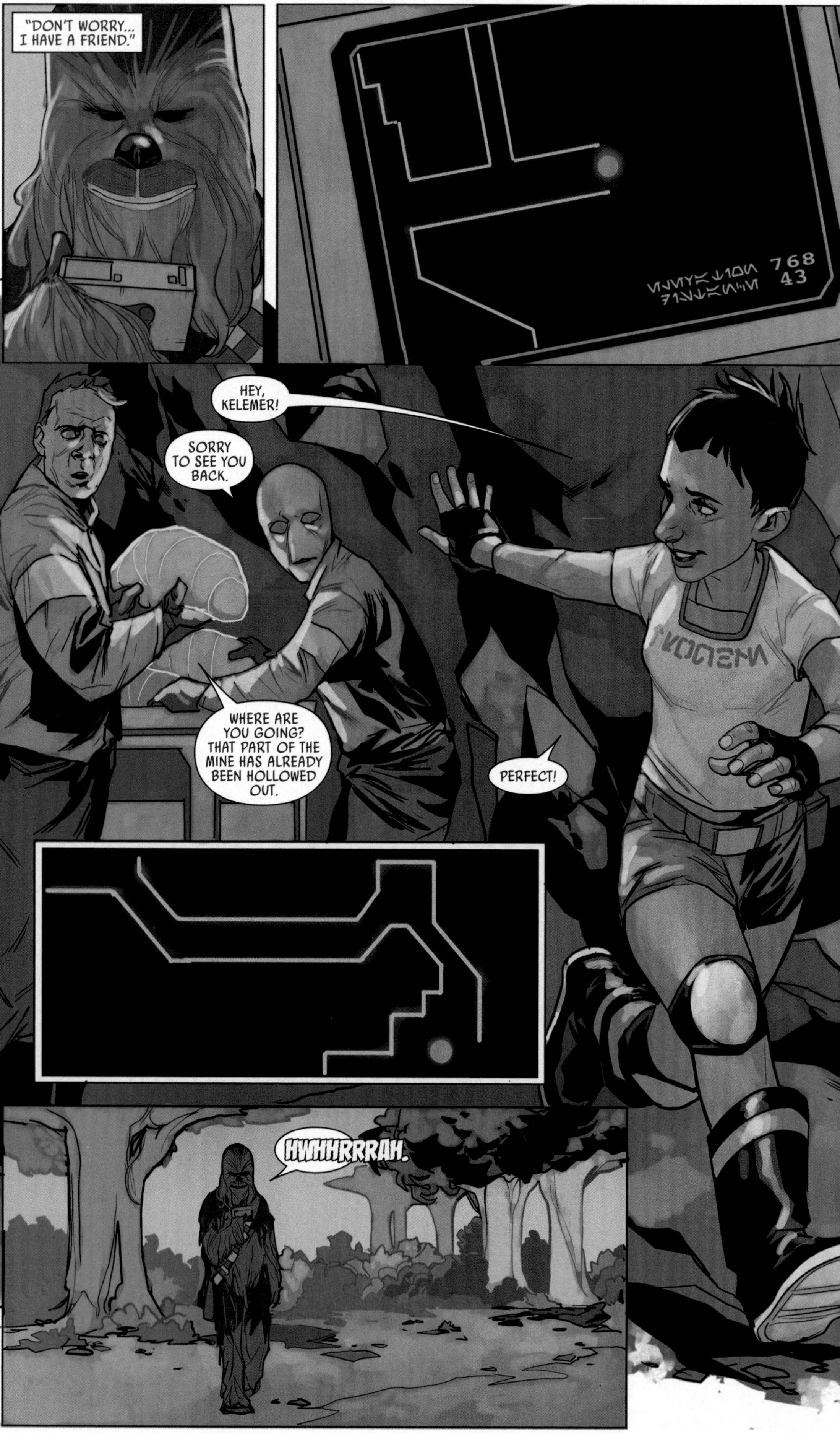
"DON'T WORRY... I HAVE A FRIEND."
768
43
HEY, KELEMER!
SORRY TO SEE YOU BACK.
WHERE ARE YOU GOING? THAT PART OF THE MINE HAS ALREADY BEEN HOLLOWED OUT.
PERFECT!
HWHHRRRAH.

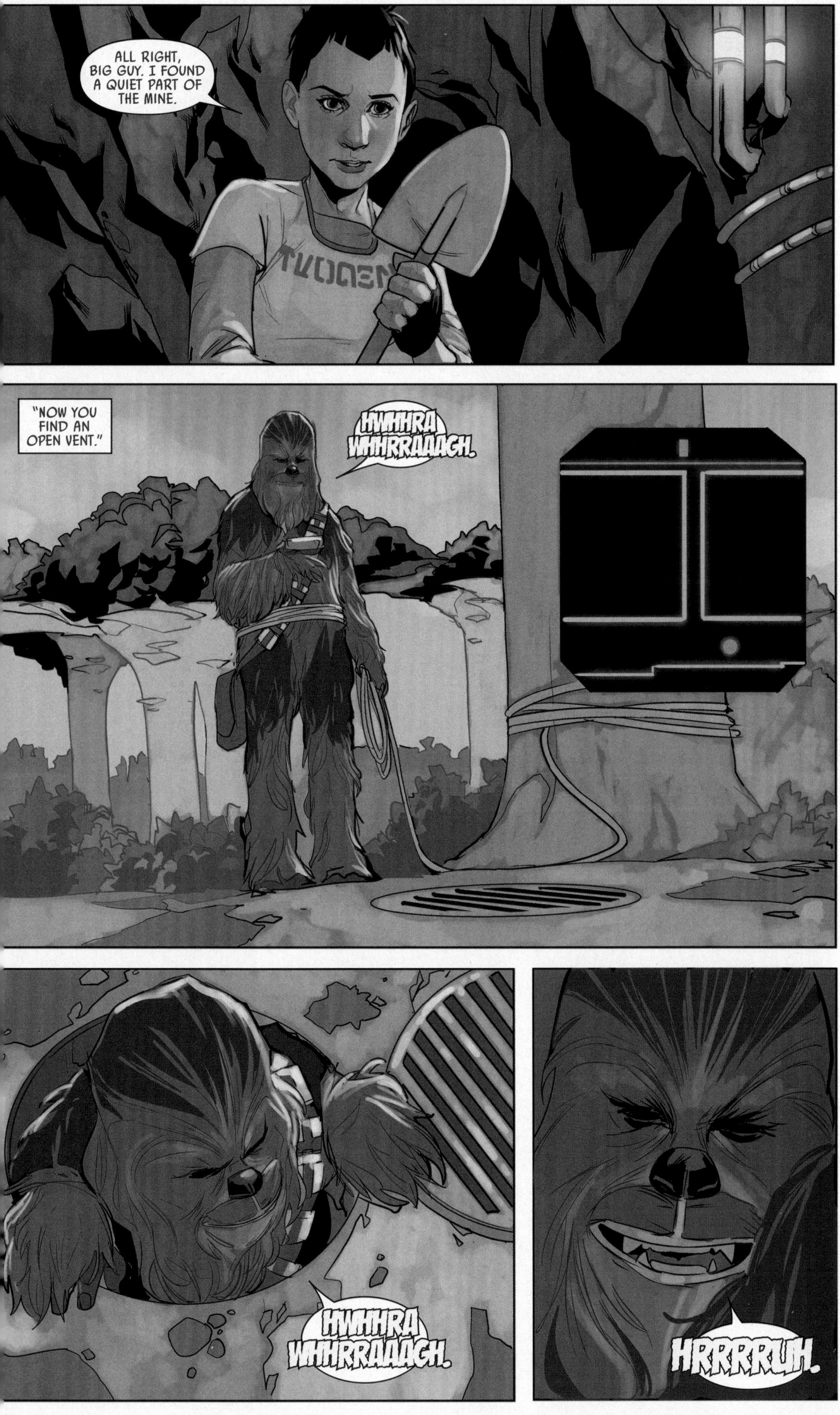
ALL RIGHT, BIG GUY. I FOUND A QUIET PART OF THE MINE.
"NOW YOU FIND AN OPEN VENT."
HWHHRA WHHRRAAAGH.
HWHHRA WHHRRAAAGH.
HRRRRUH.

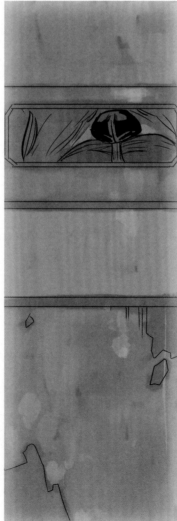

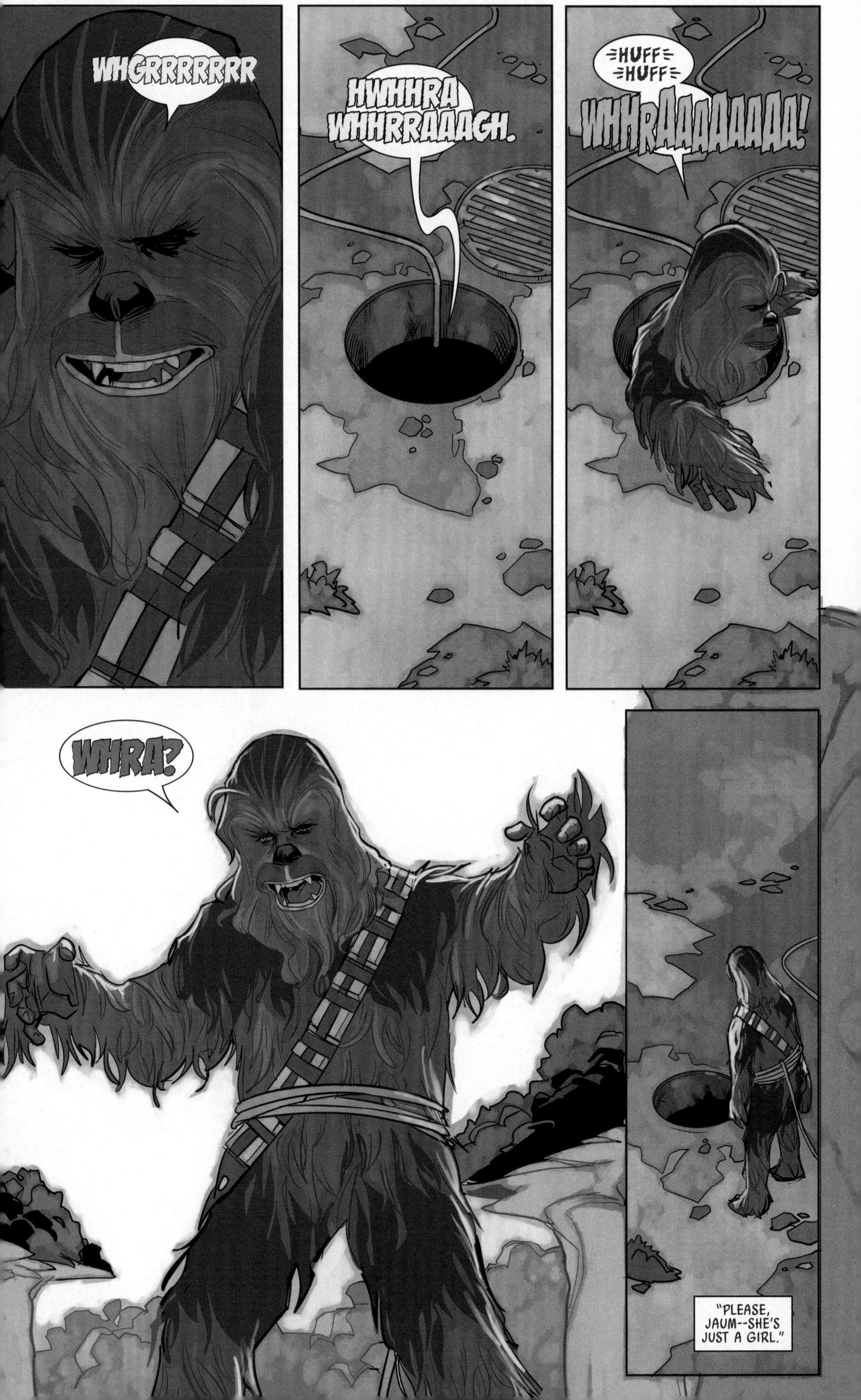
WHGRRRRRRR
HWHHRA WHHRRAAAGH.
HUFF HUFF
WHHRAAAAAAA!
WHRA?
"PLEASE, JAUM--SHE'S JUST A GIRL."

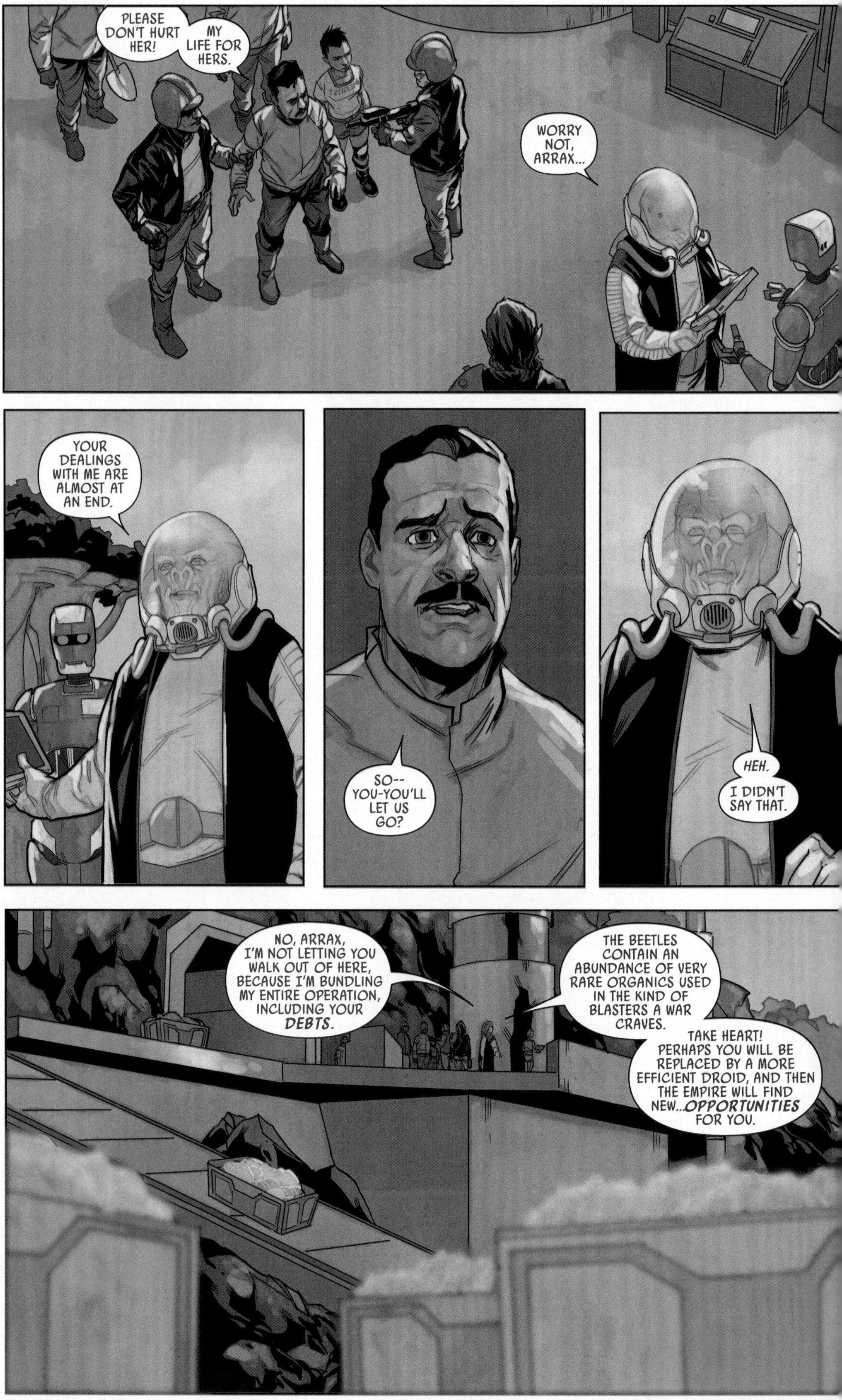

PLEASE DON'T HURT HER!
MY LIFE FOR HERS.
WORRY NOT, ARRAX...
YOUR DEALINGS WITH ME ARE ALMOST AT AN END.
SO-- YOU-YOU'LL LET US GO?
HEH.
I DIDN'T SAY THAT.
NO, ARRAX, I'M NOT LETTING YOU WALK OUT OF HERE, BECAUSE I'M BUNDLING MY ENTIRE OPERATION, INCLUDING YOUR *DEBTS.*
THE BEETLES CONTAIN AN ABUNDANCE OF VERY RARE ORGANICS USED IN THE KIND OF BLASTERS A WAR CRAVES.
TAKE HEART! PERHAPS YOU WILL BE REPLACED BY A MORE EFFICIENT DROID, AND THEN THE EMPIRE WILL FIND NEW...*OPPORTUNITIES* FOR YOU.

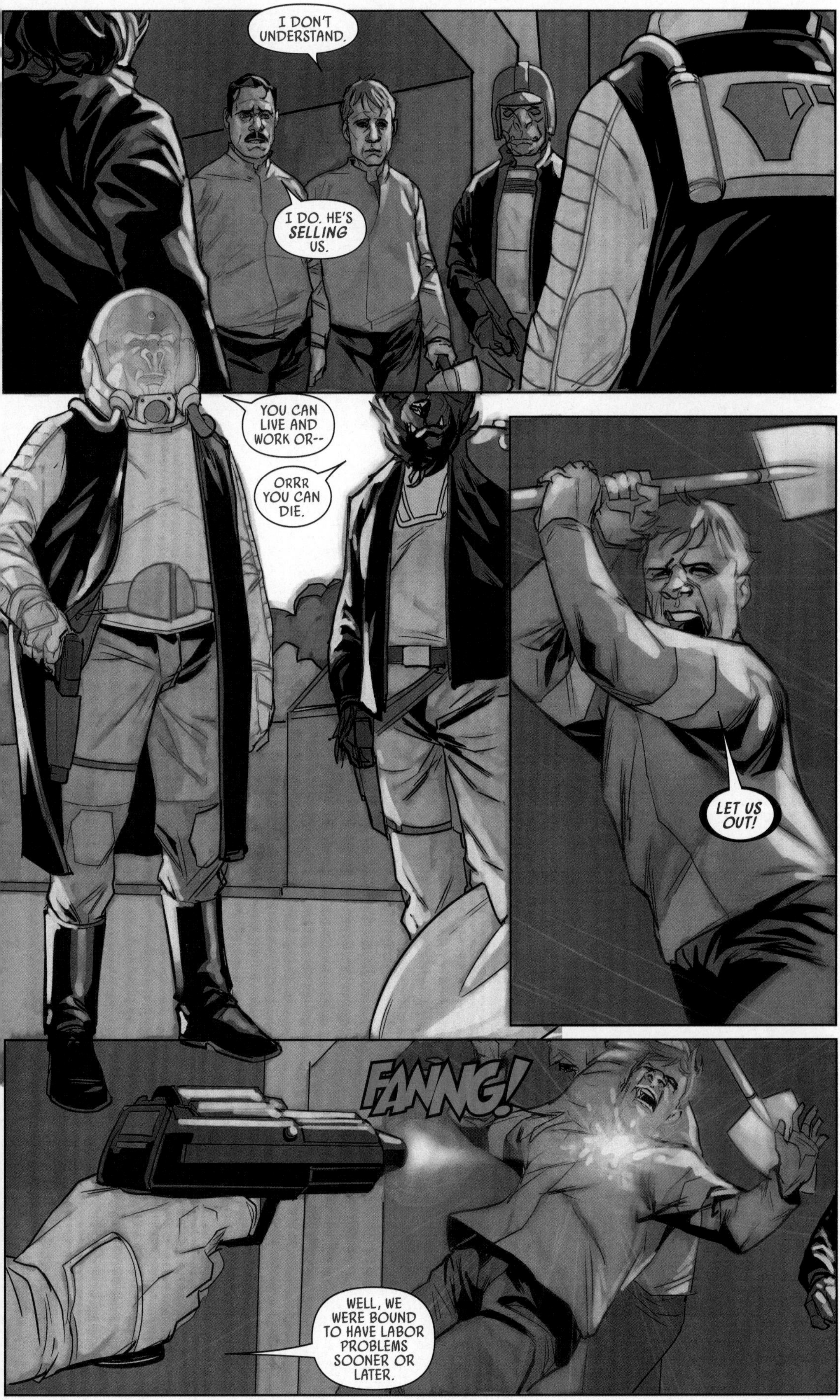

I DON'T UNDERSTAND.
I DO. HE'S SELLING US.
YOU CAN LIVE AND WORK OR--
ORRR YOU CAN DIE.
LET US OUT!
FANNG!
WELL, WE WERE BOUND TO HAVE LABOR PROBLEMS SOONER OR LATER.

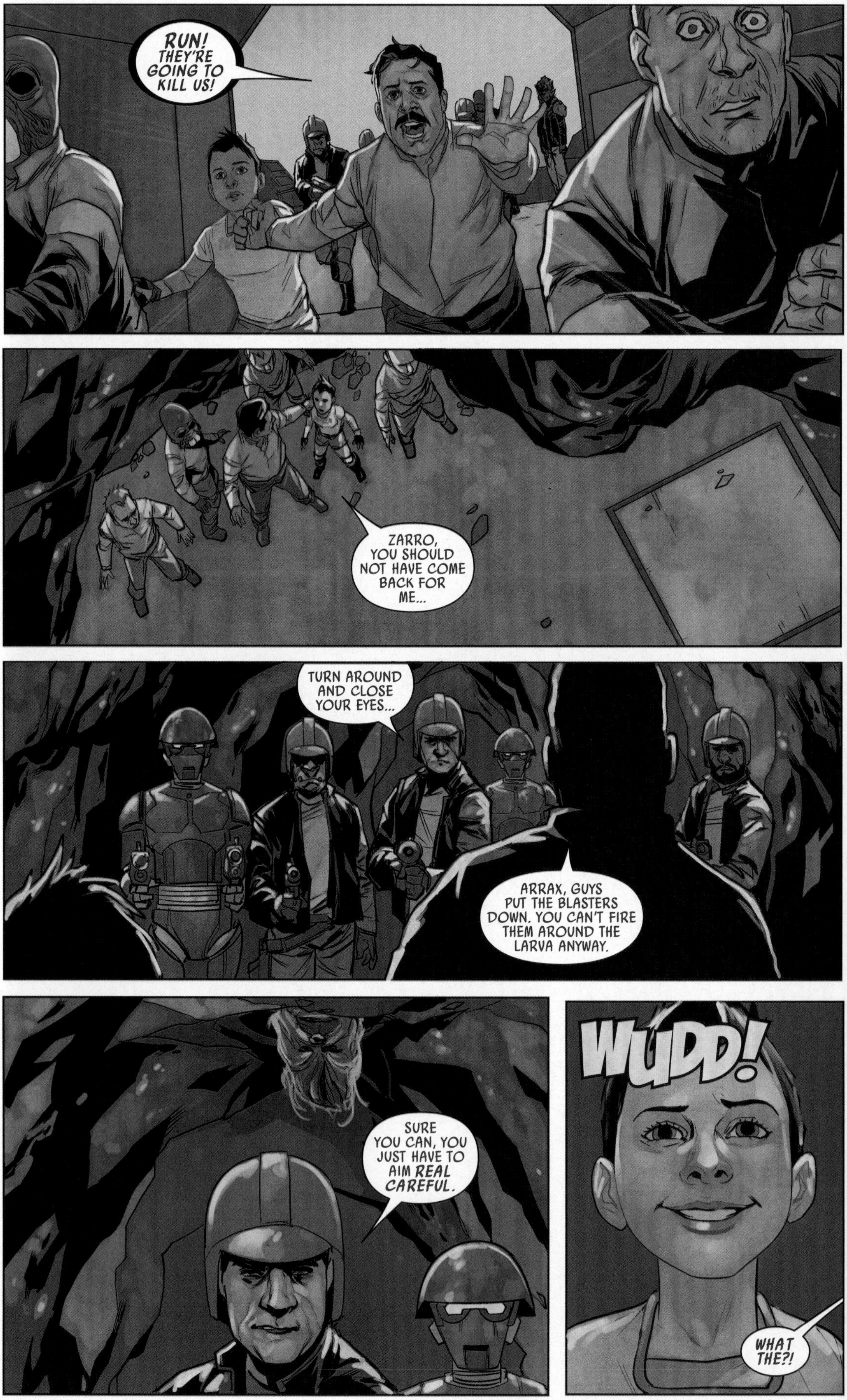
RUN! THEY'RE GOING TO KILL US!
ZARRO, YOU SHOULD NOT HAVE COME BACK FOR ME...
TURN AROUND AND CLOSE YOUR EYES...
ARRAX, GUYS PUT THE BLASTERS DOWN. YOU CAN'T FIRE THEM AROUND THE LARVA ANYWAY.
SURE YOU CAN, YOU JUST HAVE TO AIM REAL CAREFUL.
WUDD!
WHAT THE?!

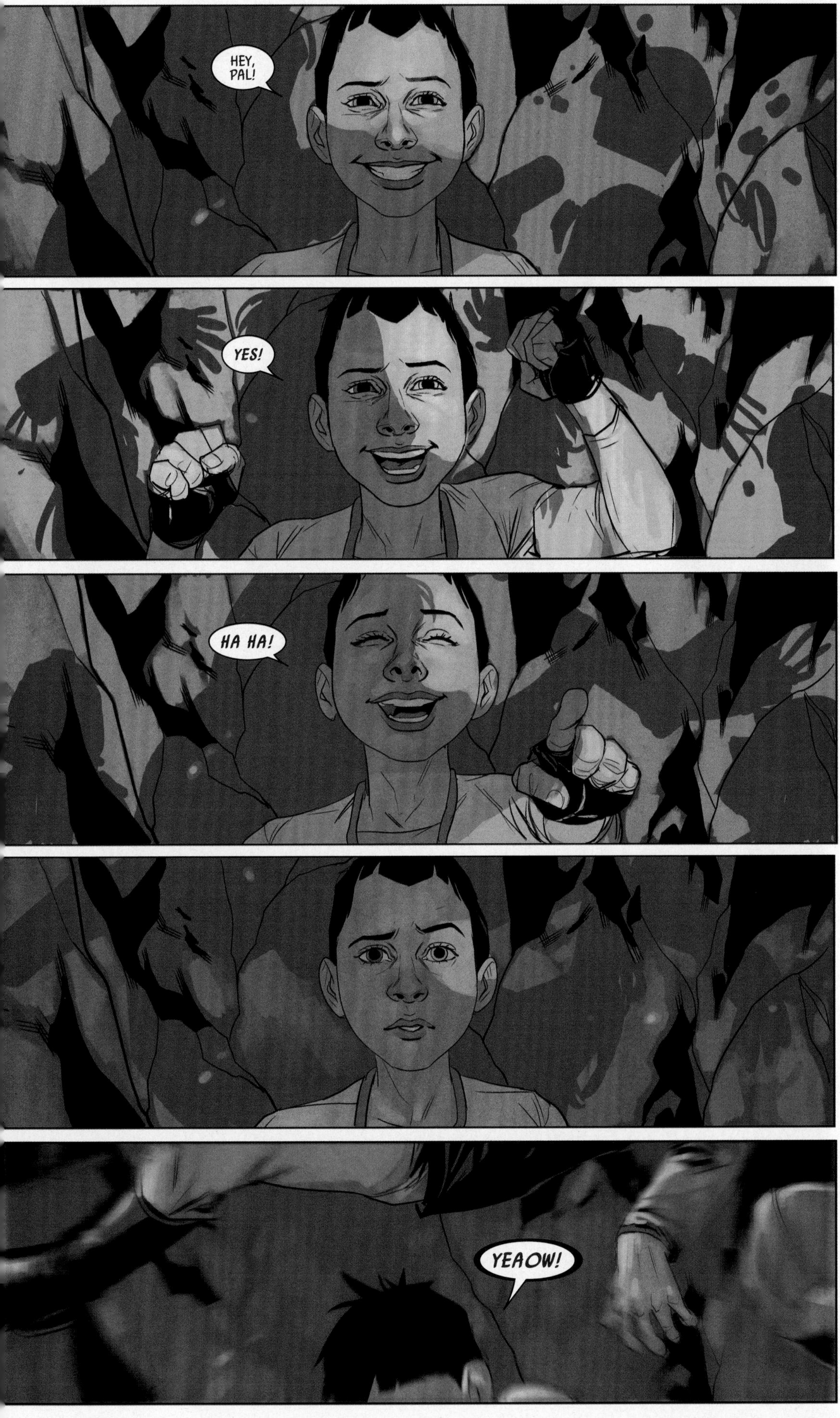
HEY, PAL!
YES!
HA HA!
YEAOW!

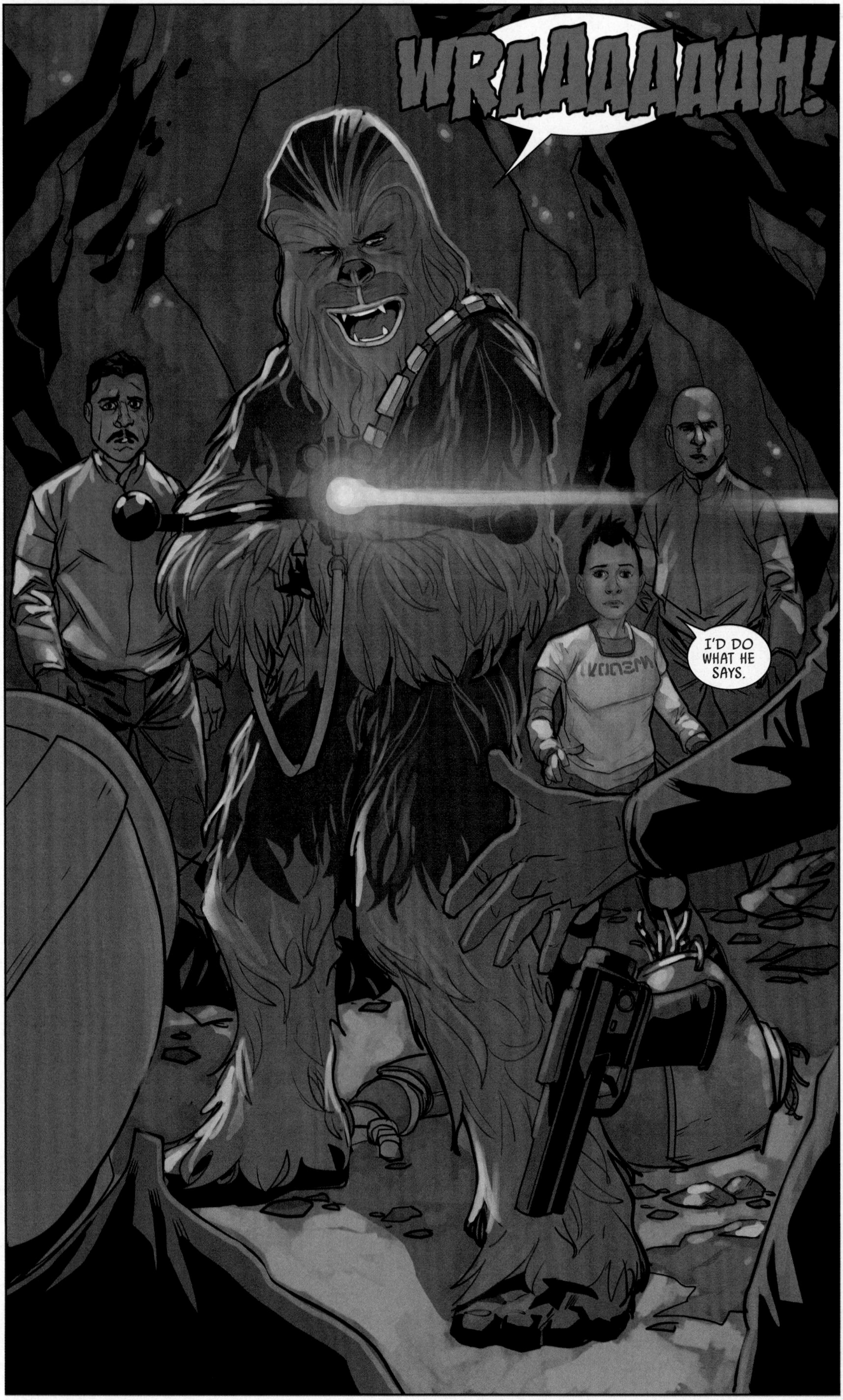
WRAAAAAAH!
I'D DO WHAT HE SAYS.

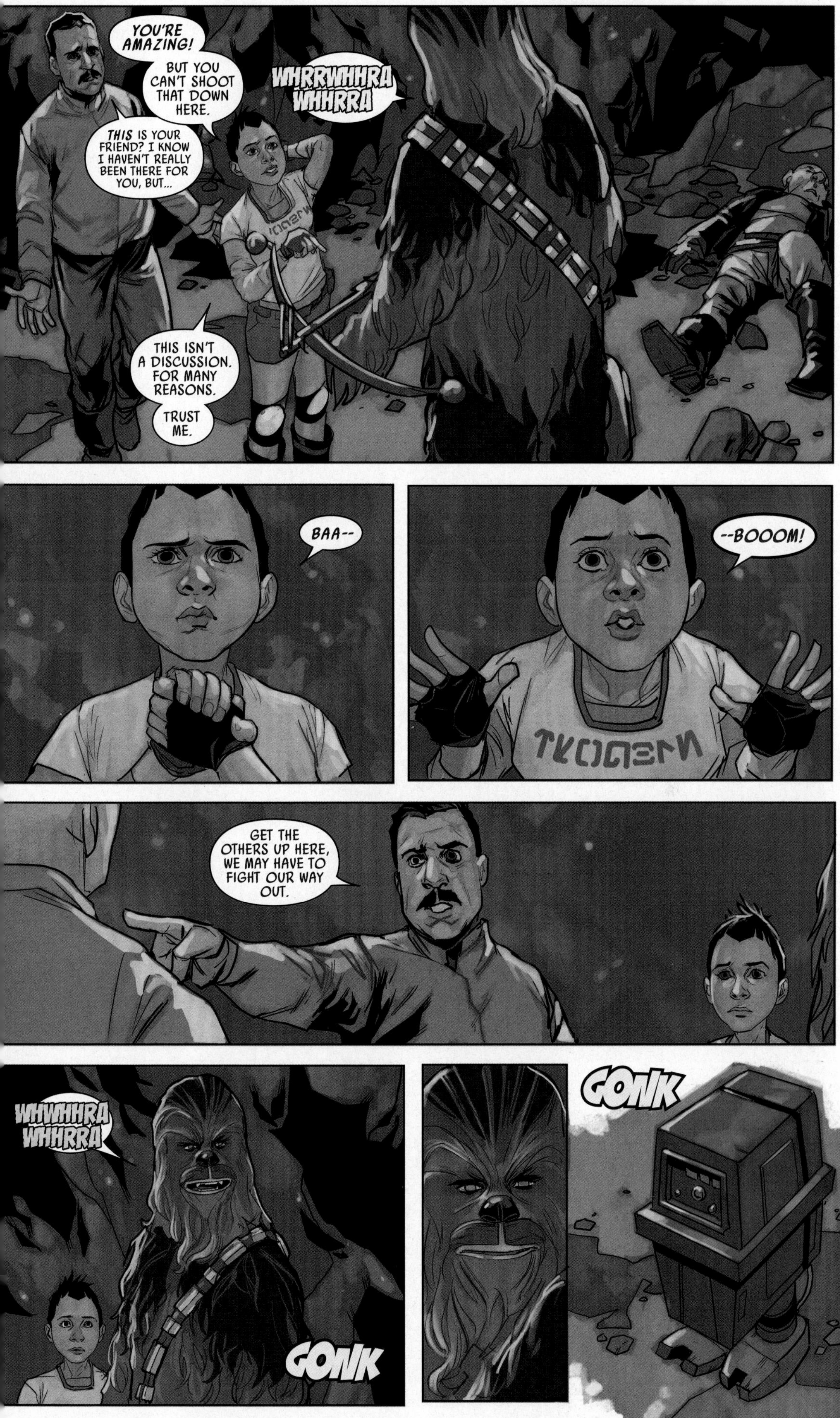
YOU'RE AMAZING!
BUT YOU CAN'T SHOOT THAT DOWN HERE.
WHRRWHHRA WHHRRA
THIS IS YOUR FRIEND? I KNOW I HAVEN'T REALLY BEEN THERE FOR YOU, BUT...
THIS ISN'T A DISCUSSION. FOR MANY REASONS.
TRUST ME.
BAA--
--BOOOM!
GET THE OTHERS UP HERE, WE MAY HAVE TO FIGHT OUR WAY OUT.
WHWHHRA WHHRRA
GONK
GONK

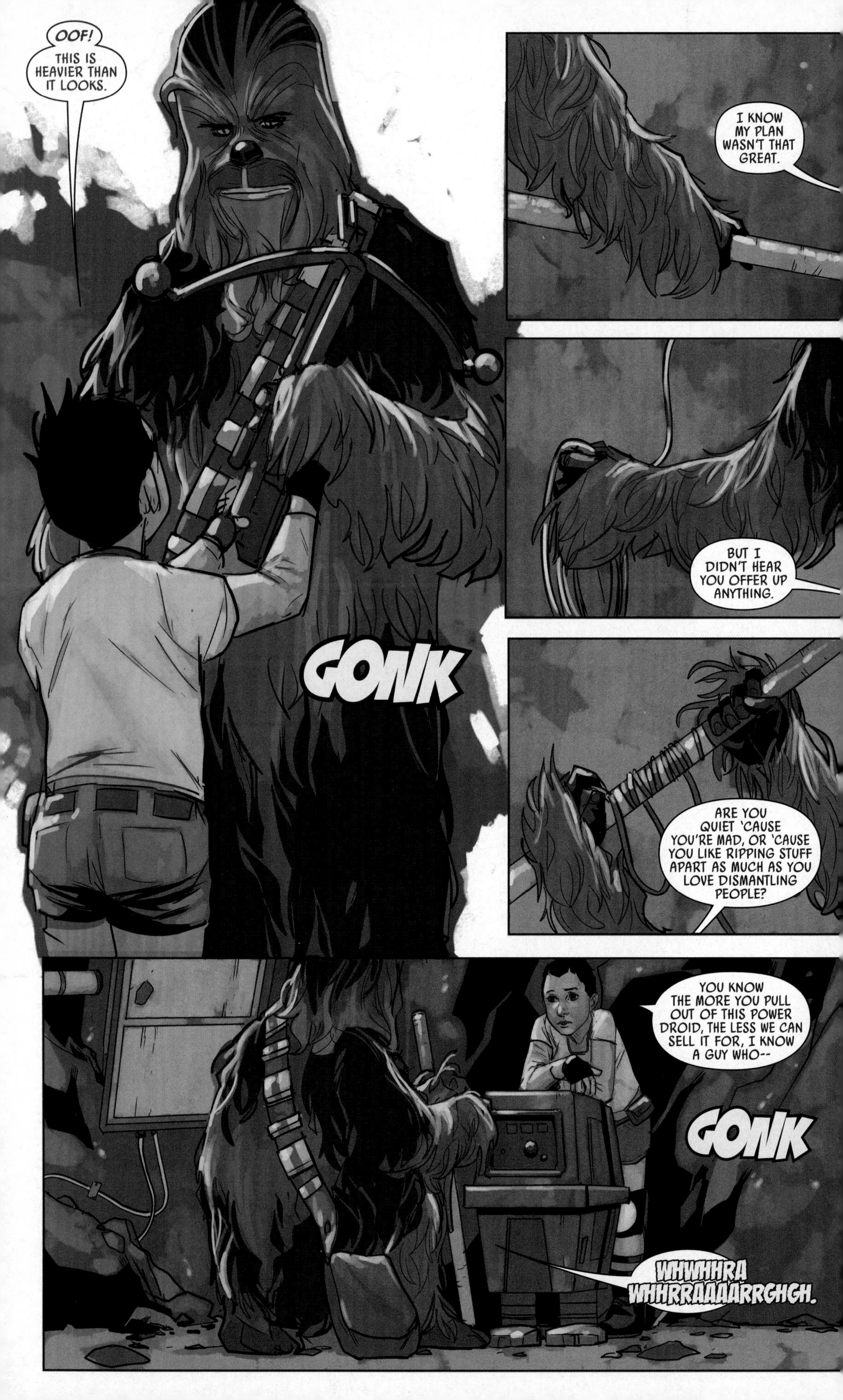
OOF!
THIS IS HEAVIER THAN IT LOOKS.
I KNOW MY PLAN WASN'T THAT GREAT.
BUT I DIDN'T HEAR YOU OFFER UP ANYTHING.
GONK
ARE YOU QUIET 'CAUSE YOU'RE MAD, OR 'CAUSE YOU LIKE RIPPING STUFF APART AS MUCH AS YOU LOVE DISMANTLING PEOPLE?
YOU KNOW THE MORE YOU PULL OUT OF THIS POWER DROID, THE LESS WE CAN SELL IT FOR, I KNOW A GUY WHO--
GONK
WHWHHRA WHHRRAAAARRGHGH.

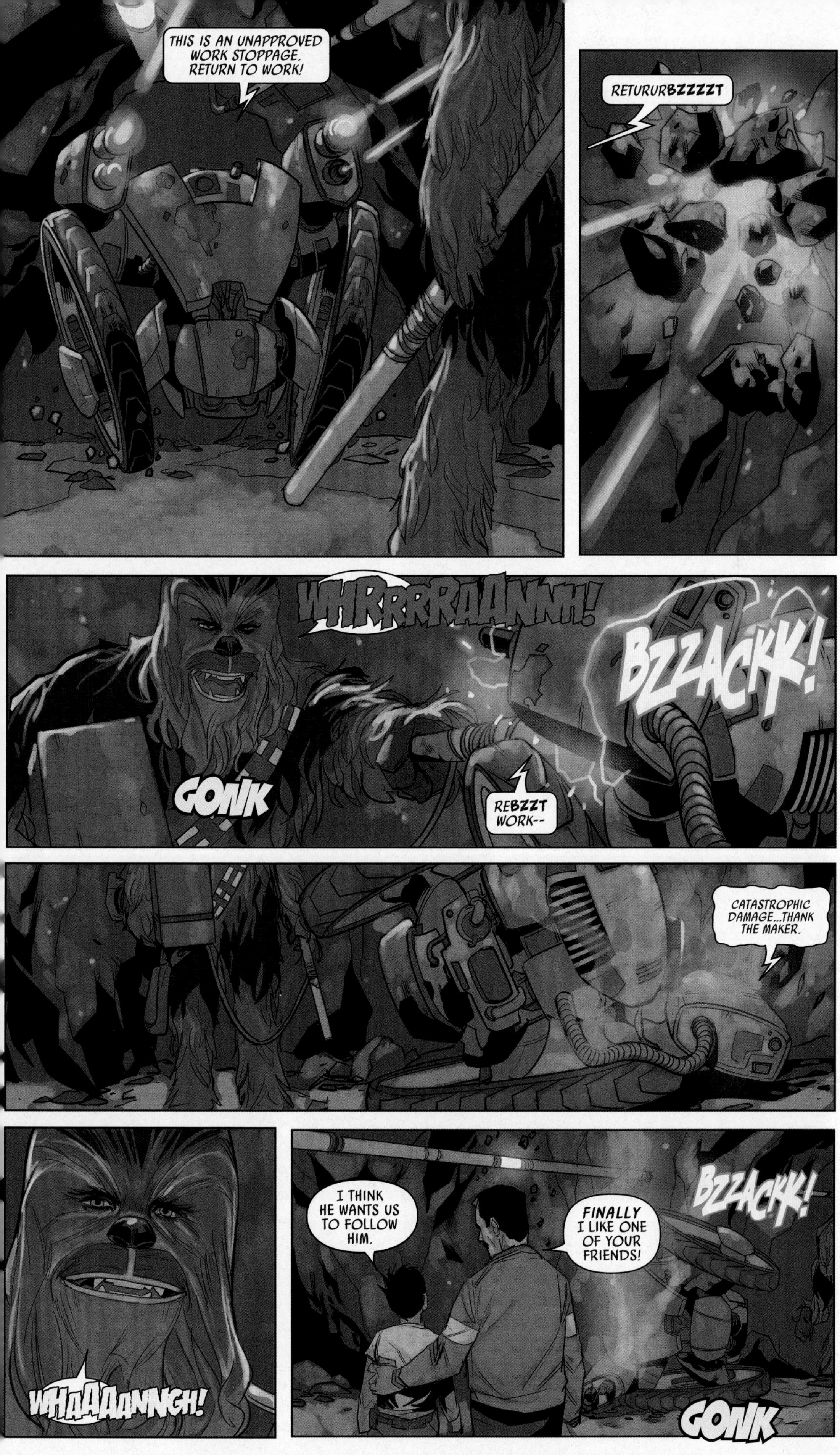
THIS IS AN UNAPPROVED WORK STOPPAGE. RETURN TO WORK!
RETURURBZZZZT
WHRRRRAANNH!
BZZACKK!
GONK
REBZZT WORK--
CATASTROPHIC DAMAGE...THANK THE MAKER.
WHAAAANNGH!
I THINK HE WANTS US TO FOLLOW HIM.
FINALLY I LIKE ONE OF YOUR FRIENDS!
BZZACKK!
GONK

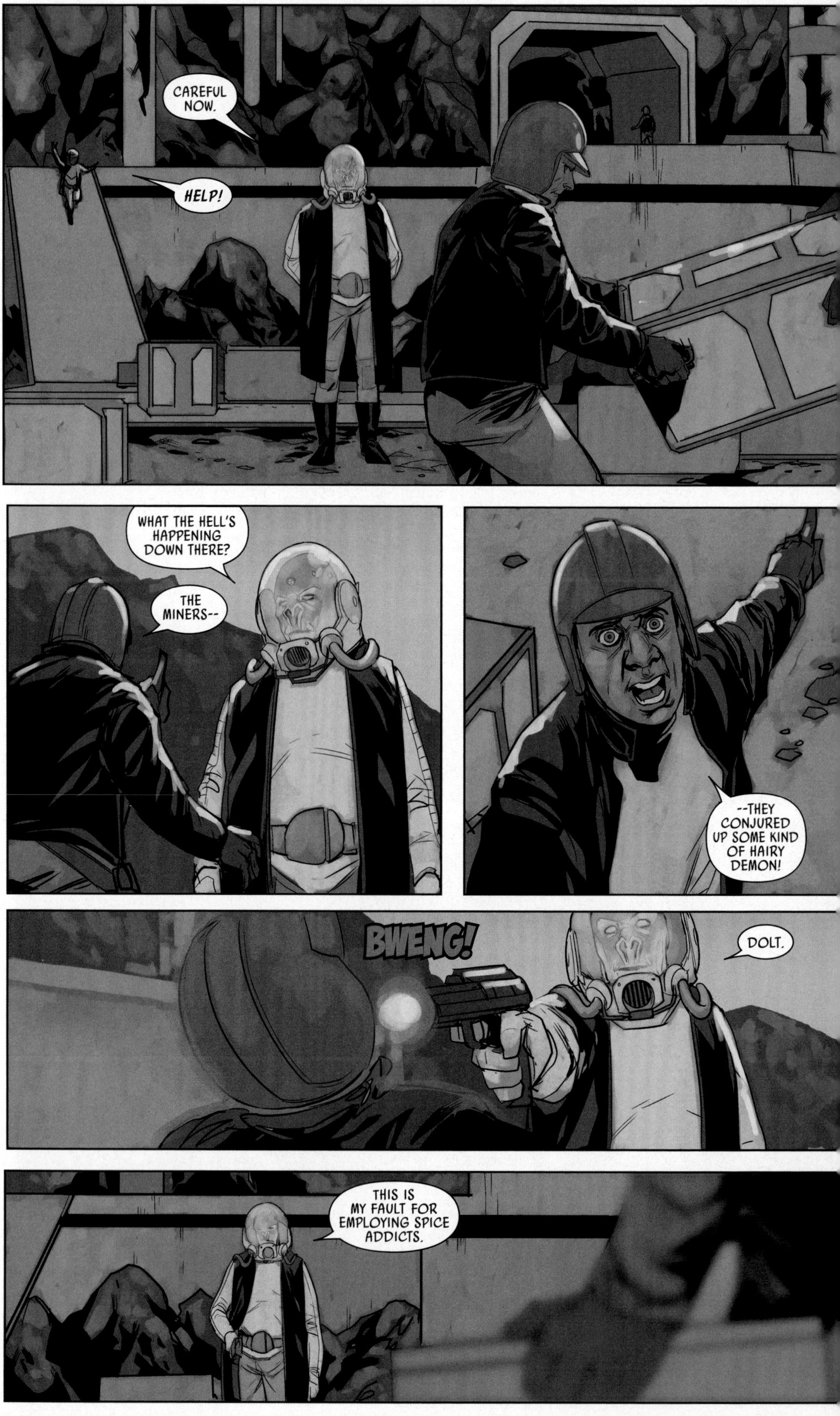
CAREFUL NOW.
HELP!
WHAT THE HELL'S HAPPENING DOWN THERE?
THE MINERS--
--THEY CONJURED UP SOME KIND OF HAIRY DEMON!
BWENG!
DOLT.
THIS IS MY FAULT FOR EMPLOYING SPICE ADDICTS.

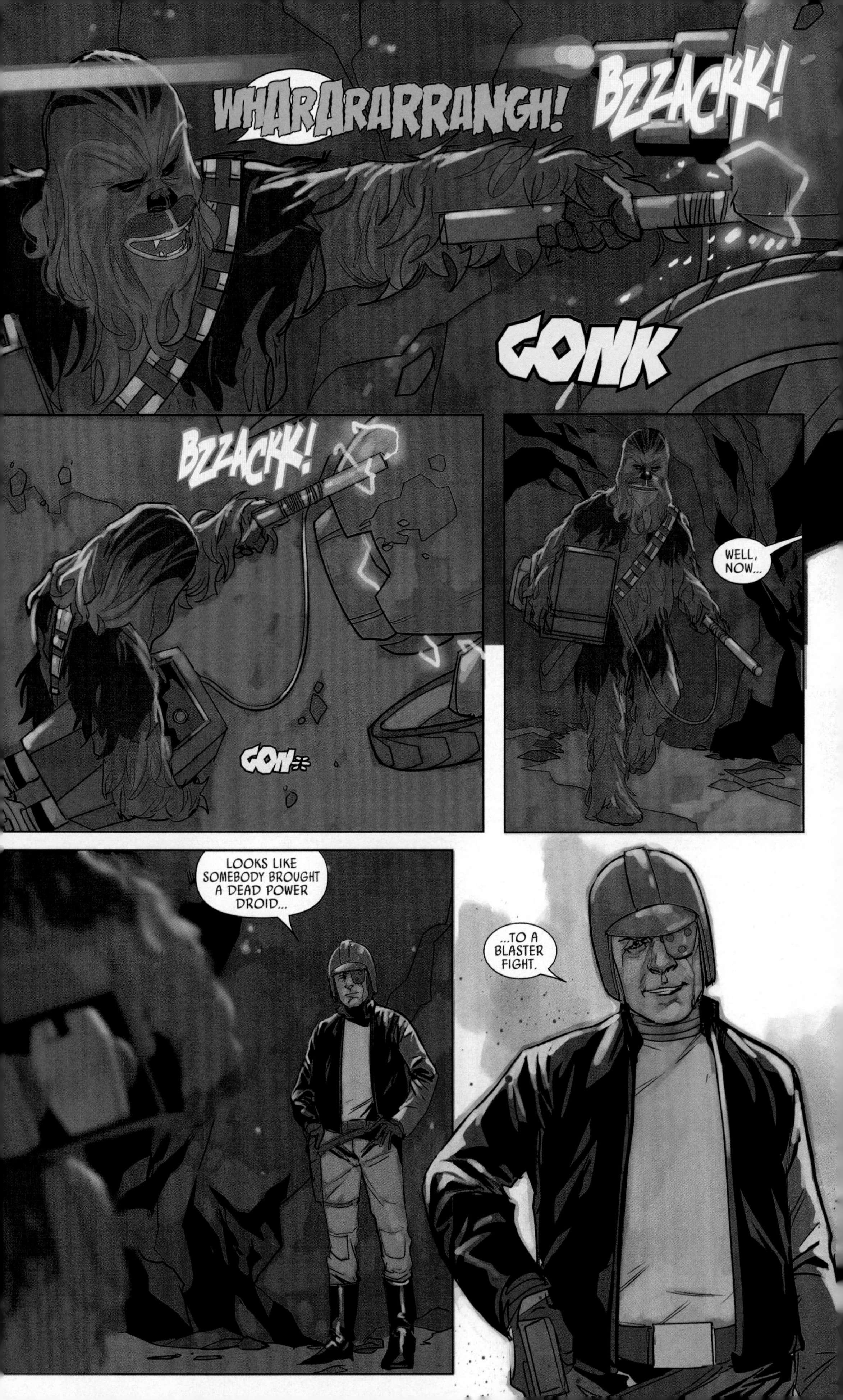
WHARARARRANGH!
BZZACKK!
GONK
BZZACKK!
GON-
WELL, NOW...
LOOKS LIKE SOMEBODY BROUGHT A DEAD POWER DROID...
...TO A BLASTER FIGHT.

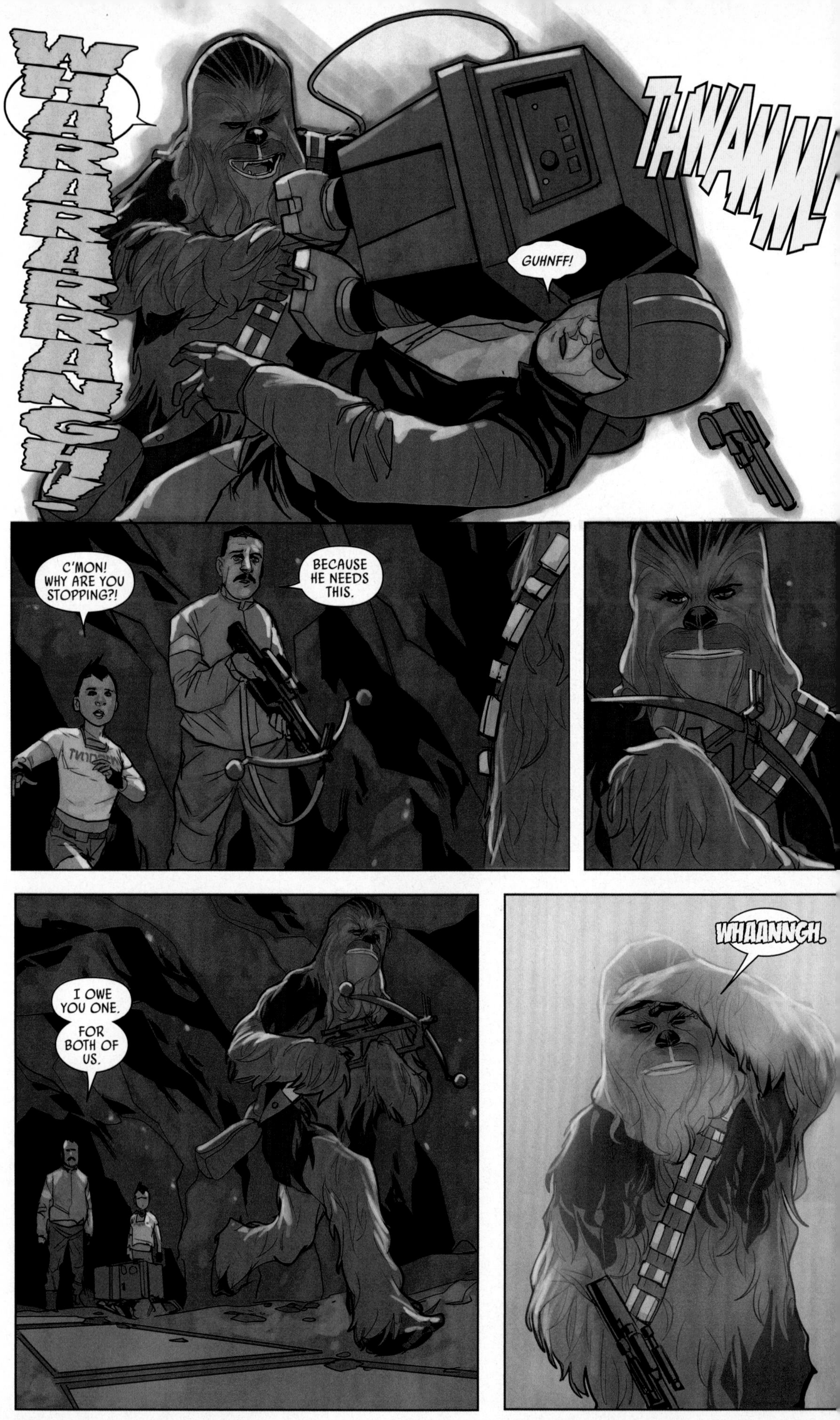
WHARAWARAAAGH!
THWAMM!
GUHNFF!
C'MON! WHY ARE YOU STOPPING?!
BECAUSE HE NEEDS THIS.
I OWE YOU ONE.
FOR BOTH OF US.
WHAANNGH.

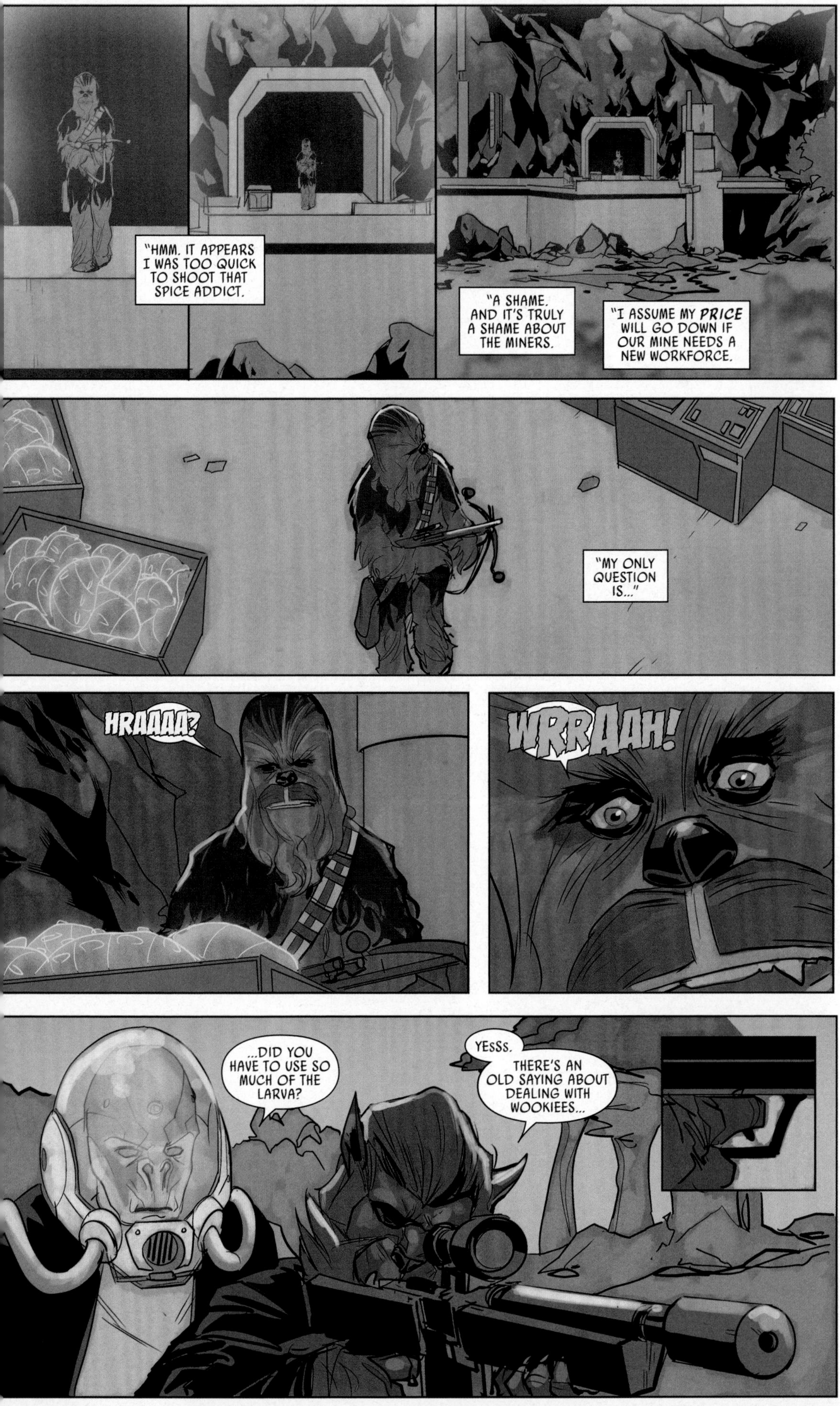
"HMM. IT APPEARS I WAS TOO QUICK TO SHOOT THAT SPICE ADDICT.
"A SHAME. AND IT'S TRULY A SHAME ABOUT THE MINERS.
"I ASSUME MY PRICE WILL GO DOWN IF OUR MINE NEEDS A NEW WORKFORCE.
"MY ONLY QUESTION IS..."
HRAAAA?
WRRAAH!
...DID YOU HAVE TO USE SO MUCH OF THE LARVA?
YESSS.
THERE'S AN OLD SAYING ABOUT DEALING WITH WOOKIEES...

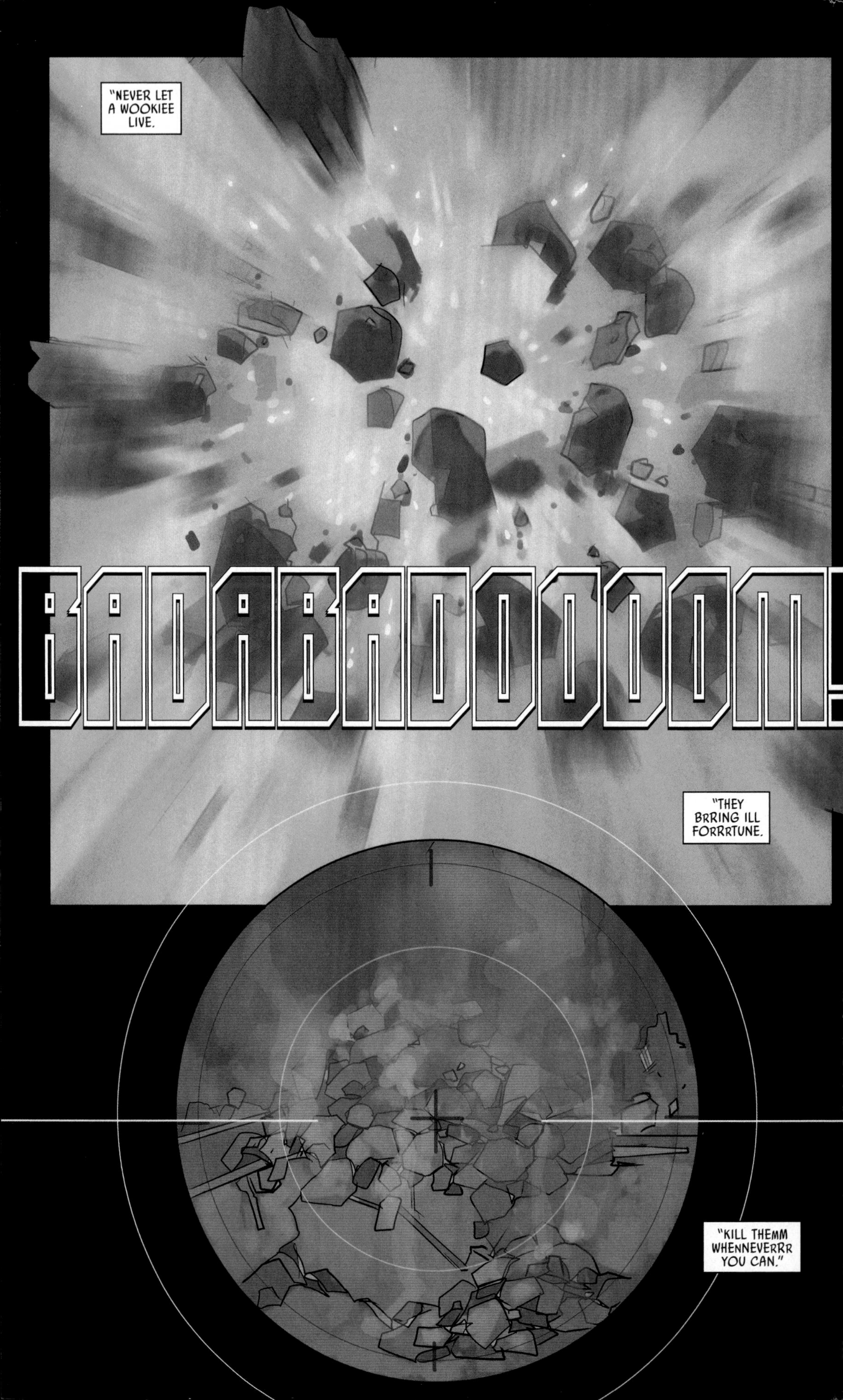
"NEVER LET A WOOKIEE LIVE.
BADABADOOOOM!
"THEY BRRING ILL FORRRTUNE.
"KILL THEMM WHENNEVERRR YOU CAN."

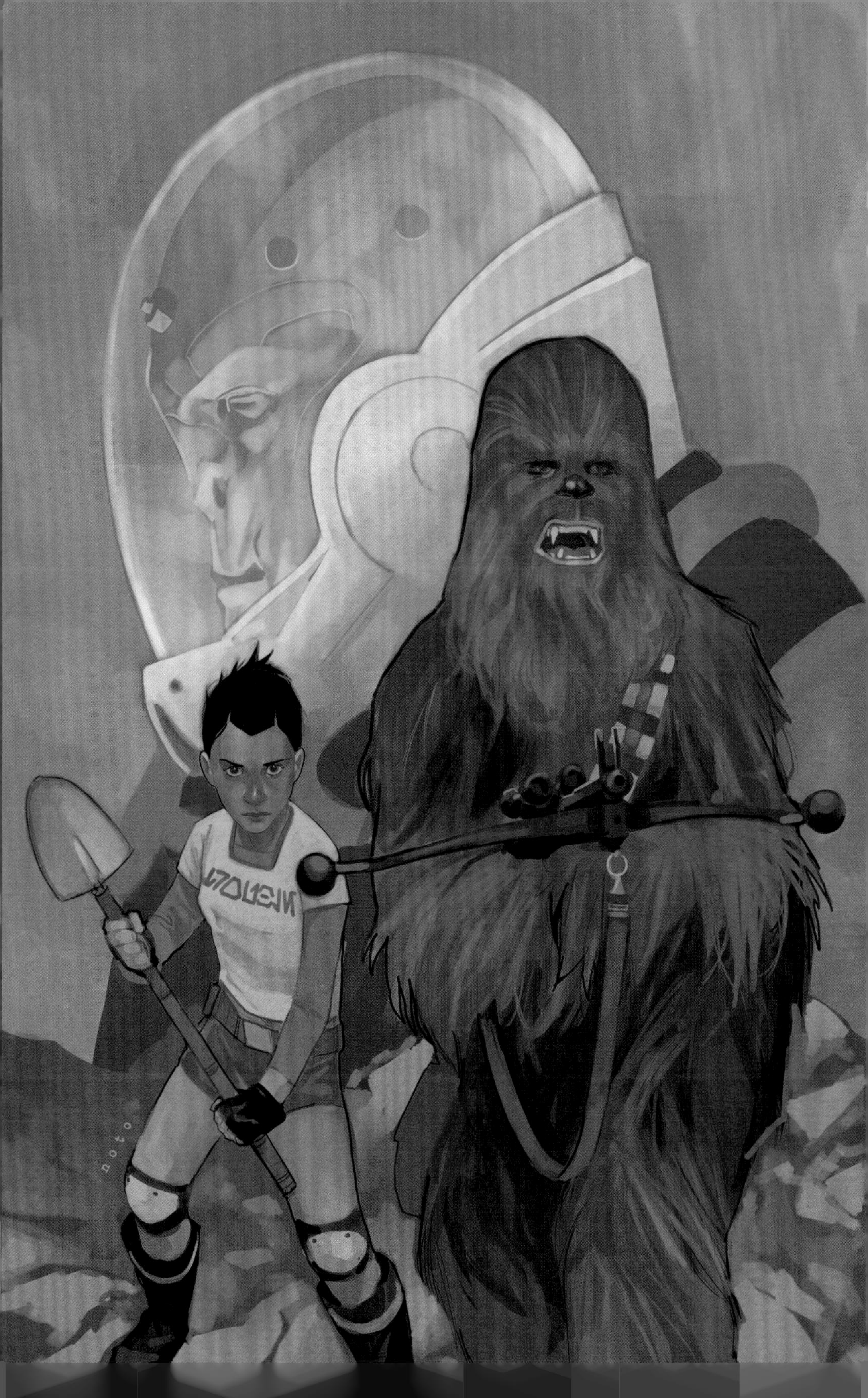

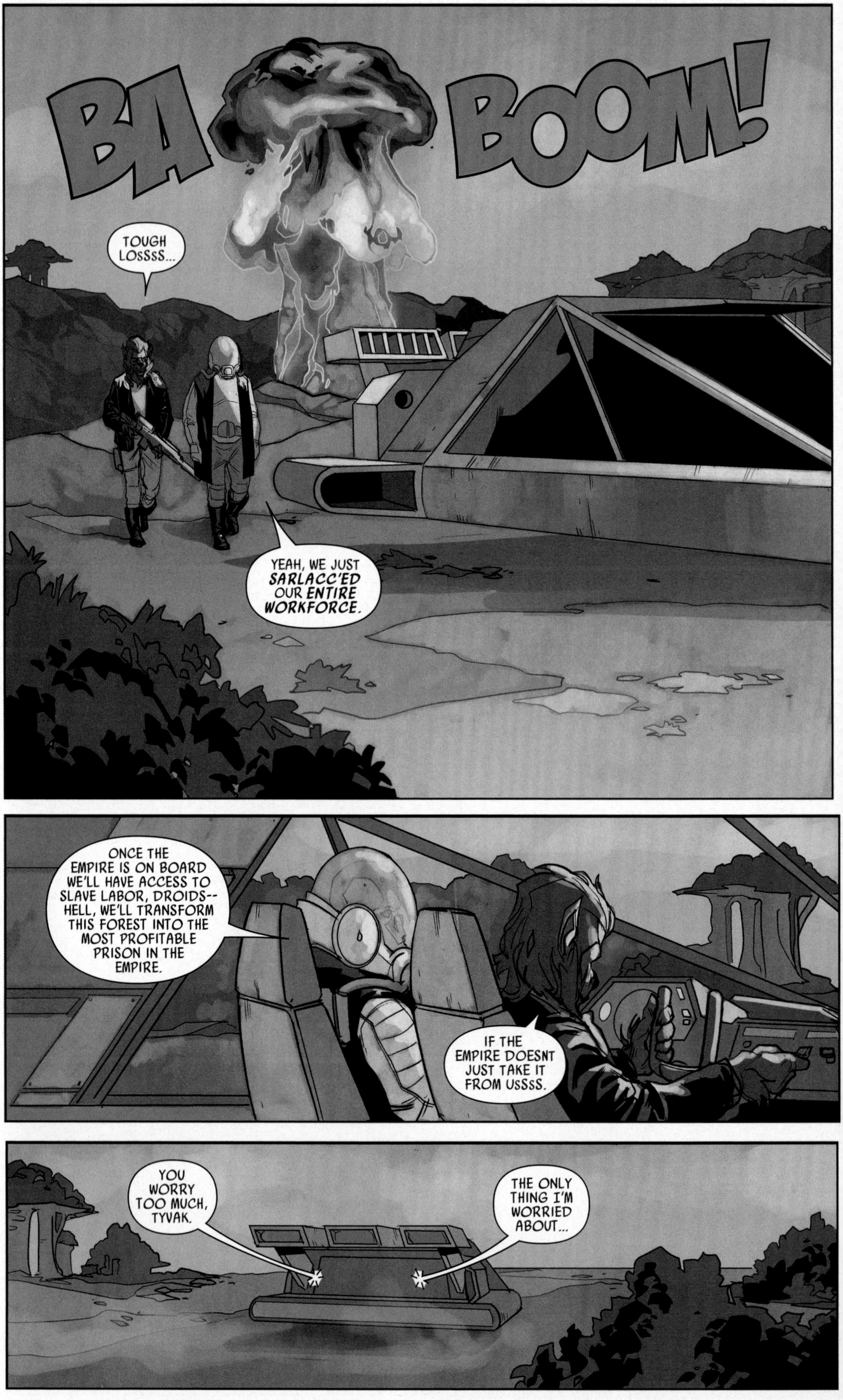
BA BOOM!
TOUGH LOSSSS...
YEAH, WE JUST *SARLACC'ED* OUR *ENTIRE WORKFORCE.*
ONCE THE EMPIRE IS ON BOARD WE'LL HAVE ACCESS TO SLAVE LABOR, DROIDS-- HELL, WE'LL TRANSFORM THIS FOREST INTO THE MOST PROFITABLE PRISON IN THE EMPIRE.
IF THE EMPIRE DOESNT JUST TAKE IT FROM USSSS.
YOU WORRY TOO MUCH, TYVAK.
THE ONLY THING I'M WORRIED ABOUT...

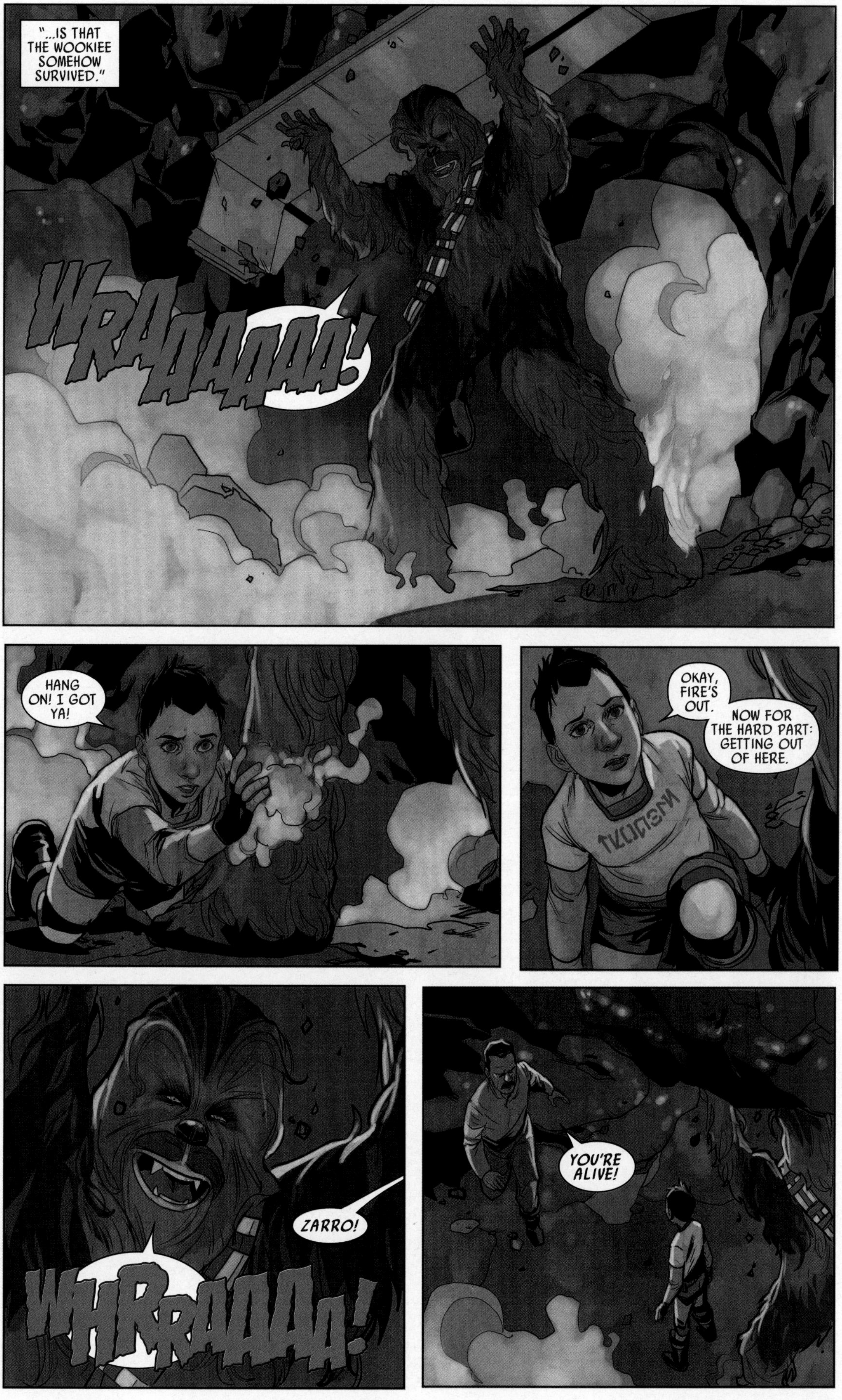
"...IS THAT THE WOOKIEE SOMEHOW SURVIVED."
WRAAAAAA!
HANG ON! I GOT YA!
OKAY, FIRE'S OUT.
NOW FOR THE HARD PART: GETTING OUT OF HERE.
ZARRO!
WHRRAAAAA!
YOU'RE ALIVE!

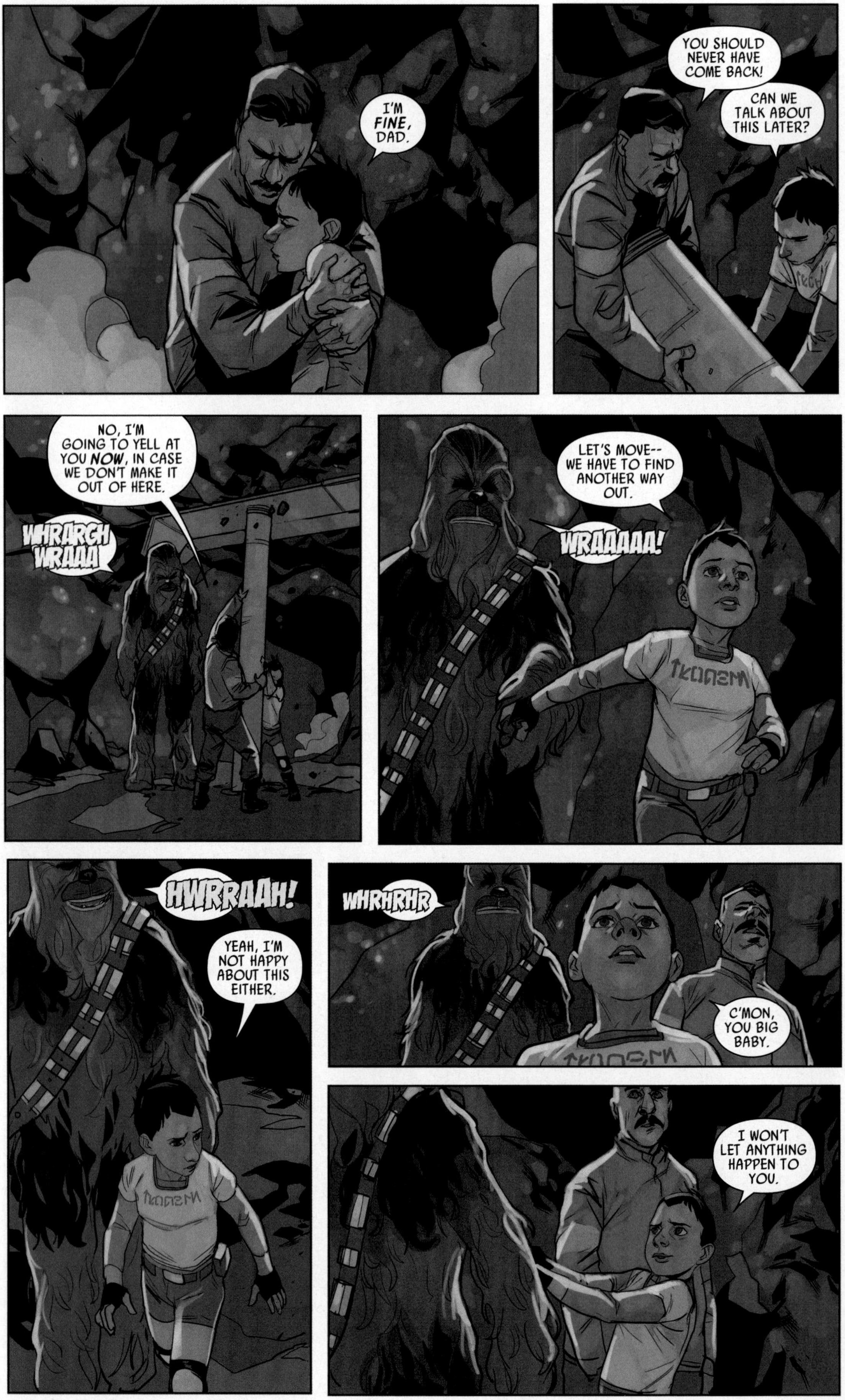
I'M
FINE,
DAD.
YOU SHOULD NEVER HAVE COME BACK!
CAN WE TALK ABOUT THIS LATER?
NO, I'M GOING TO YELL AT YOU NOW, IN CASE WE DON'T MAKE IT OUT OF HERE.
WHRARGH WRAAA
LET'S MOVE-- WE HAVE TO FIND ANOTHER WAY OUT.
WRAAAAA!
HWRRAAH!
YEAH, I'M NOT HAPPY ABOUT THIS EITHER.
WHRHRHR
C'MON, YOU BIG BABY.
I WON'T LET ANYTHING HAPPEN TO YOU.

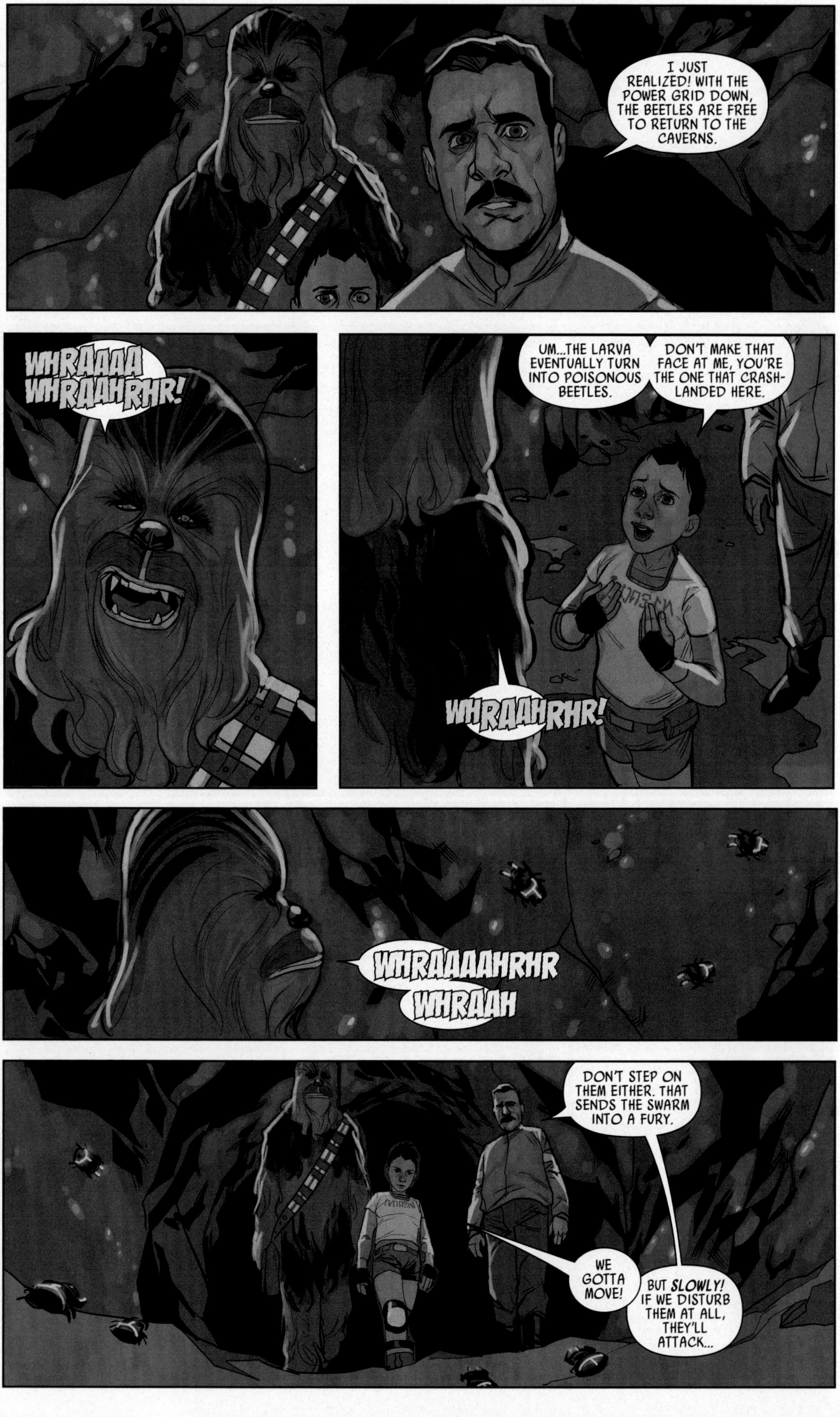
I JUST REALIZED! WITH THE POWER GRID DOWN, THE BEETLES ARE FREE TO RETURN TO THE CAVERNS.
WHRAAAA WHRAAHRHR!
UM...THE LARVA EVENTUALLY TURN INTO POISONOUS BEETLES.
DON'T MAKE THAT FACE AT ME, YOU'RE THE ONE THAT CRASH-LANDED HERE.
WHRAAHRHR!
WHRAAAAHRHR
WHRAAH
DON'T STEP ON THEM EITHER. THAT SENDS THE SWARM INTO A FURY.
WE GOTTA MOVE!
BUT *SLOWLY!* IF WE DISTURB THEM AT ALL, THEY'LL ATTACK...

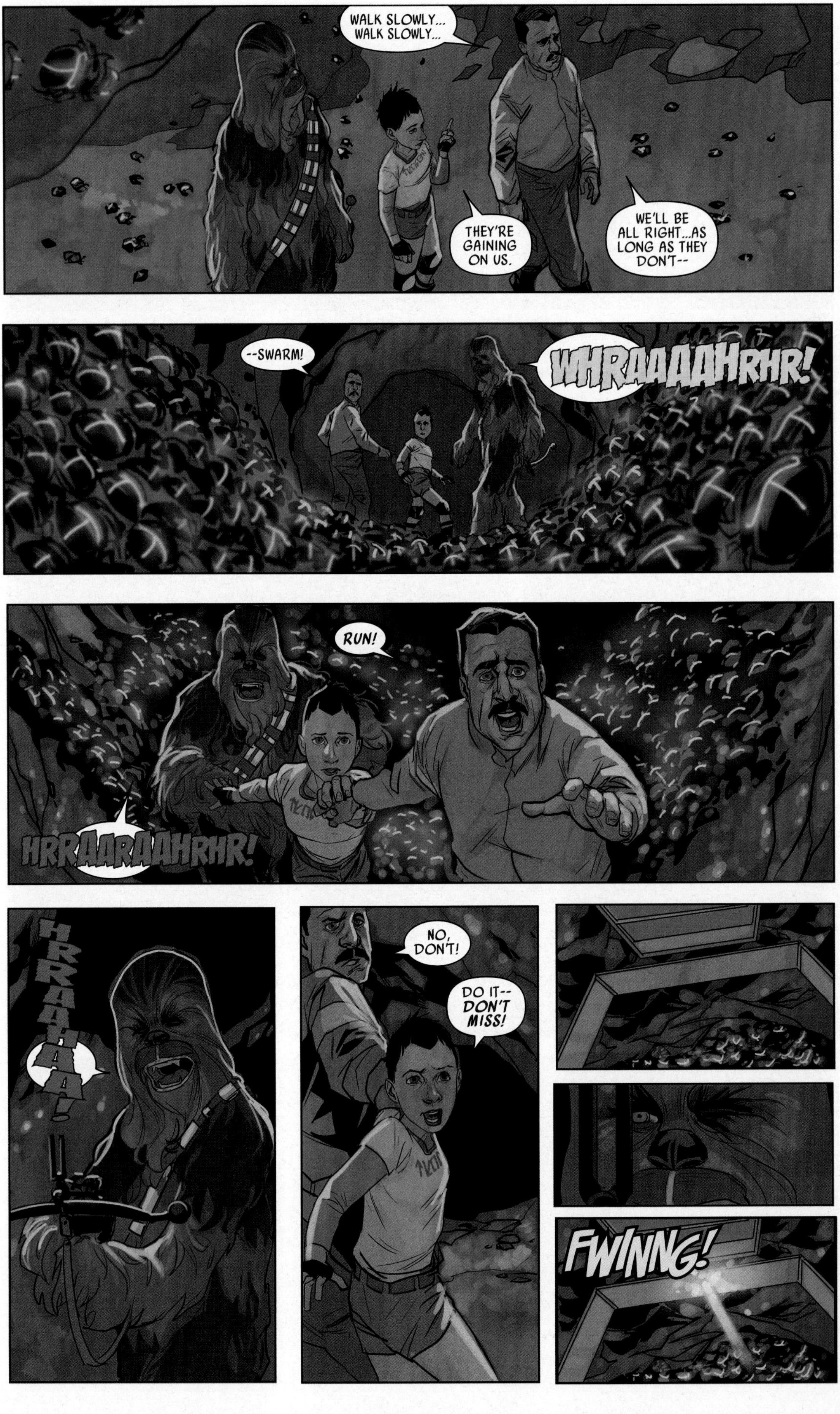
WALK SLOWLY... WALK SLOWLY...
THEY'RE GAINING ON US.
WE'LL BE ALL RIGHT...AS LONG AS THEY DON'T--
--SWARM!
WHRAAAAHRHR!
RUN!
HRRAARAAHRHR!
HRRAAAHAA!
NO, DON'T!
DO IT-- DON'T MISS!
FWINNG!

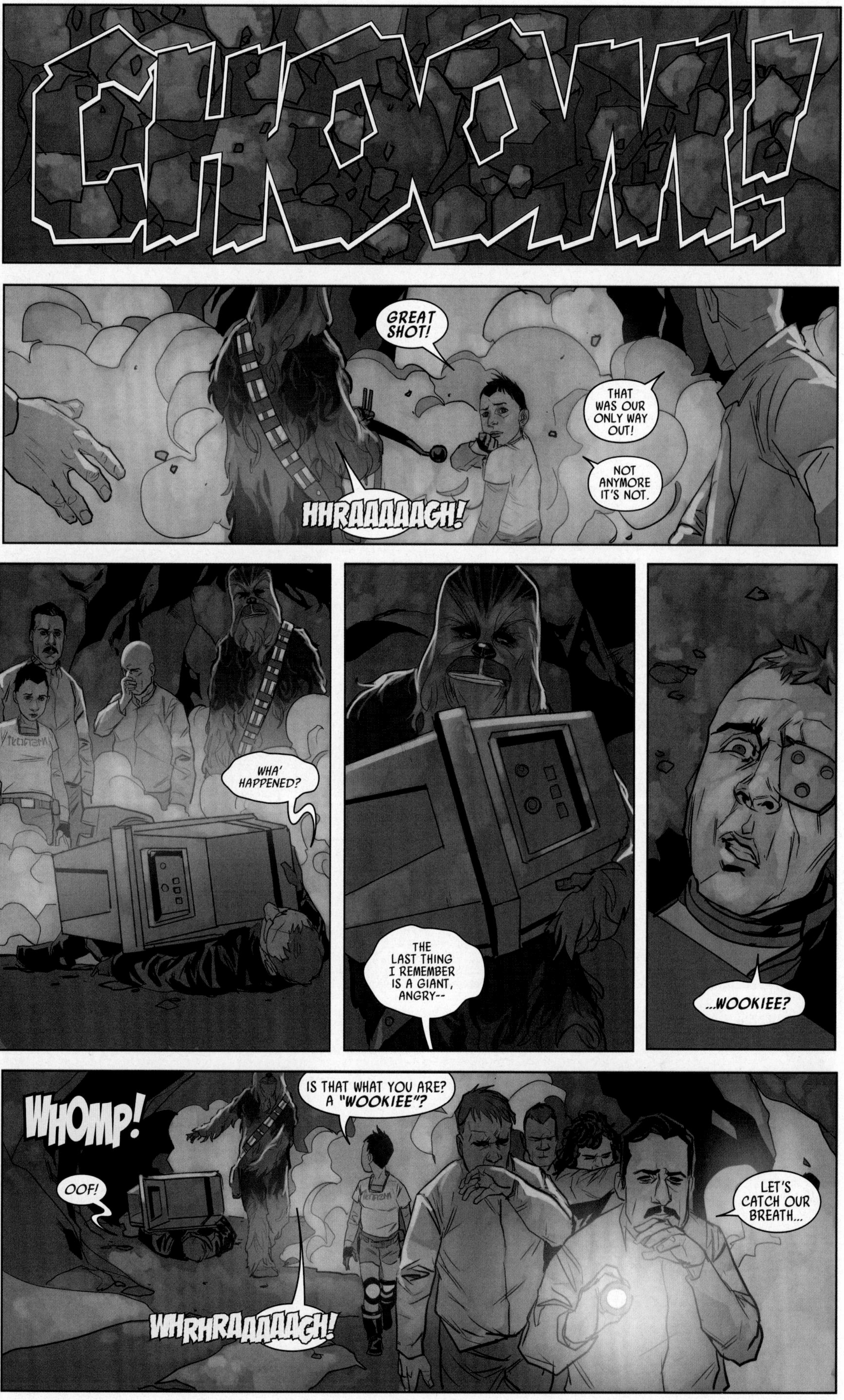
CHOOM!
GREAT SHOT!
THAT WAS OUR ONLY WAY OUT!
NOT ANYMORE IT'S NOT.
HHRAAAAAGH!
WHA' HAPPENED?
THE LAST THING I REMEMBER IS A GIANT, ANGRY--
...WOOKIEE?
WHOMP!
OOF!
IS THAT WHAT YOU ARE? A "WOOKIEE"?
WHRHRAAAAAGH!
LET'S CATCH OUR BREATH...

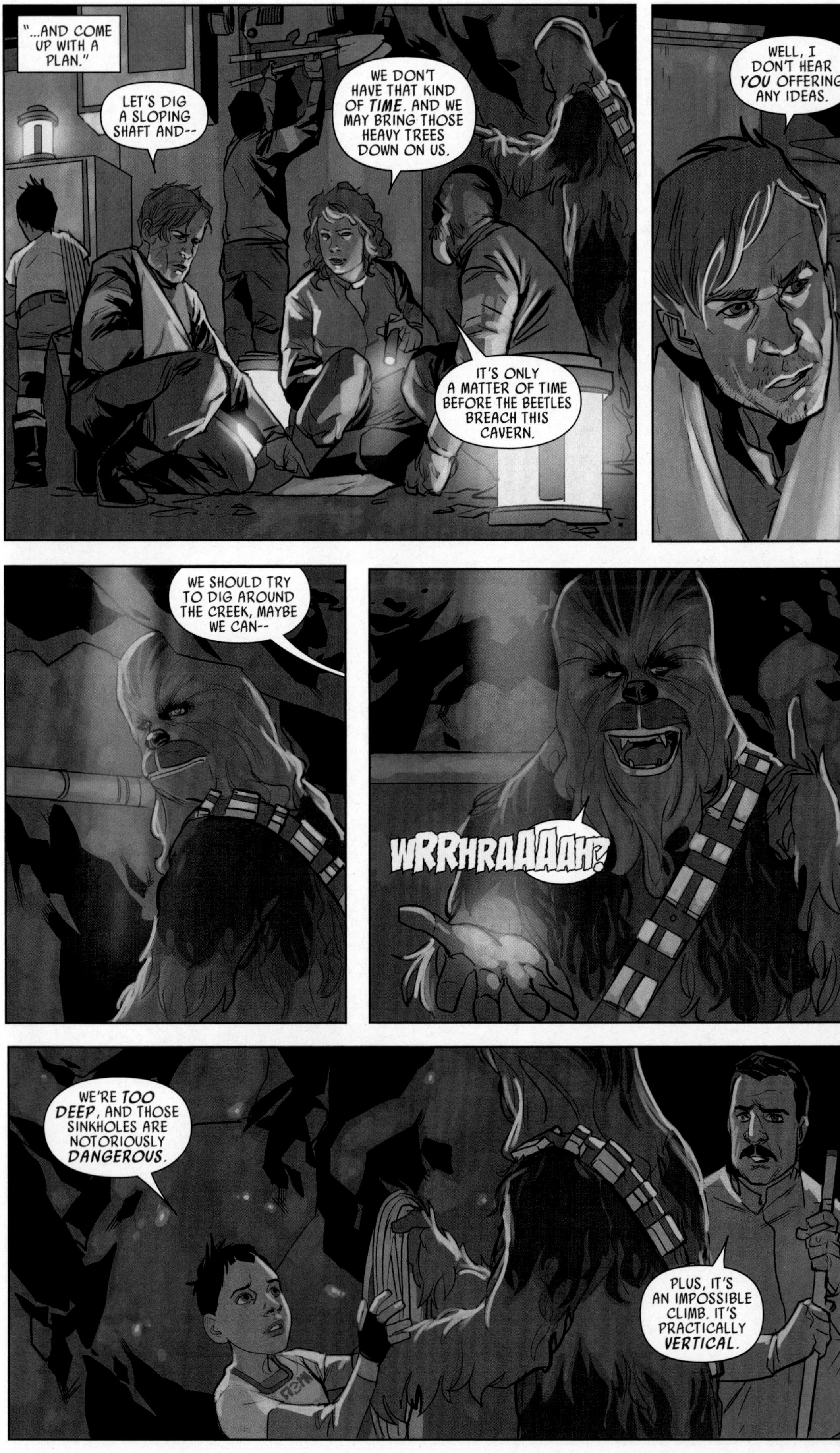
"...AND COME UP WITH A PLAN."
LET'S DIG A SLOPING SHAFT AND--
WE DON'T HAVE THAT KIND OF TIME. AND WE MAY BRING THOSE HEAVY TREES DOWN ON US.
IT'S ONLY A MATTER OF TIME BEFORE THE BEETLES BREACH THIS CAVERN.
WELL, I DON'T HEAR YOU OFFERING ANY IDEAS.
WE SHOULD TRY TO DIG AROUND THE CREEK, MAYBE WE CAN--
WRRHRAAAAH?
WE'RE TOO DEEP, AND THOSE SINKHOLES ARE NOTORIOUSLY DANGEROUS.
PLUS, IT'S AN IMPOSSIBLE CLIMB. IT'S PRACTICALLY VERTICAL.

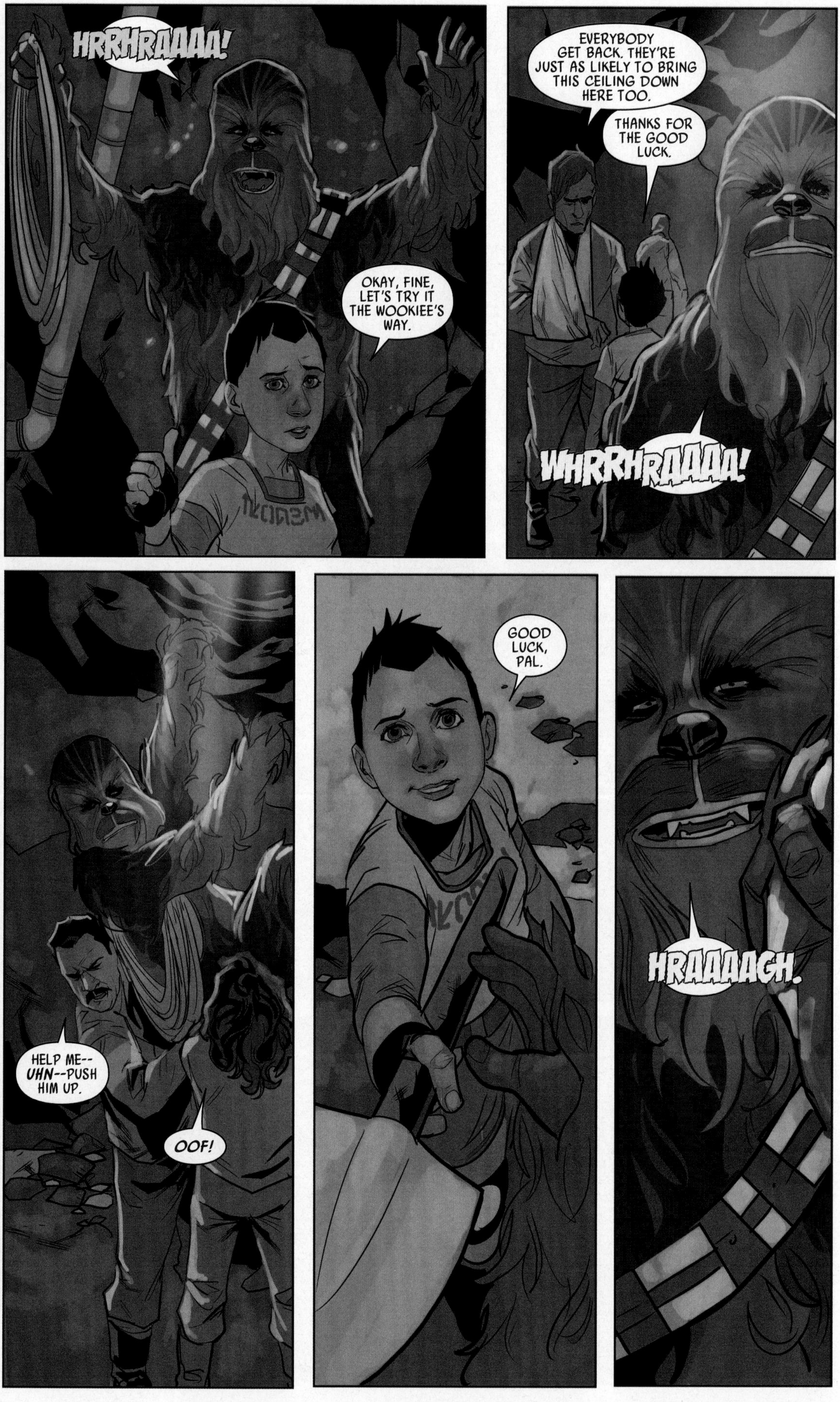
HRRHRAAAA!
OKAY, FINE, LET'S TRY IT THE WOOKIEE'S WAY.
EVERYBODY GET BACK. THEY'RE JUST AS LIKELY TO BRING THIS CEILING DOWN HERE TOO.
THANKS FOR THE GOOD LUCK.
WHRRHRAAAA!
HELP ME-- *UHN*--PUSH HIM UP.
OOF!
GOOD LUCK, PAL.
HRAAAAGH.

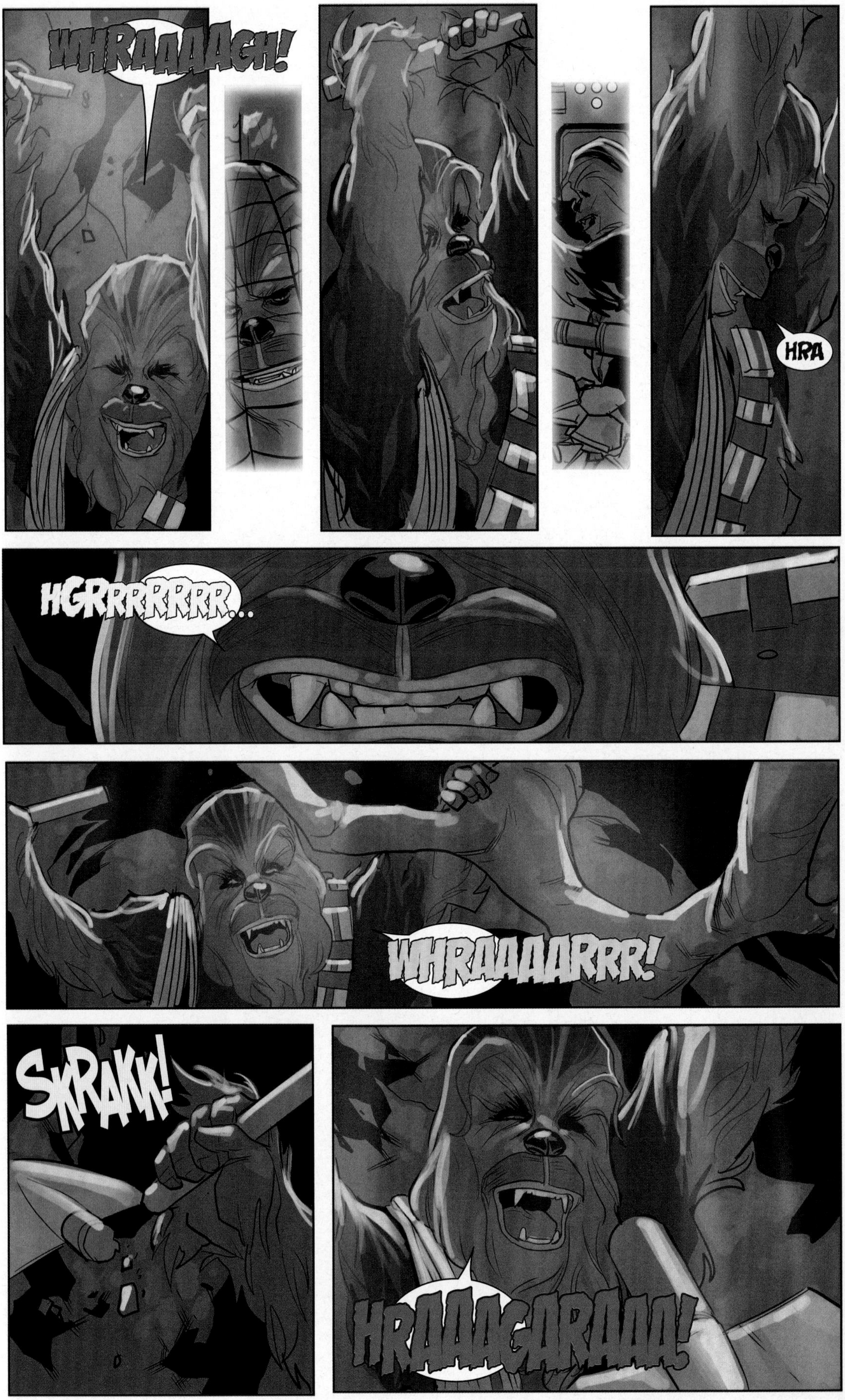
WHRAAAAGH!
HRA
HGRRRRRRR...
WHRAAAARRR!
SKRAKK!
HRAAAGARAAA!

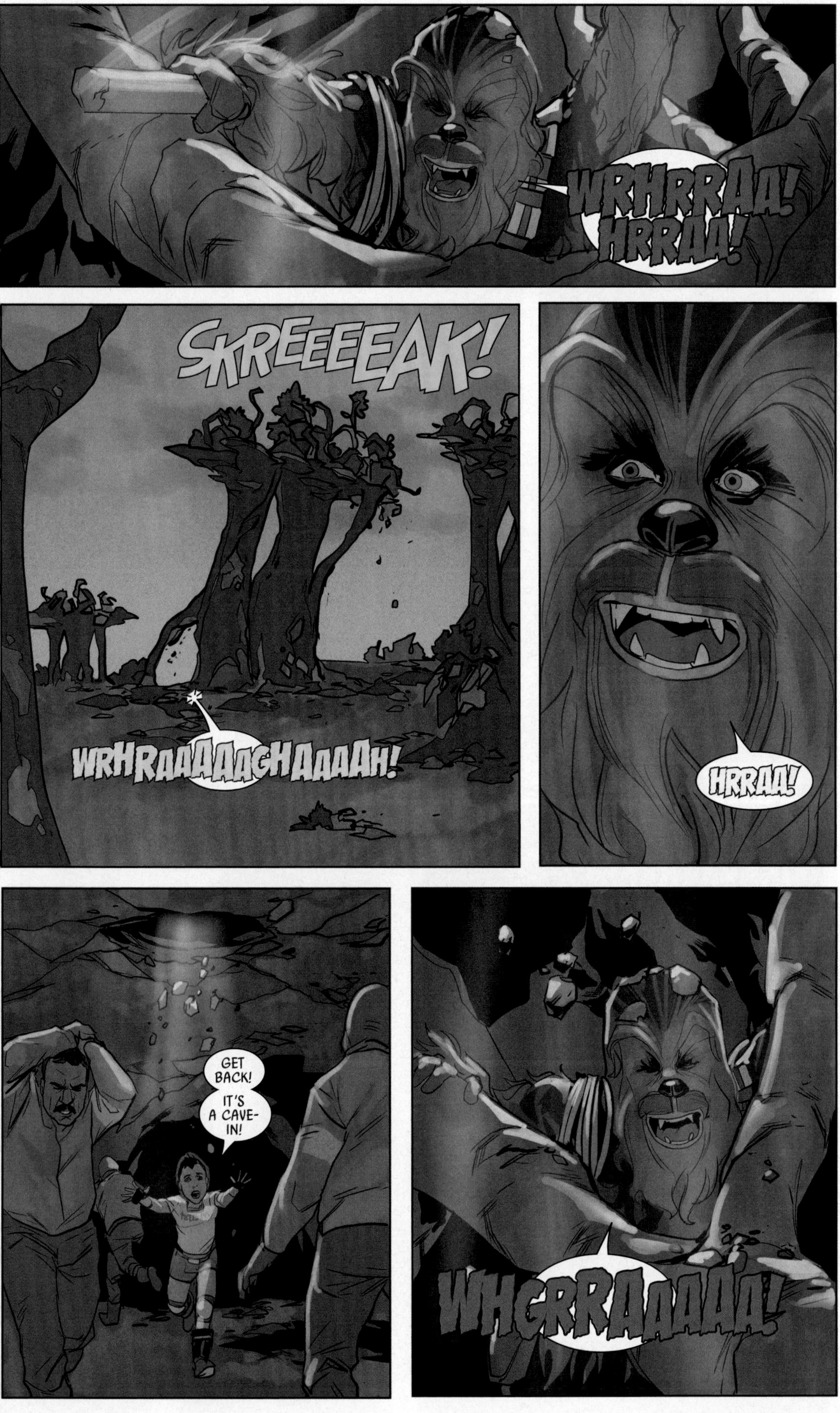
WRHRRAA! HRRAA!
SKREEEEAK!
WRHRAAAAAGHAAAAH!
HRRAA!
GET BACK! IT'S A CAVE-IN!
WHGRRAAAAAA!

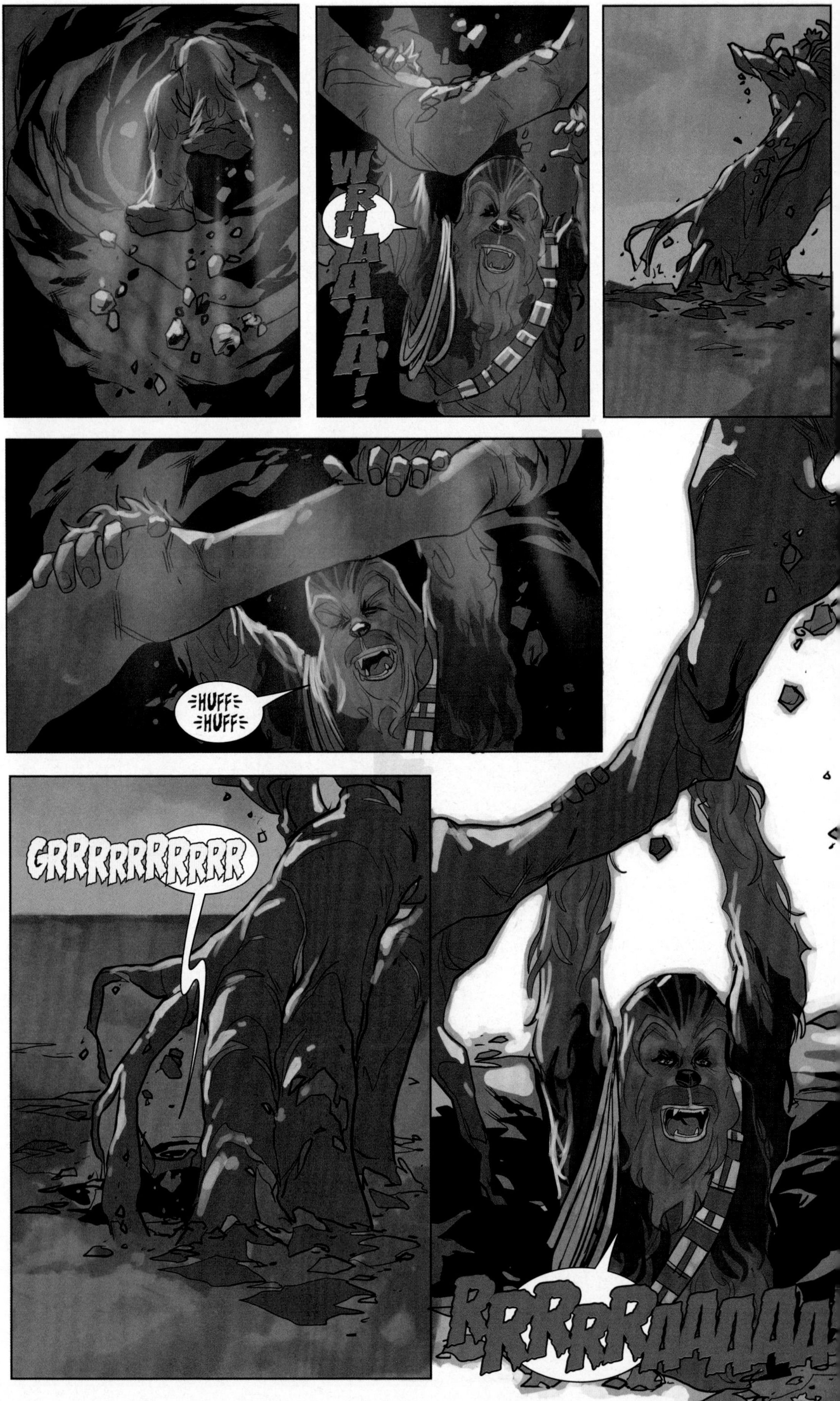
WRHAAAA!
HUFF HUFF
GRRRRRRRRRR
RRRRRAAAAA

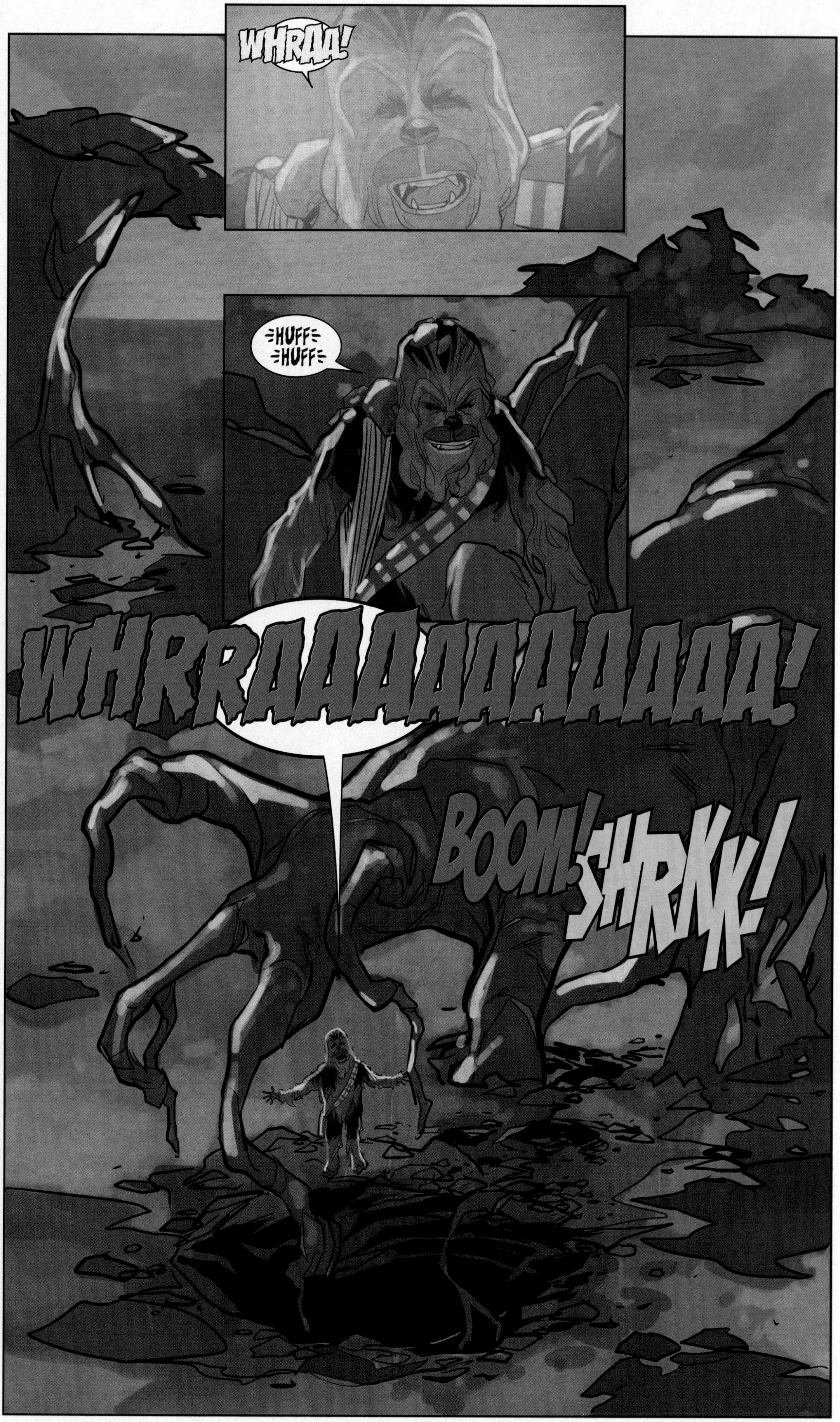
WHRAA!
HUFF
HUFF
WHRRAAAAAAAAAAA!
BOOM!
SHRKK!

WHRAA RAAAH WRAH AAAHG
YOU OKAY? ARE YOU HURT?
WOOKIEE?
YES!
HE DID IT!
WE'RE SAVED!

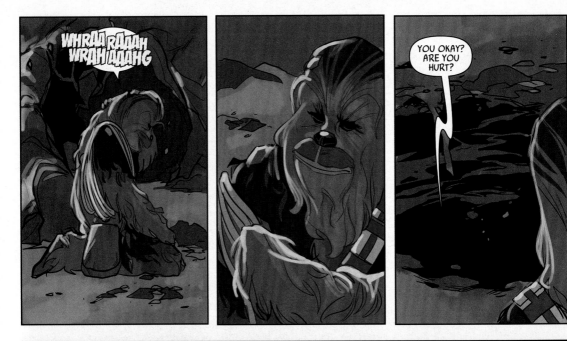

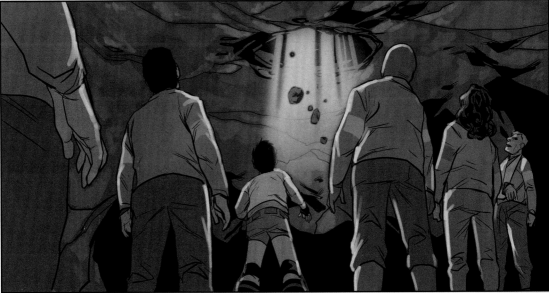

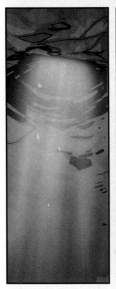

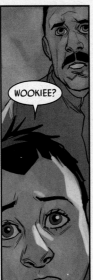

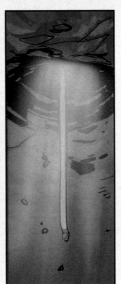

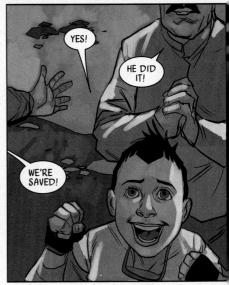

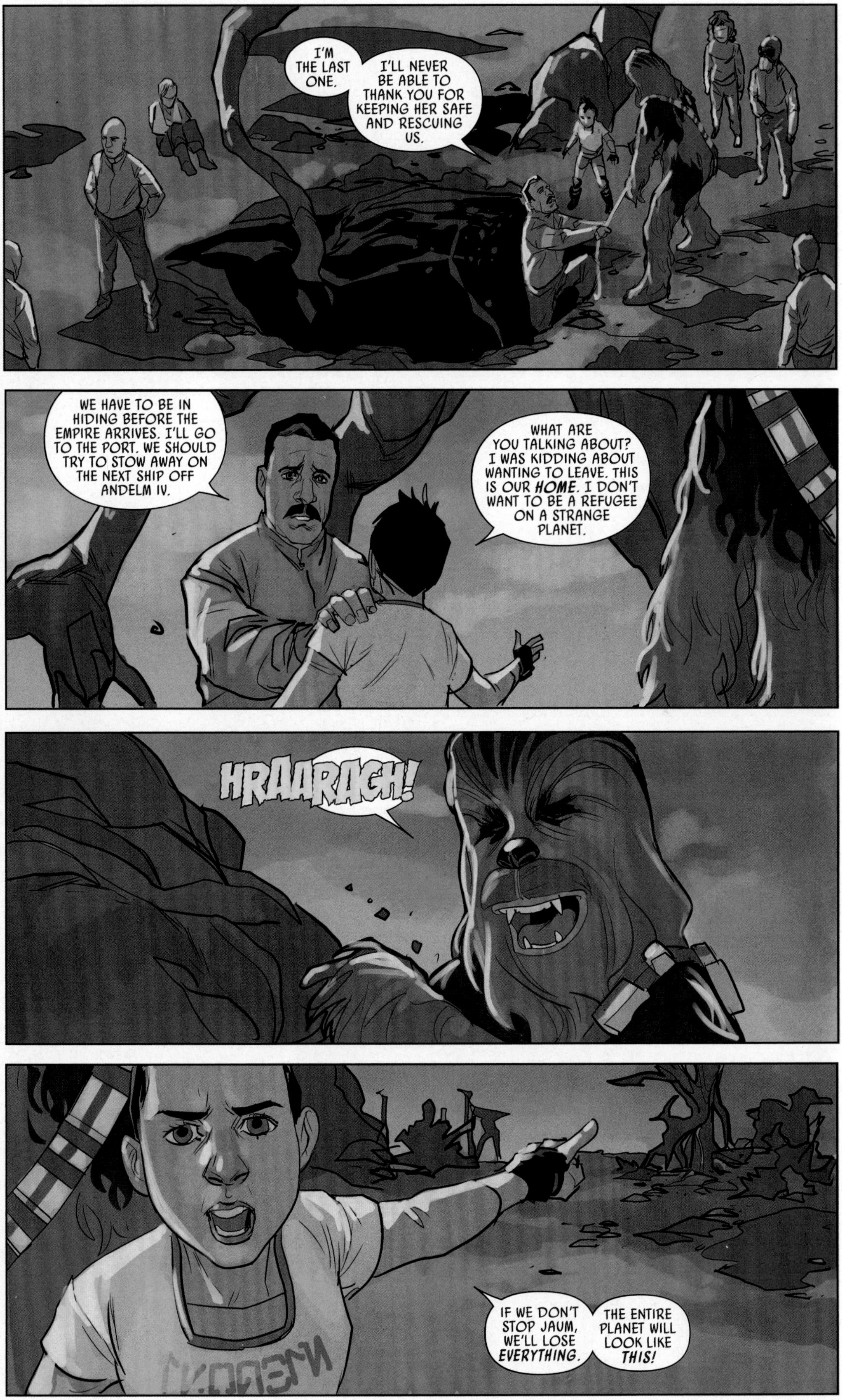
I'M THE LAST ONE.
I'LL NEVER BE ABLE TO THANK YOU FOR KEEPING HER SAFE AND RESCUING US.
WE HAVE TO BE IN HIDING BEFORE THE EMPIRE ARRIVES. I'LL GO TO THE PORT. WE SHOULD TRY TO STOW AWAY ON THE NEXT SHIP OFF ANDELM IV.
WHAT ARE YOU TALKING ABOUT? I WAS KIDDING ABOUT WANTING TO LEAVE. THIS IS OUR *HOME*. I DON'T WANT TO BE A REFUGEE ON A STRANGE PLANET.
HRAARAGH!
IF WE DON'T STOP JAUM, WE'LL LOSE *EVERYTHING*.
THE ENTIRE PLANET WILL LOOK LIKE *THIS!*

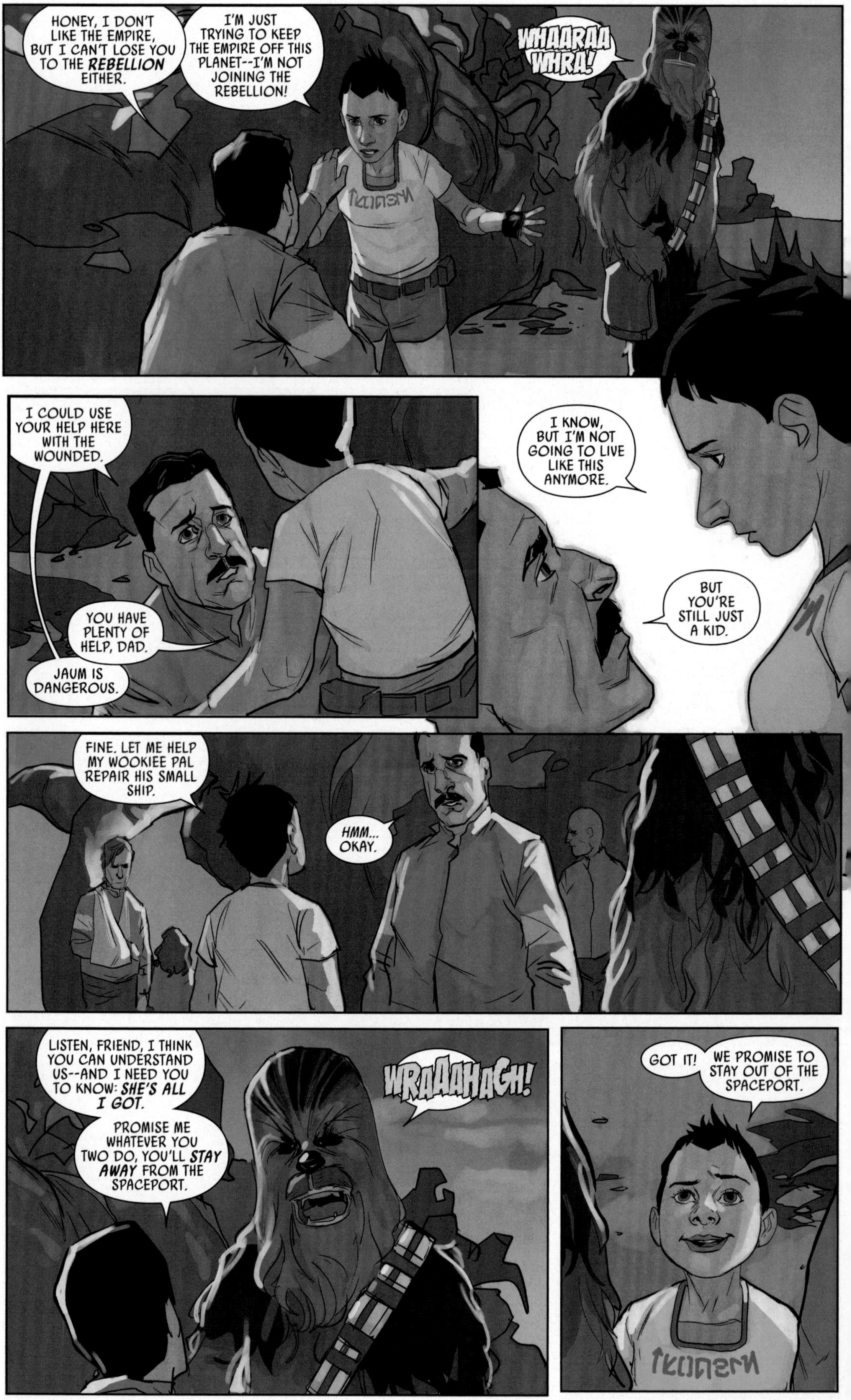
HONEY, I DON'T LIKE THE EMPIRE, BUT I CAN'T LOSE YOU TO THE REBELLION EITHER.
I'M JUST TRYING TO KEEP THE EMPIRE OFF THIS PLANET--I'M NOT JOINING THE REBELLION!
WHAARAA WHRA!
I COULD USE YOUR HELP HERE WITH THE WOUNDED.
YOU HAVE PLENTY OF HELP, DAD.
JAUM IS DANGEROUS.
I KNOW, BUT I'M NOT GOING TO LIVE LIKE THIS ANYMORE.
BUT YOU'RE STILL JUST A KID.
FINE. LET ME HELP MY WOOKIEE PAL REPAIR HIS SMALL SHIP.
HMM... OKAY.
LISTEN, FRIEND, I THINK YOU CAN UNDERSTAND US--AND I NEED YOU TO KNOW: SHE'S ALL I GOT.
PROMISE ME WHATEVER YOU TWO DO, YOU'LL STAY AWAY FROM THE SPACEPORT.
WRAAAHAGH!
GOT IT!
WE PROMISE TO STAY OUT OF THE SPACEPORT.

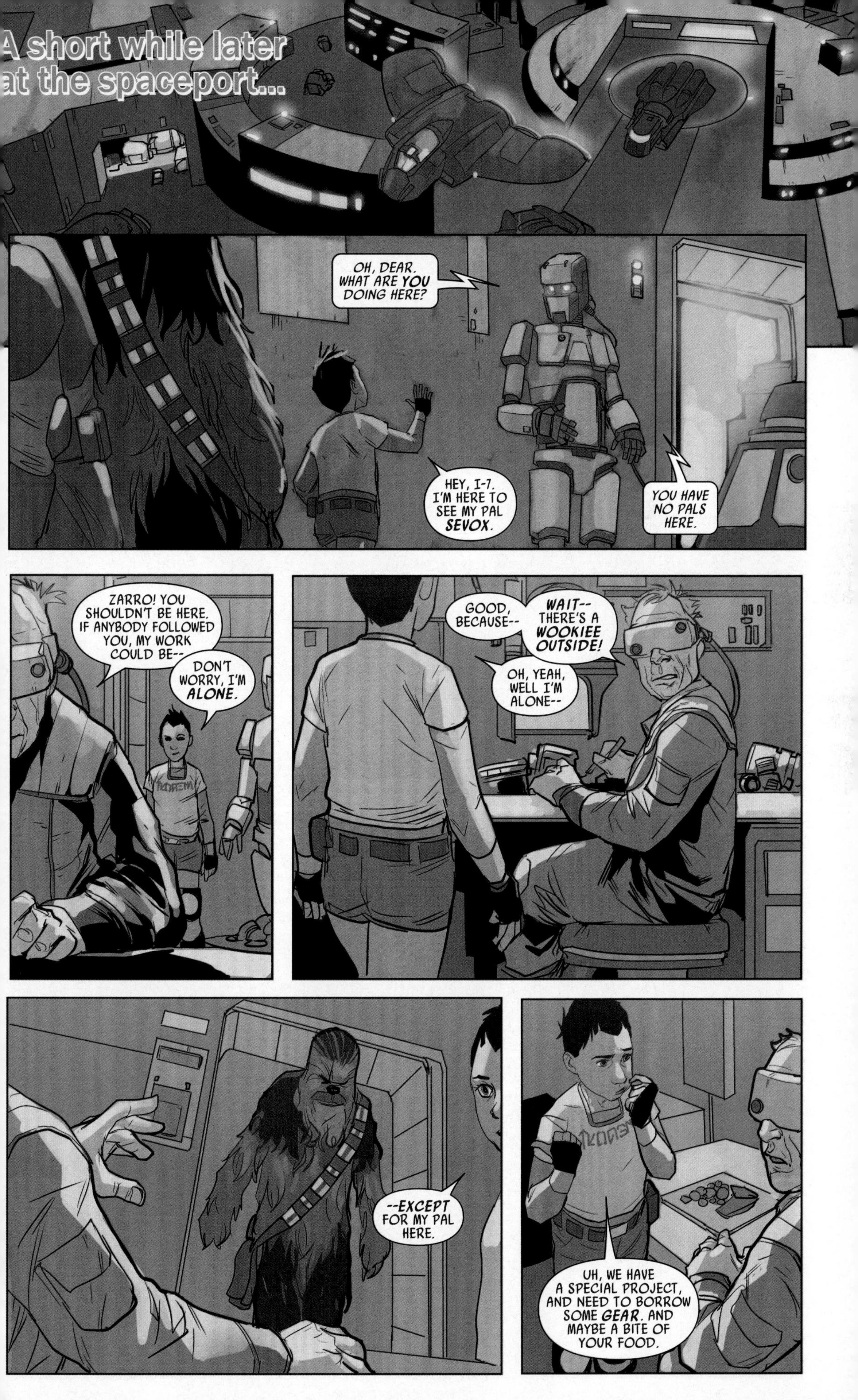
A short while later at the spaceport...
OH, DEAR. WHAT ARE YOU DOING HERE?
HEY, I-7. I'M HERE TO SEE MY PAL SEVOX.
YOU HAVE NO PALS HERE.
ZARRO! YOU SHOULDN'T BE HERE. IF ANYBODY FOLLOWED YOU, MY WORK COULD BE--
DON'T WORRY, I'M ALONE.
GOOD, BECAUSE--
WAIT-- THERE'S A WOOKIEE OUTSIDE!
OH, YEAH, WELL I'M ALONE--
--EXCEPT FOR MY PAL HERE.
UH, WE HAVE A SPECIAL PROJECT, AND NEED TO BORROW SOME GEAR. AND MAYBE A BITE OF YOUR FOOD.

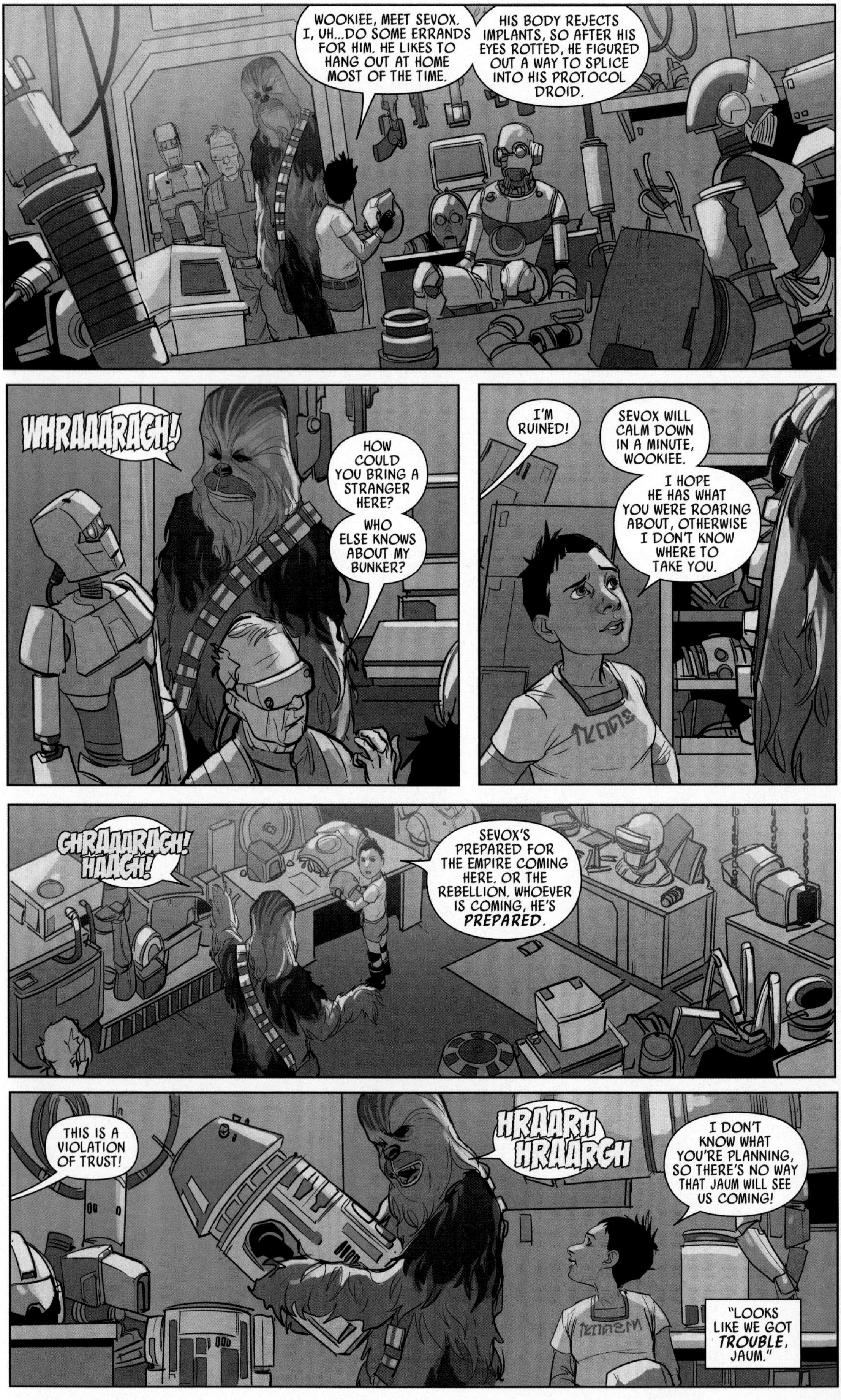
WOOKIEE, MEET SEVOX. I, UH...DO SOME ERRANDS FOR HIM. HE LIKES TO HANG OUT AT HOME MOST OF THE TIME.
HIS BODY REJECTS IMPLANTS, SO AFTER HIS EYES ROTTED, HE FIGURED OUT A WAY TO SPLICE INTO HIS PROTOCOL DROID.
WHRAAARAGH!
HOW COULD YOU BRING A STRANGER HERE?
WHO ELSE KNOWS ABOUT MY BUNKER?
I'M RUINED!
SEVOX WILL CALM DOWN IN A MINUTE, WOOKIEE.
I HOPE HE HAS WHAT YOU WERE ROARING ABOUT, OTHERWISE I DON'T KNOW WHERE TO TAKE YOU.
GHRAAARAGH! HAAGH!
SEVOX'S PREPARED FOR THE EMPIRE COMING HERE. OR THE REBELLION. WHOEVER IS COMING, HE'S PREPARED.
THIS IS A VIOLATION OF TRUST!
HRAARH HRAARGH
I DON'T KNOW WHAT YOU'RE PLANNING, SO THERE'S NO WAY THAT JAUM WILL SEE US COMING!
"LOOKS LIKE WE GOT TROUBLE, JAUM."

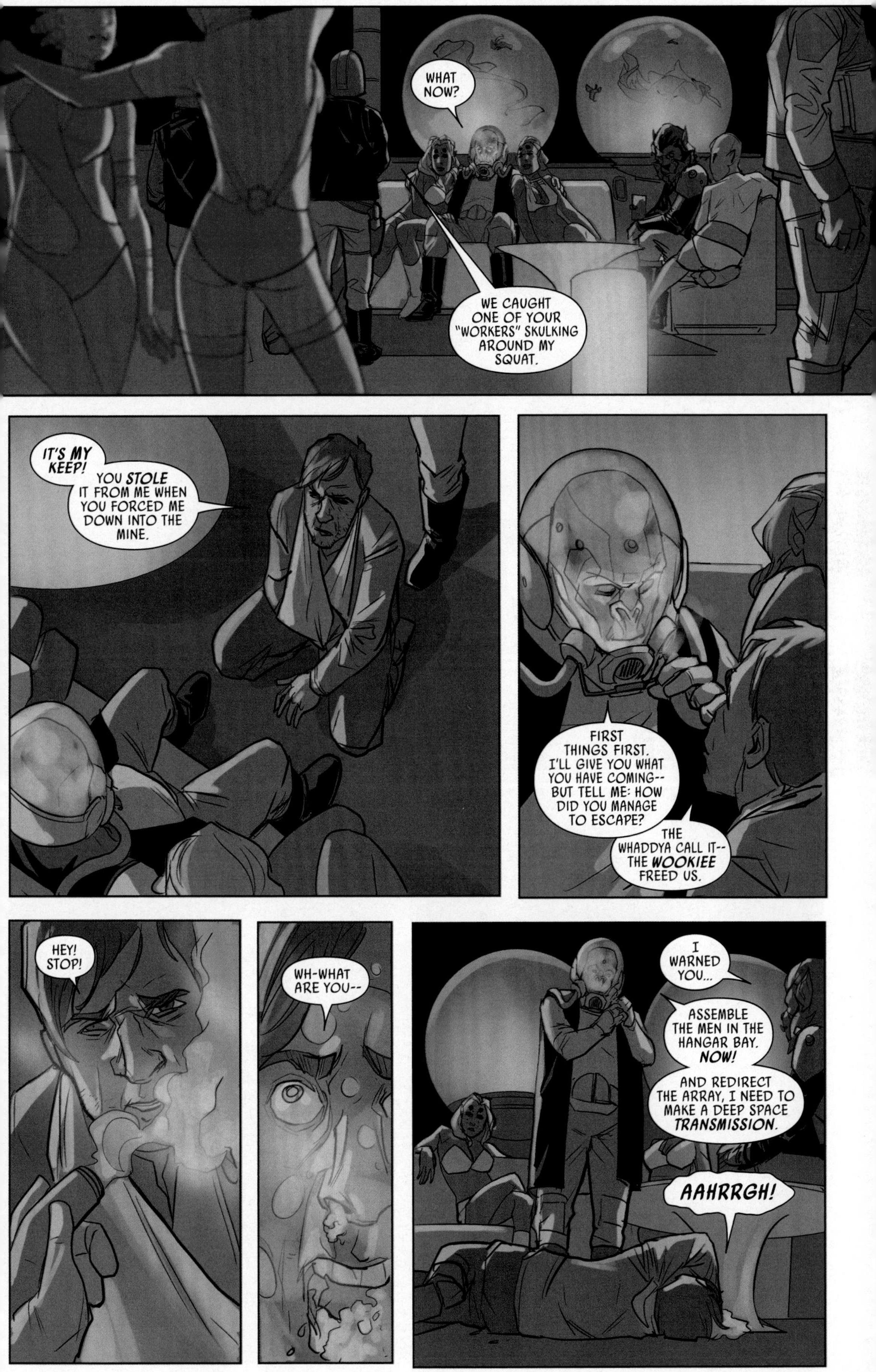
WHAT NOW?
WE CAUGHT ONE OF YOUR "WORKERS" SKULKING AROUND MY SQUAT.
IT'S MY KEEP!
YOU STOLE IT FROM ME WHEN YOU FORCED ME DOWN INTO THE MINE.
FIRST THINGS FIRST. I'LL GIVE YOU WHAT YOU HAVE COMING-- BUT TELL ME: HOW DID YOU MANAGE TO ESCAPE?
THE WHADDYA CALL IT-- THE WOOKIEE FREED US.
HEY! STOP!
WH-WHAT ARE YOU--
I WARNED YOU...
ASSEMBLE THE MEN IN THE HANGAR BAY. NOW!
AND REDIRECT THE ARRAY, I NEED TO MAKE A DEEP SPACE TRANSMISSION.
AAHRRGH!

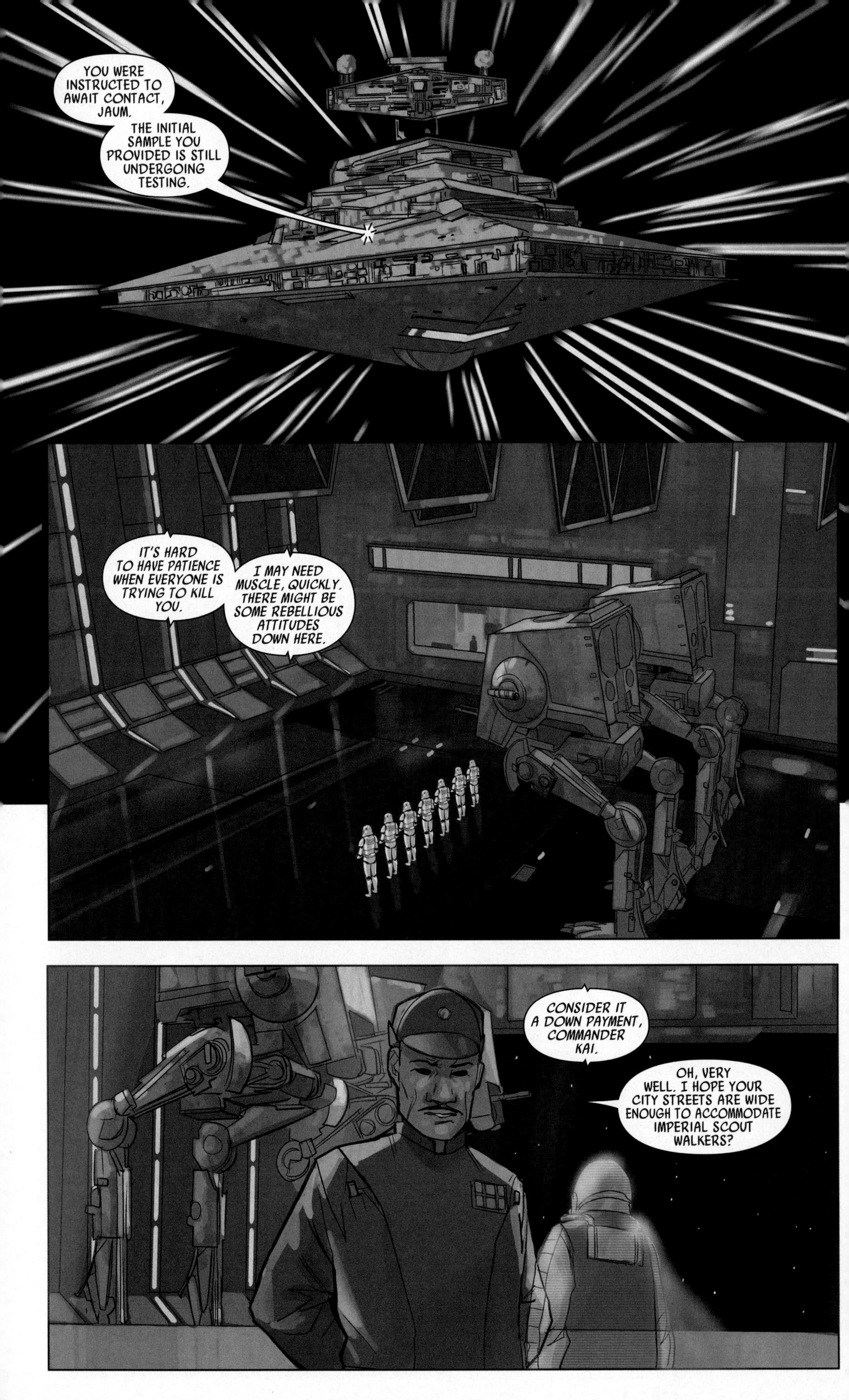
YOU WERE INSTRUCTED TO AWAIT CONTACT, JAUM.
THE INITIAL SAMPLE YOU PROVIDED IS STILL UNDERGOING TESTING.
IT'S HARD TO HAVE PATIENCE WHEN EVERYONE IS TRYING TO KILL YOU.
I MAY NEED MUSCLE, QUICKLY. THERE MIGHT BE SOME REBELLIOUS ATTITUDES DOWN HERE.
CONSIDER IT A DOWN PAYMENT, COMMANDER KAI.
OH, VERY WELL. I HOPE YOUR CITY STREETS ARE WIDE ENOUGH TO ACCOMMODATE IMPERIAL SCOUT WALKERS?

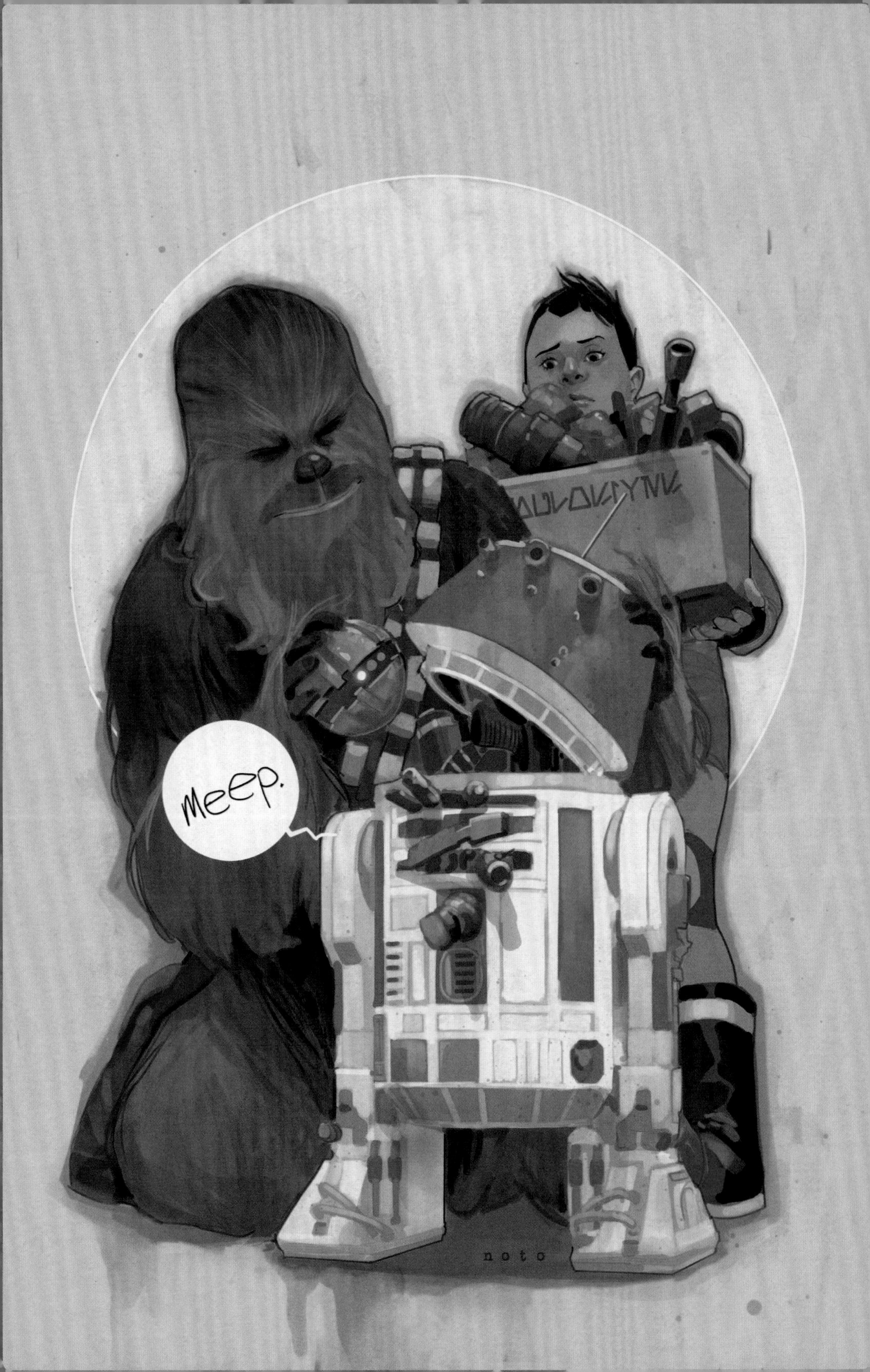
Meep.
noto

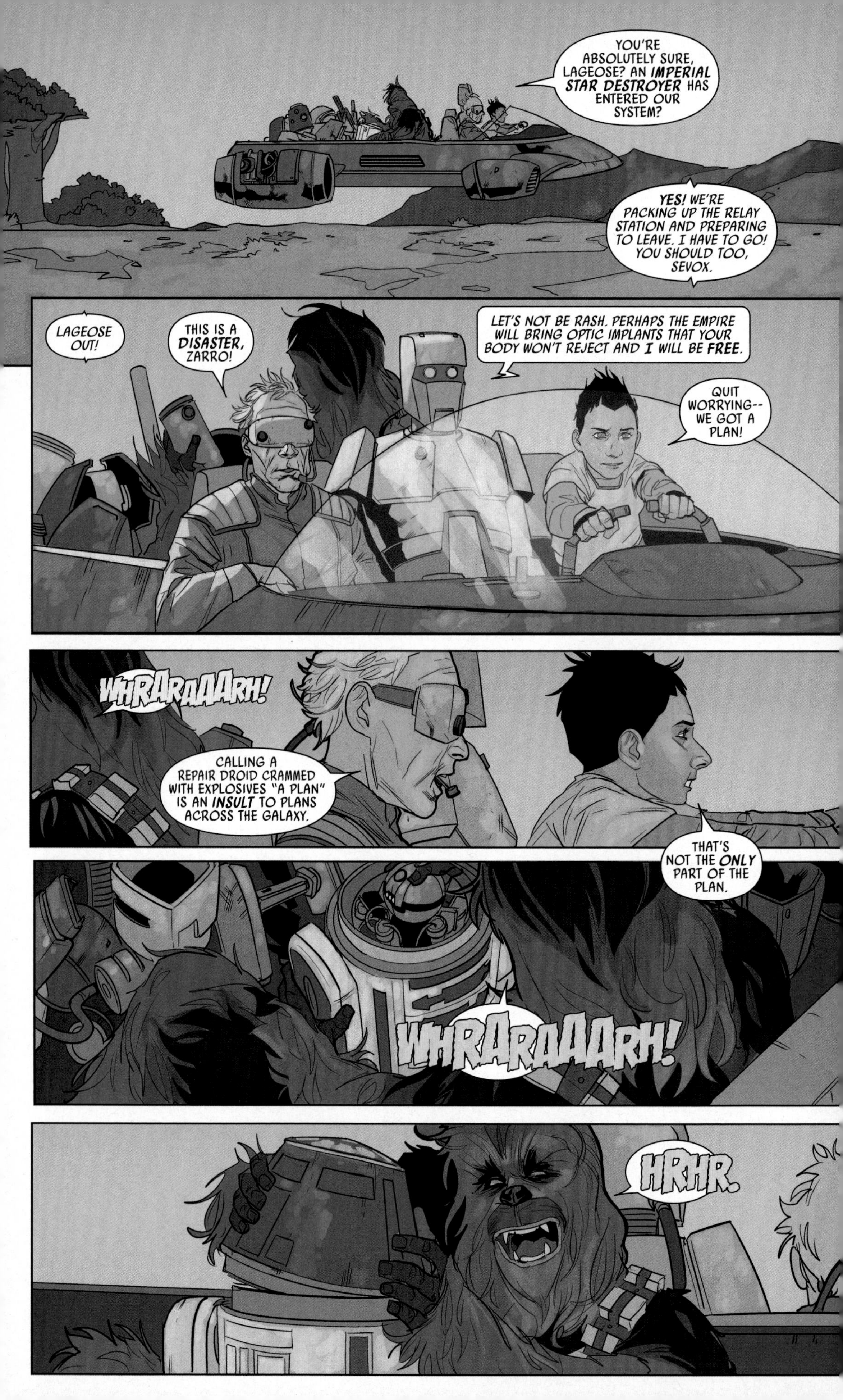
YOU'RE ABSOLUTELY SURE, LAGEOSE? AN IMPERIAL STAR DESTROYER HAS ENTERED OUR SYSTEM?
YES! WE'RE PACKING UP THE RELAY STATION AND PREPARING TO LEAVE. I HAVE TO GO! YOU SHOULD TOO, SEVOX.
LAGEOSE OUT!
THIS IS A DISASTER, ZARRO!
LET'S NOT BE RASH. PERHAPS THE EMPIRE WILL BRING OPTIC IMPLANTS THAT YOUR BODY WON'T REJECT AND I WILL BE FREE.
QUIT WORRYING-- WE GOT A PLAN!
WHRARAAARH!
CALLING A REPAIR DROID CRAMMED WITH EXPLOSIVES "A PLAN" IS AN INSULT TO PLANS ACROSS THE GALAXY.
THAT'S NOT THE ONLY PART OF THE PLAN.
WHRARAAARH!
HRHR.

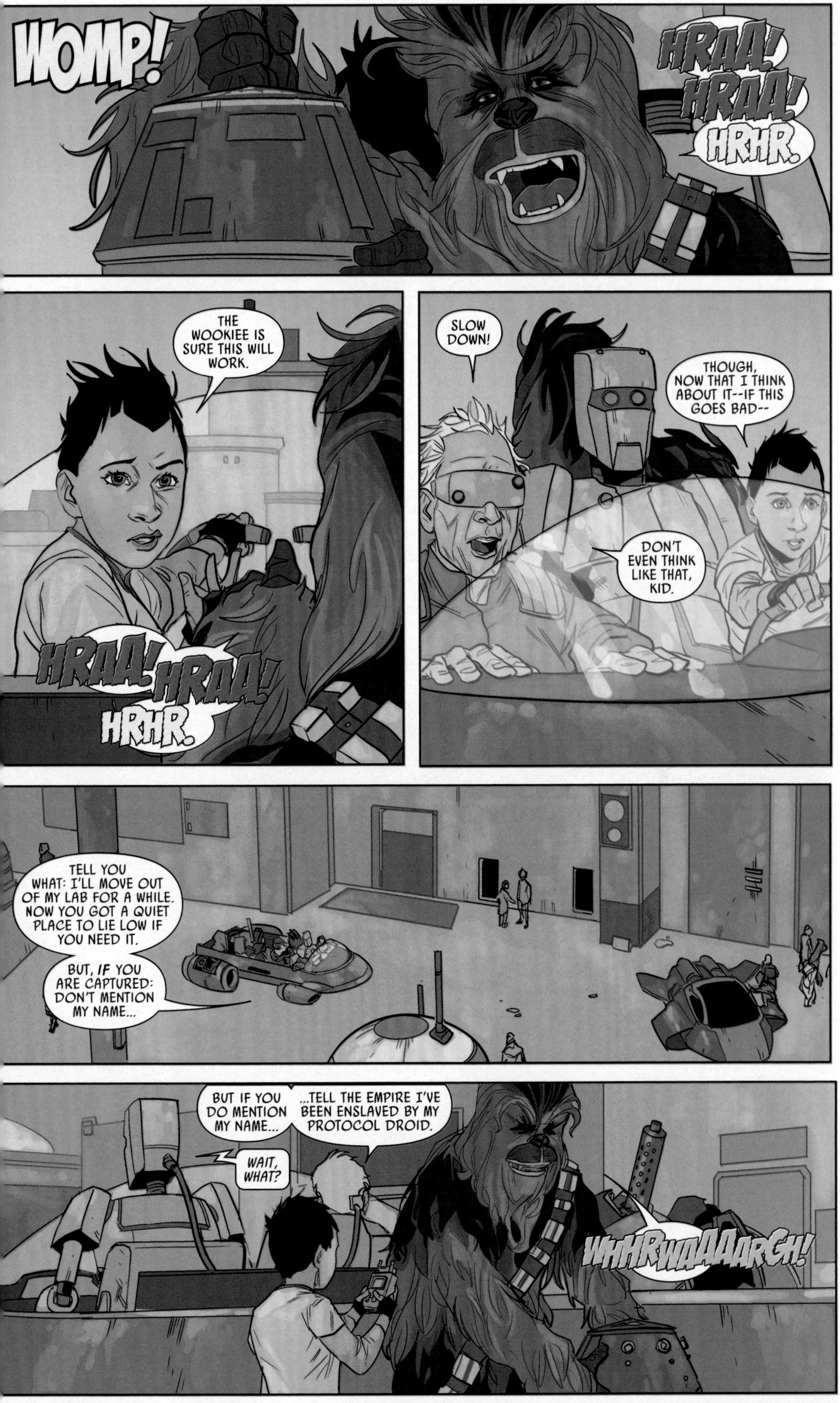
WOMP!
HRAA! HRAA! HRHR.
THE WOOKIEE IS SURE THIS WILL WORK.
HRAA! HRAA! HRHR.
SLOW DOWN!
THOUGH, NOW THAT I THINK ABOUT IT--IF THIS GOES BAD--
DON'T EVEN THINK LIKE THAT, KID.
TELL YOU WHAT: I'LL MOVE OUT OF MY LAB FOR A WHILE. NOW YOU GOT A QUIET PLACE TO LIE LOW IF YOU NEED IT.
BUT, IF YOU ARE CAPTURED: DON'T MENTION MY NAME...
BUT IF YOU DO MENTION MY NAME...
...TELL THE EMPIRE I'VE BEEN ENSLAVED BY MY PROTOCOL DROID.
WAIT, WHAT?
WHHRWAAAARGH!

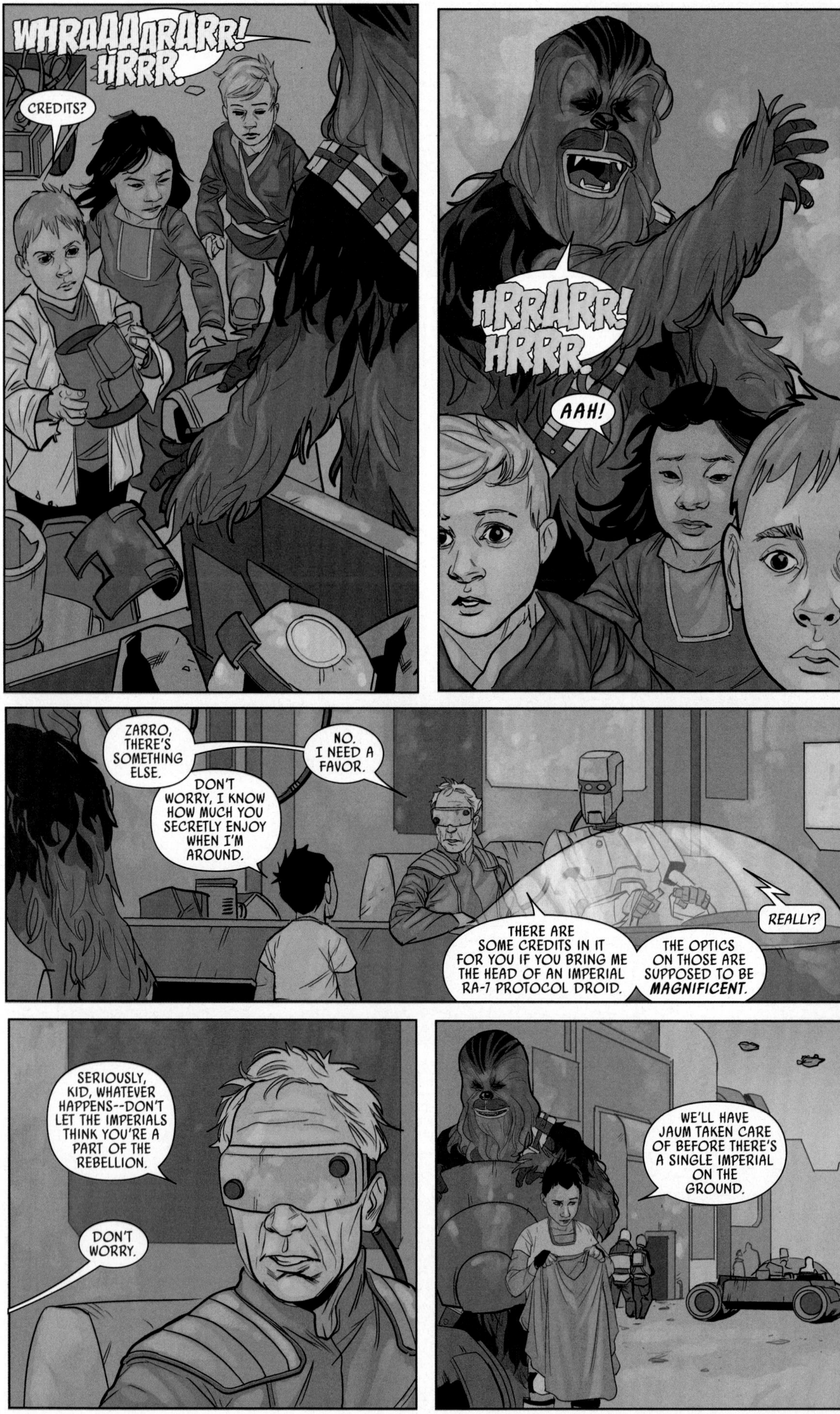
WHRAAAARARR! HRRR.
CREDITS?
HRRARR! HRRR.
AAH!
ZARRO, THERE'S SOMETHING ELSE.
NO. I NEED A FAVOR.
DON'T WORRY, I KNOW HOW MUCH YOU SECRETLY ENJOY WHEN I'M AROUND.
THERE ARE SOME CREDITS IN IT FOR YOU IF YOU BRING ME THE HEAD OF AN IMPERIAL RA-7 PROTOCOL DROID.
THE OPTICS ON THOSE ARE SUPPOSED TO BE MAGNIFICENT.
REALLY?
SERIOUSLY, KID, WHATEVER HAPPENS--DON'T LET THE IMPERIALS THINK YOU'RE A PART OF THE REBELLION.
DON'T WORRY.
WE'LL HAVE JAUM TAKEN CARE OF BEFORE THERE'S A SINGLE IMPERIAL ON THE GROUND.

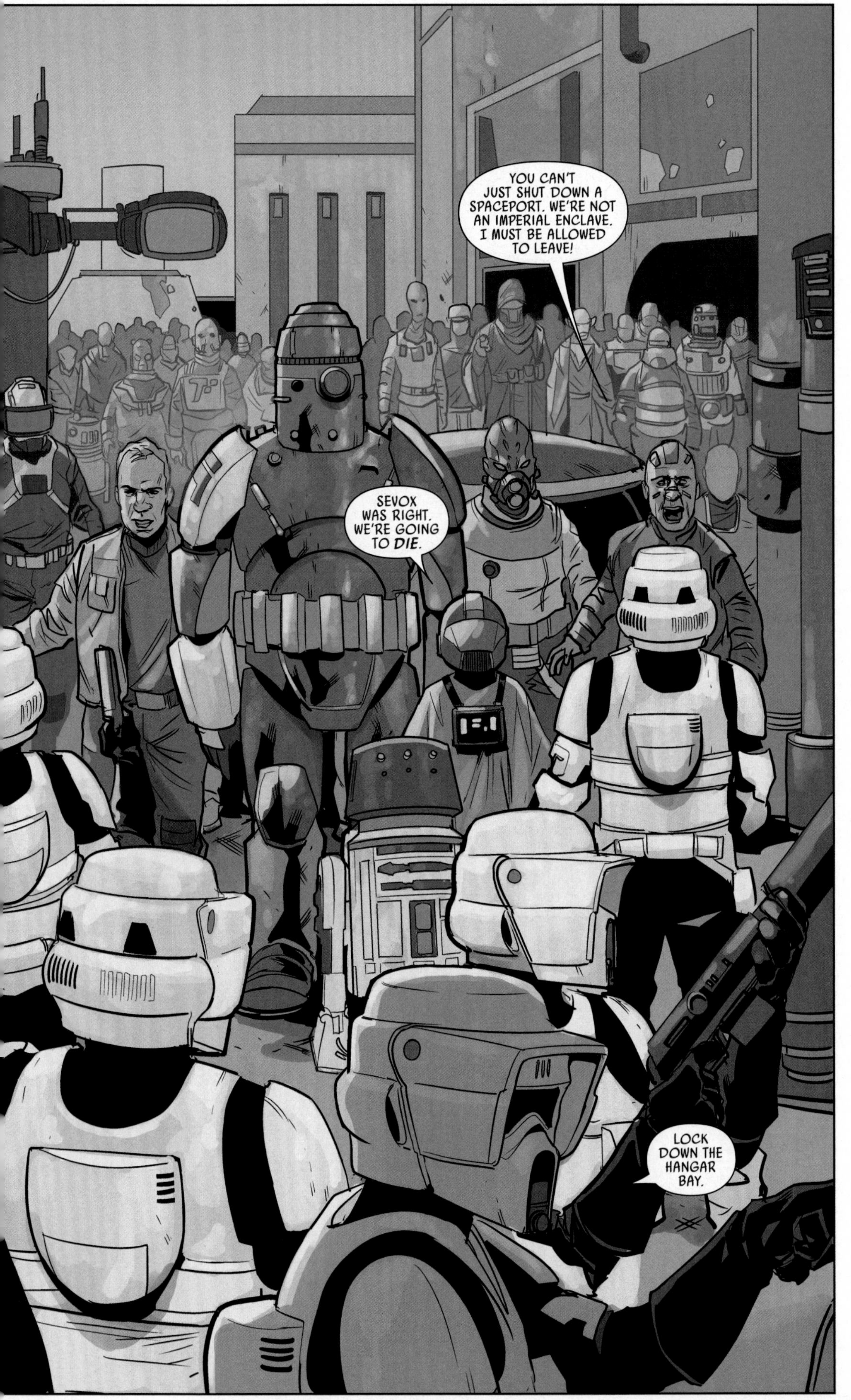
YOU CAN'T JUST SHUT DOWN A SPACEPORT. WE'RE NOT AN IMPERIAL ENCLAVE. I MUST BE ALLOWED TO LEAVE!
SEVOX WAS RIGHT. WE'RE GOING TO *DIE*.
LOCK DOWN THE HANGAR BAY.

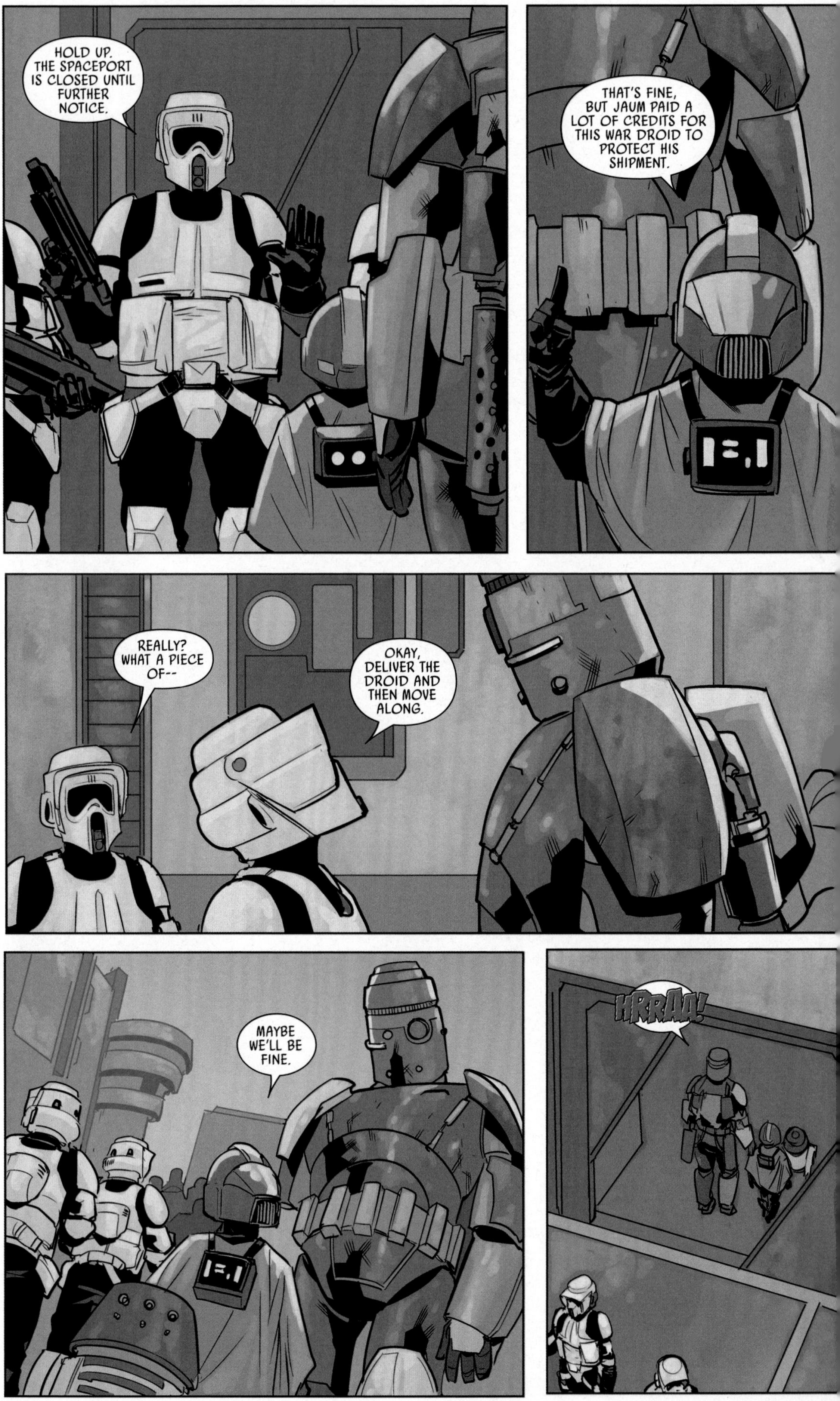
HOLD UP. THE SPACEPORT IS CLOSED UNTIL FURTHER NOTICE.
THAT'S FINE, BUT JAUM PAID A LOT OF CREDITS FOR THIS WAR DROID TO PROTECT HIS SHIPMENT.
REALLY? WHAT A PIECE OF--
OKAY, DELIVER THE DROID AND THEN MOVE ALONG.
MAYBE WE'LL BE FINE.
HRRAA!

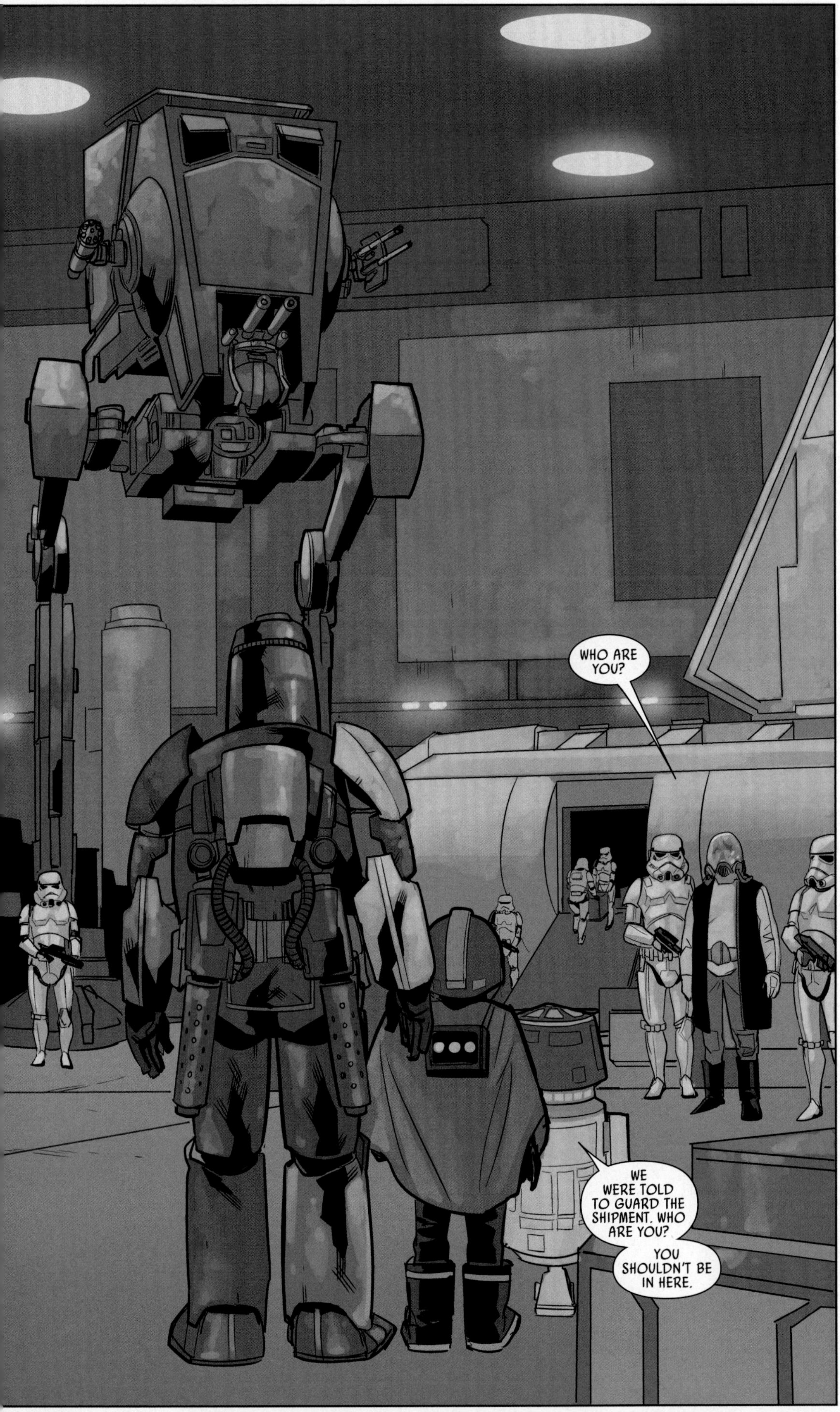
WHO ARE YOU?
WE WERE TOLD TO GUARD THE SHIPMENT. WHO ARE YOU?
YOU SHOULDN'T BE IN HERE.

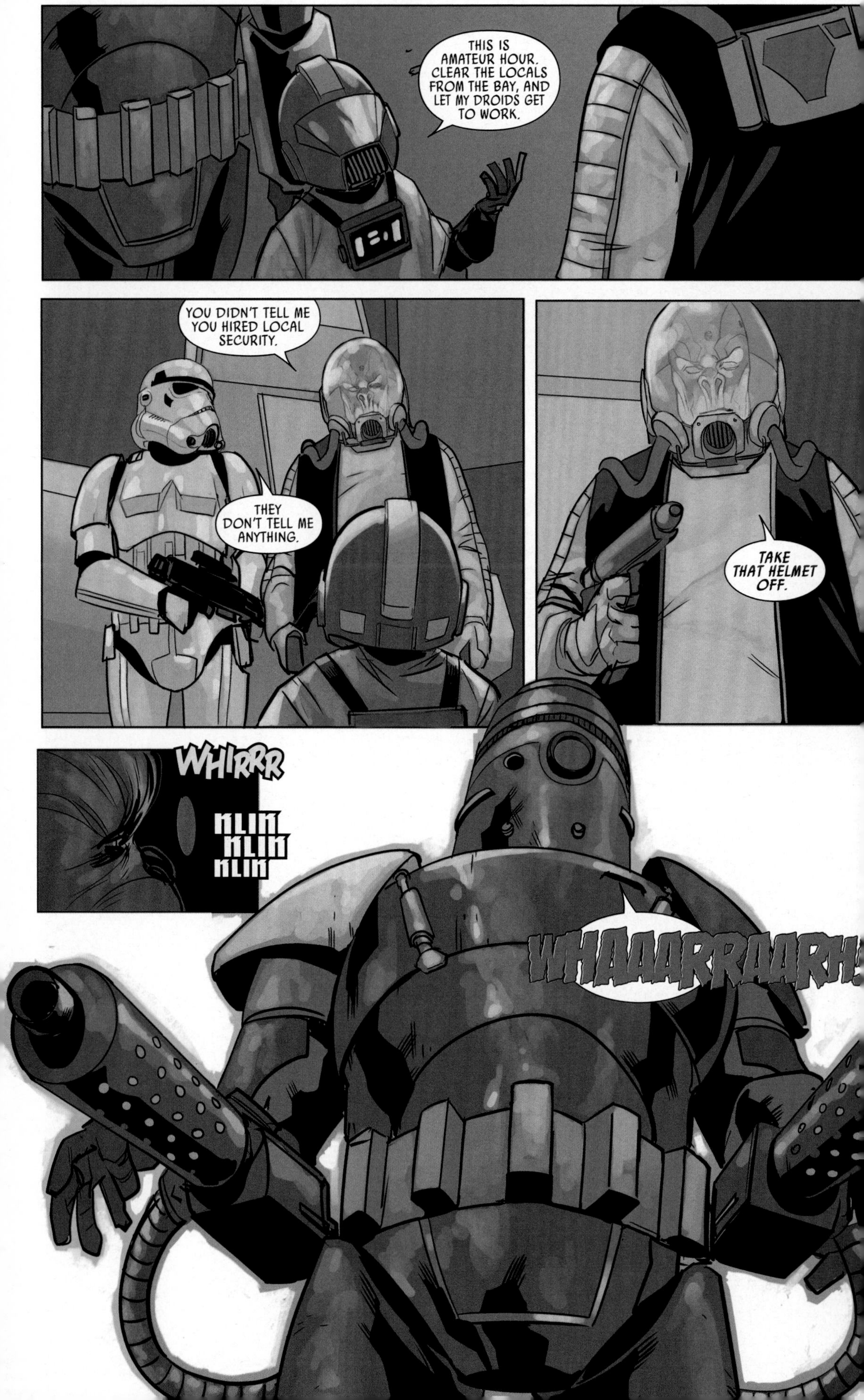
THIS IS AMATEUR HOUR. CLEAR THE LOCALS FROM THE BAY, AND LET MY DROIDS GET TO WORK.
YOU DIDN'T TELL ME YOU HIRED LOCAL SECURITY.
THEY DON'T TELL ME ANYTHING.
TAKE THAT HELMET OFF.
WHIRRR
KLIK
KLIK
KLIK
WHAAARRAARH!

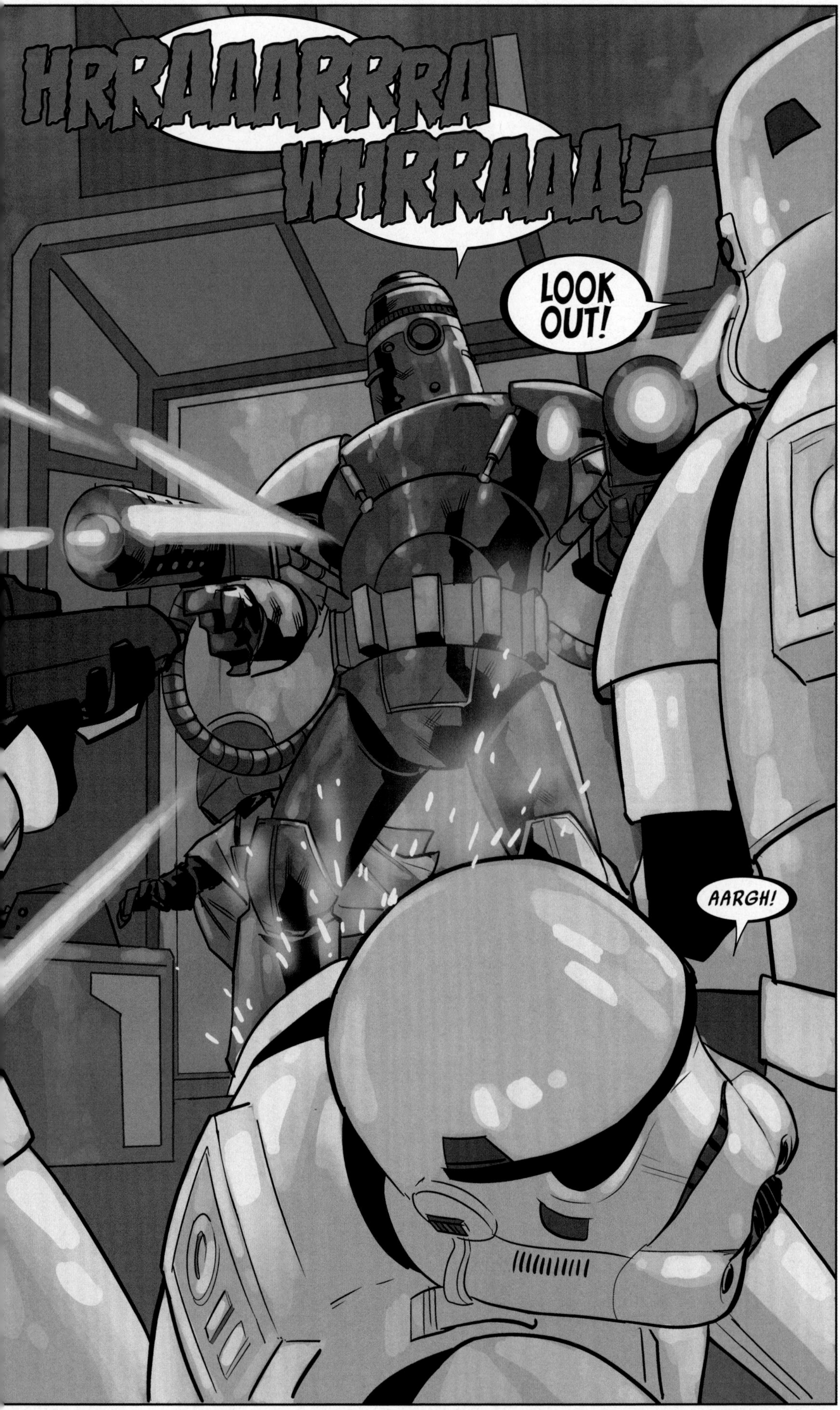
HRRAAAARRRRA WHRRAAA!
LOOK OUT!
AARGH!

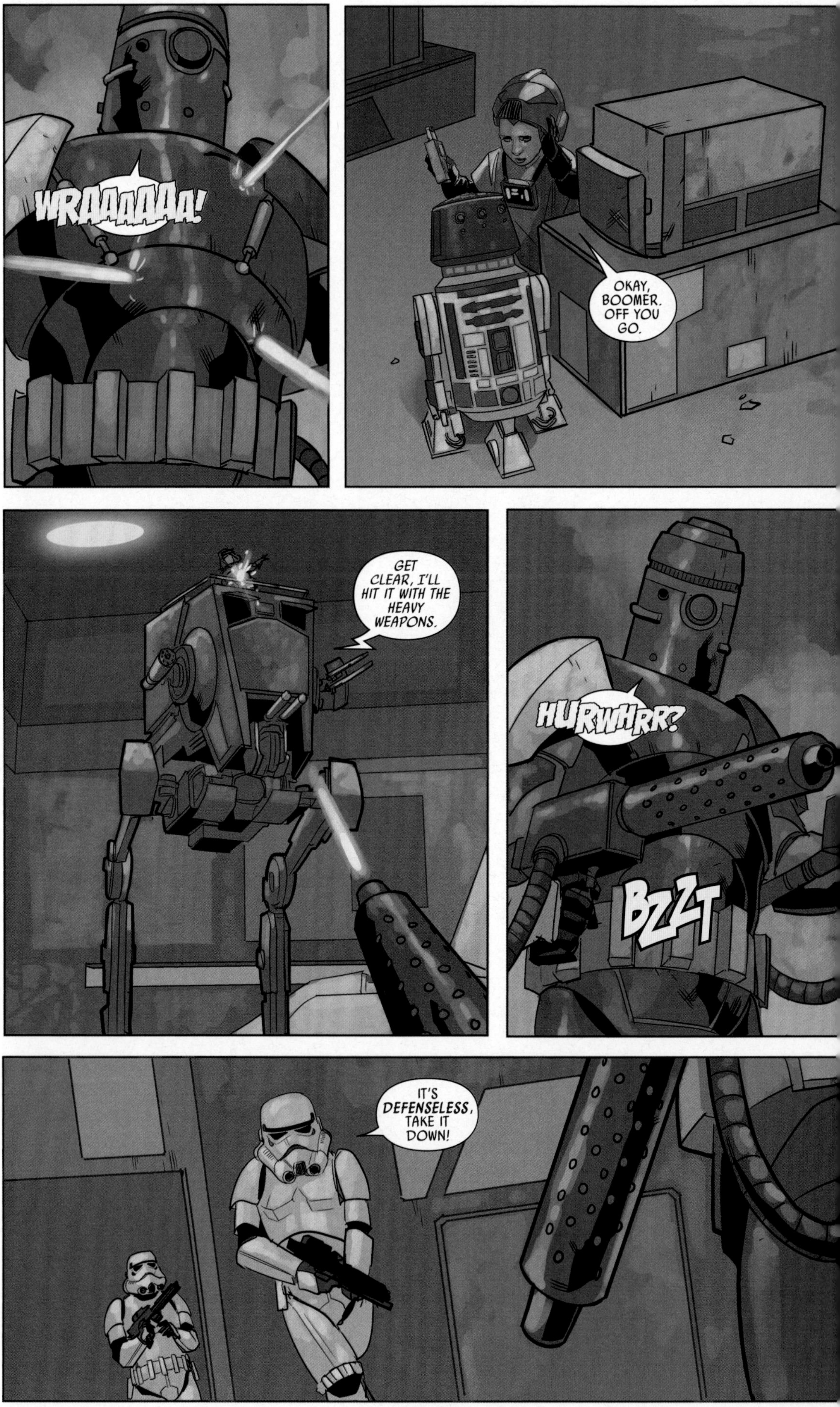
WRAAAAAA!
OKAY, BOOMER. OFF YOU GO.
GET CLEAR, I'LL HIT IT WITH THE HEAVY WEAPONS.
HURWHRR?
BZZT
IT'S DEFENSELESS, TAKE IT DOWN!

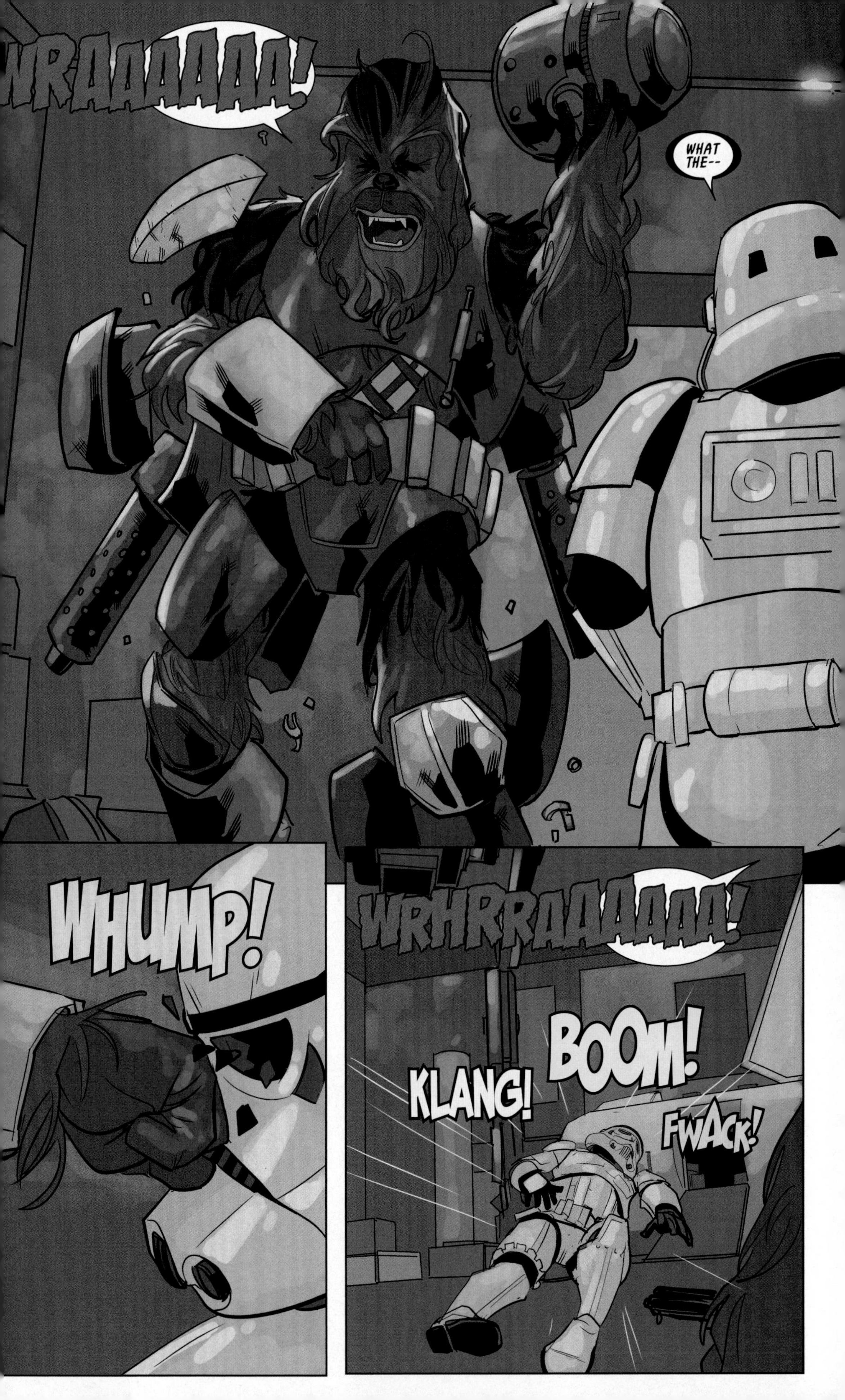
WRAAAAAA!
WHAT THE--
WHUMP!
WRHRRAAAAAA!
KLANG!
BOOM!
FWACK!

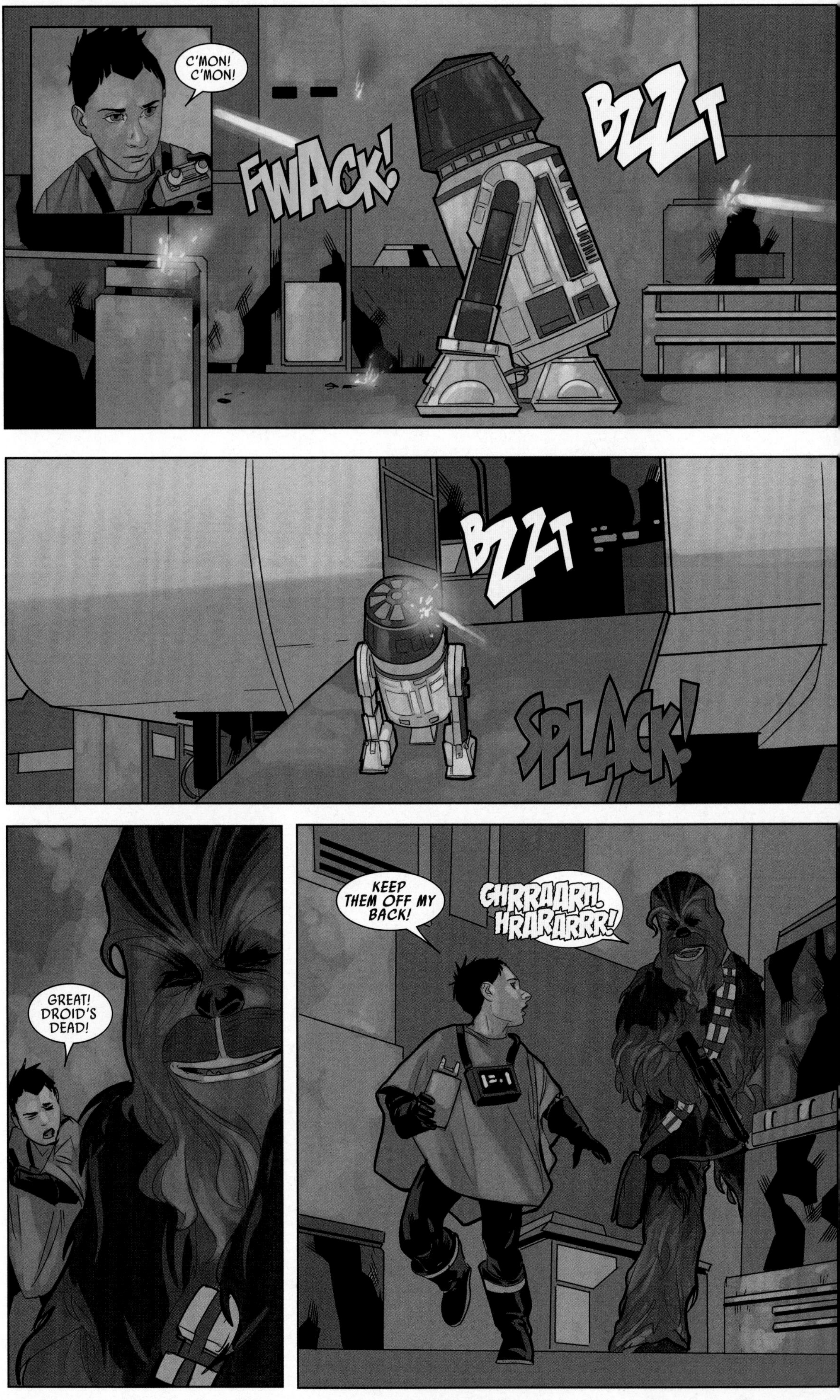
C'MON! C'MON!
FWACK!
BZZT
BZZT
SPLACK!
GREAT! DROID'S DEAD!
KEEP THEM OFF MY BACK!
GHRRAARH. HRARARRR!

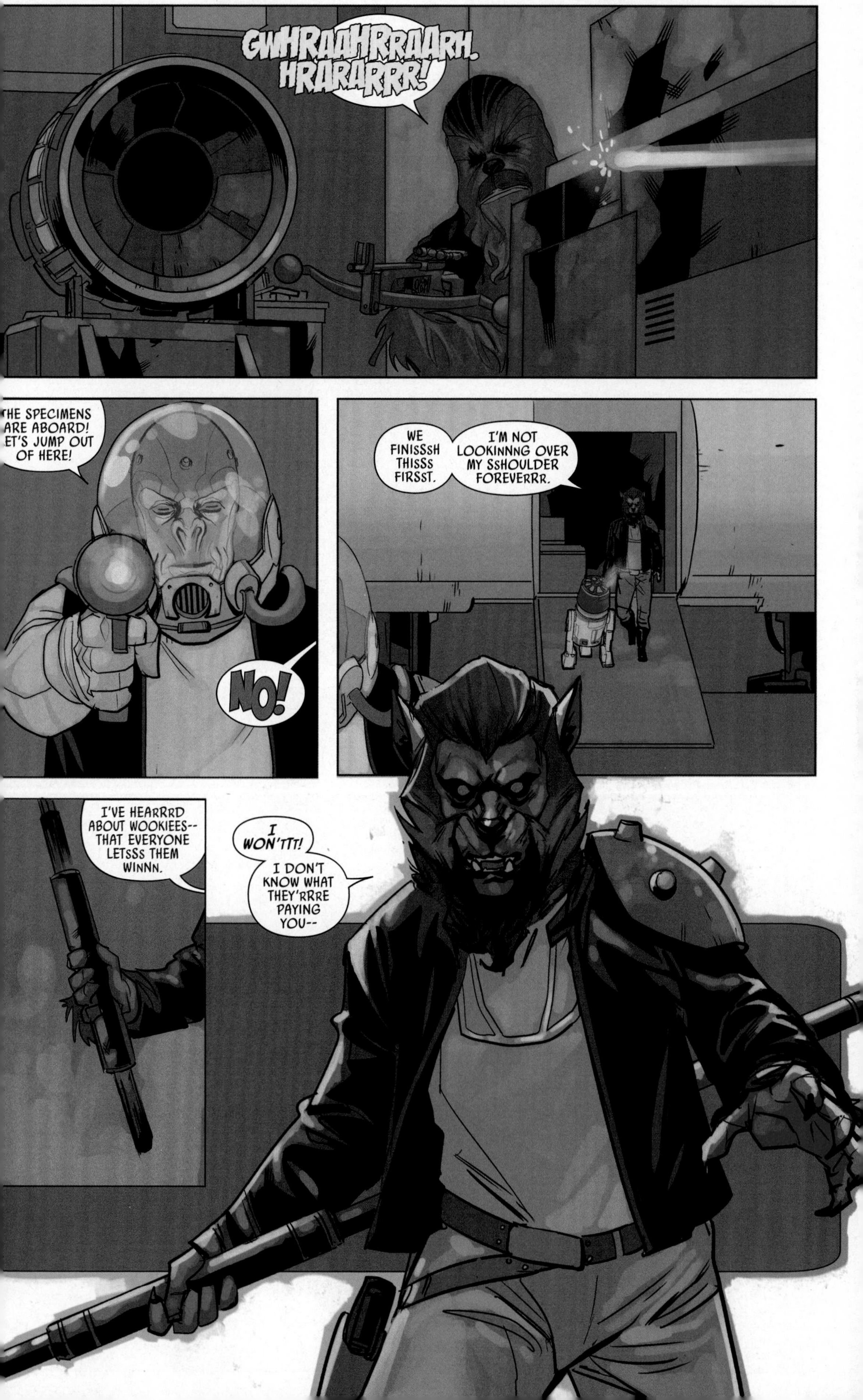
GWHRAAHRRAARH. HRARARRR!
THE SPECIMENS ARE ABOARD! LET'S JUMP OUT OF HERE!
NO!
WE FINISSSH THISSS FIRSST.
I'M NOT LOOKINNNG OVER MY SSHOULDER FOREVERRR.
I'VE HEARRRD ABOUT WOOKIEES-- THAT EVERYONE LETSSS THEM WINNN.
I WON'TTT!
I DON'T KNOW WHAT THEY'RRRE PAYING YOU--

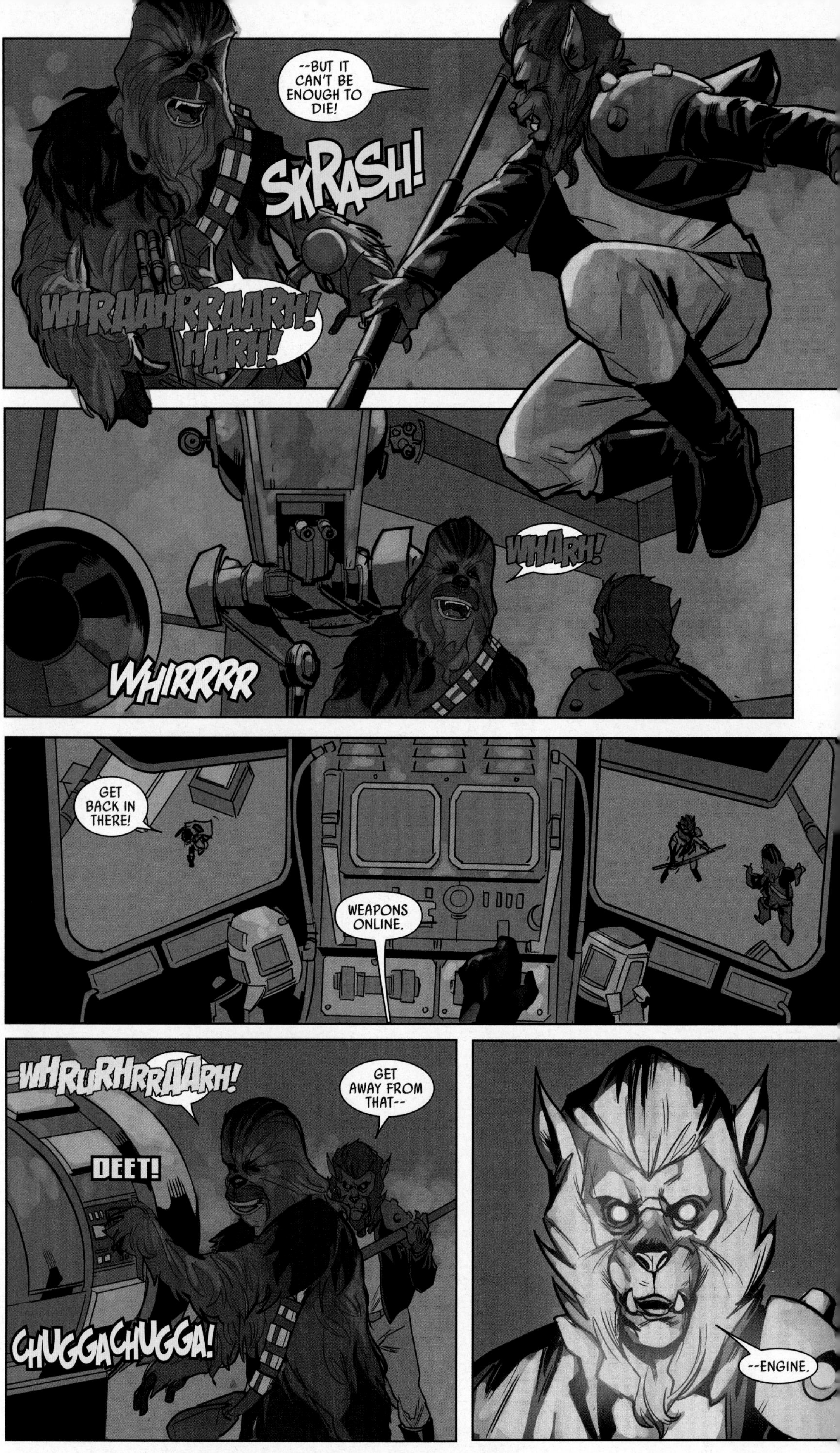
--BUT IT CAN'T BE ENOUGH TO DIE!
SKRASH!
WHRAAHRRAARH! HARH!
WHARH!
WHIRRRR
GET BACK IN THERE!
WEAPONS ONLINE.
WHRURHRRAARH!
GET AWAY FROM THAT--
DEET!
CHUGGACHUGGA!
--ENGINE.

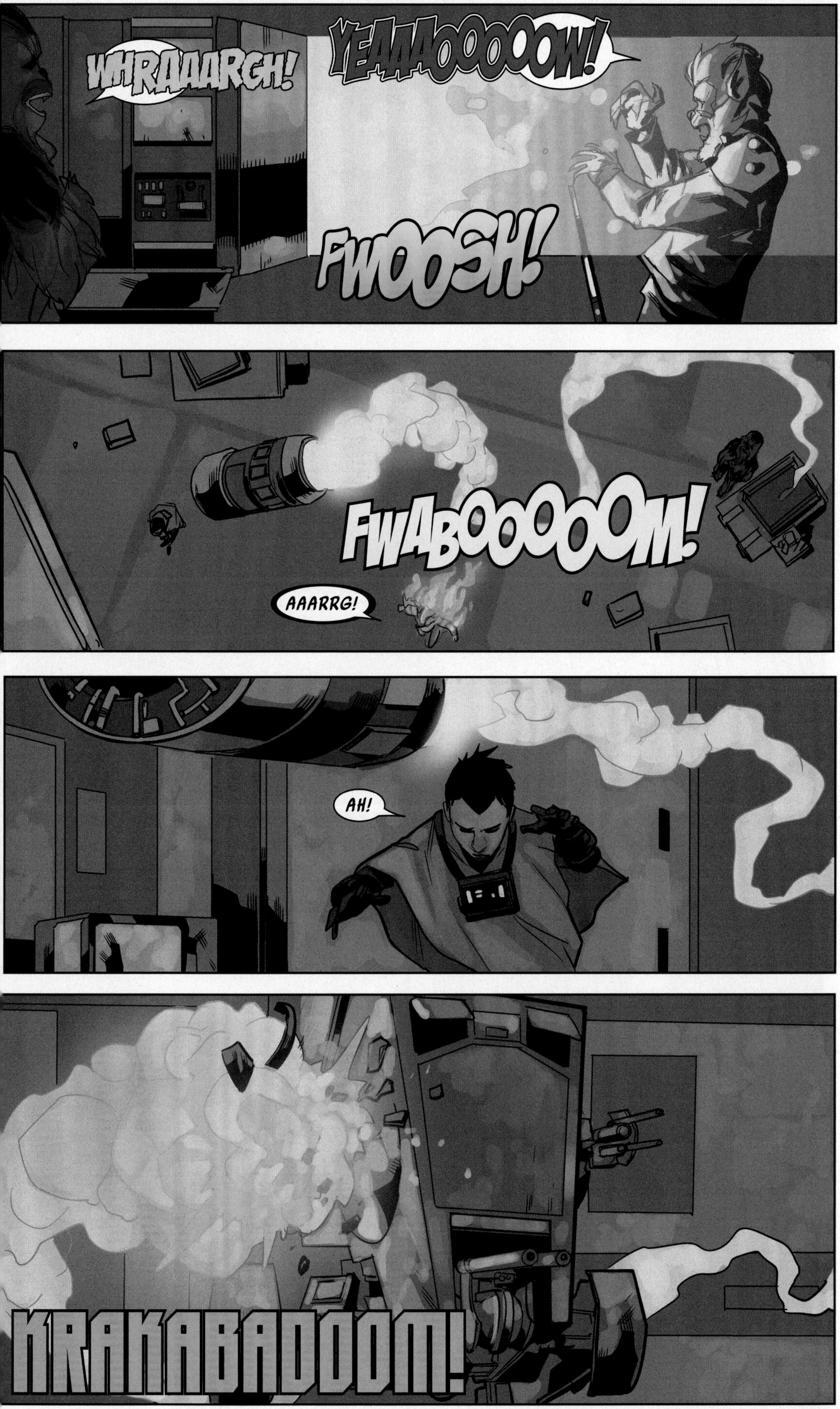
WHRAAARGH!
YEAAAOOOOOW!
FWOOSH!
FWABOOOOOOM!
AAARRG!
AH!
KRAKABADOOM!

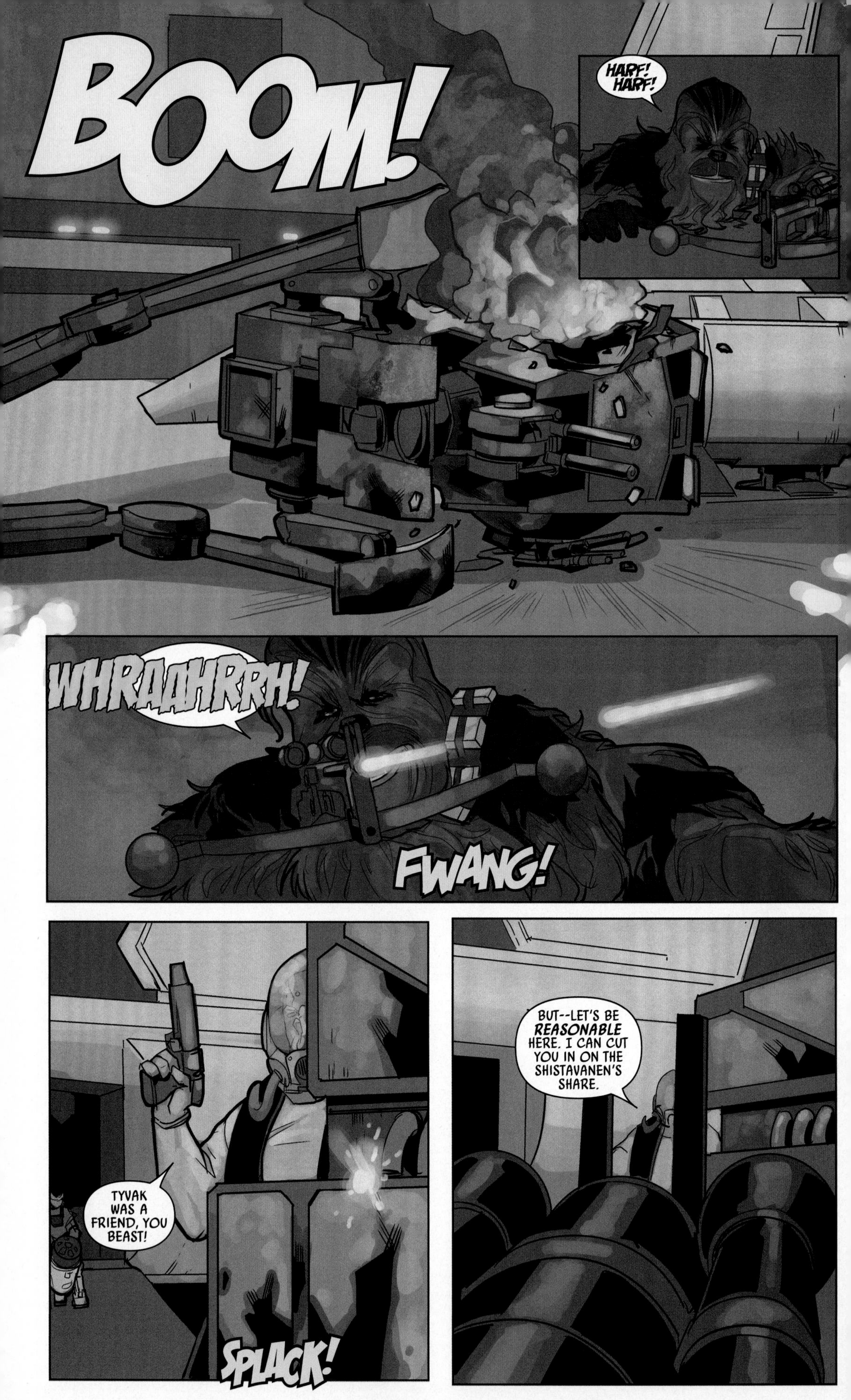
BOOM!
HARF! HARF!
WHRAAHRRH!
FWANG!
TYVAK WAS A FRIEND, YOU BEAST!
SPLACK!
BUT--LET'S BE *REASONABLE* HERE. I CAN CUT YOU IN ON THE SHISTAVANEN'S SHARE.

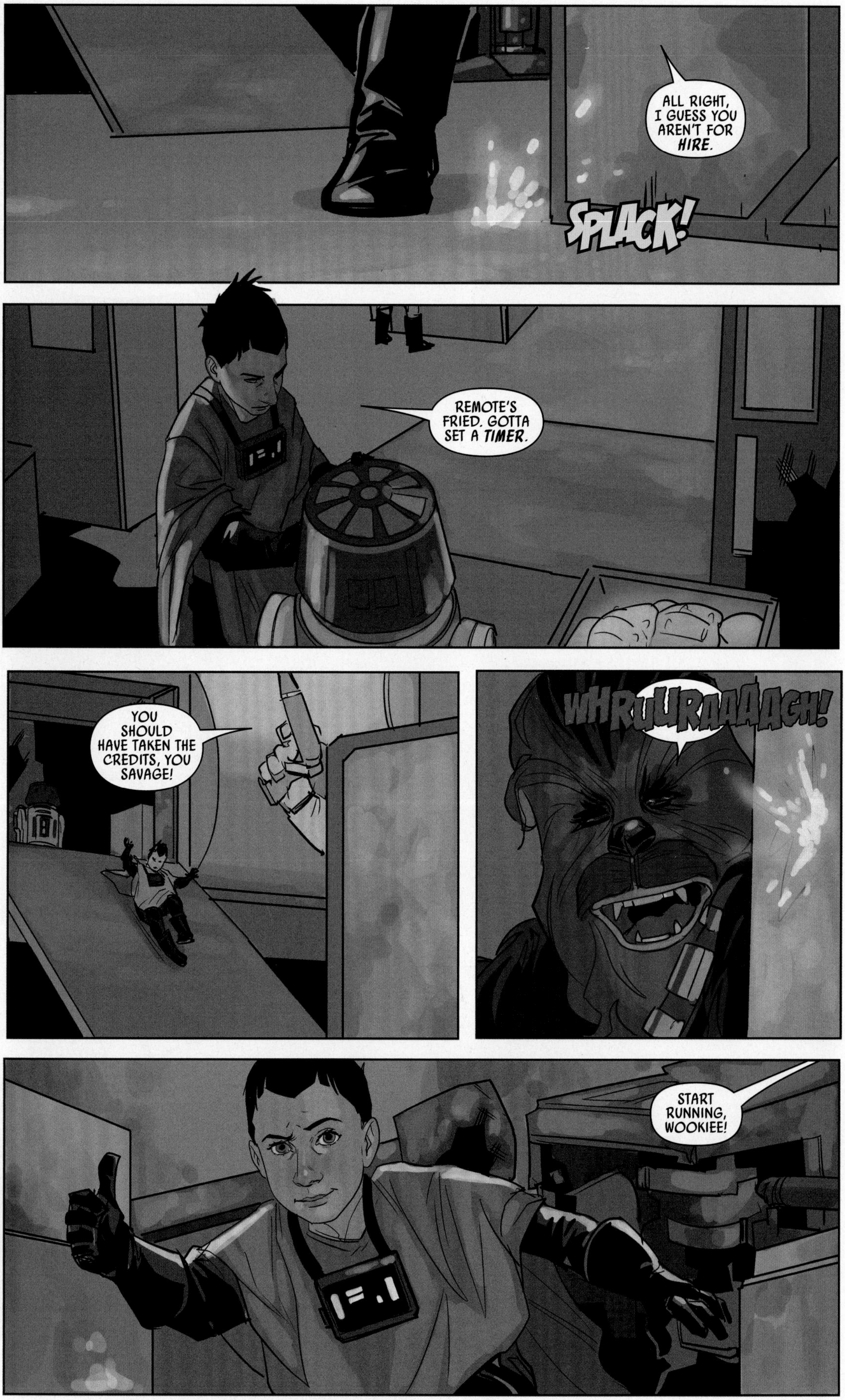
ALL RIGHT, I GUESS YOU AREN'T FOR HIRE.
SPLACK!
REMOTE'S FRIED. GOTTA SET A TIMER.
YOU SHOULD HAVE TAKEN THE CREDITS, YOU SAVAGE!
WHRUURAAAAGH!
START RUNNING, WOOKIEE!

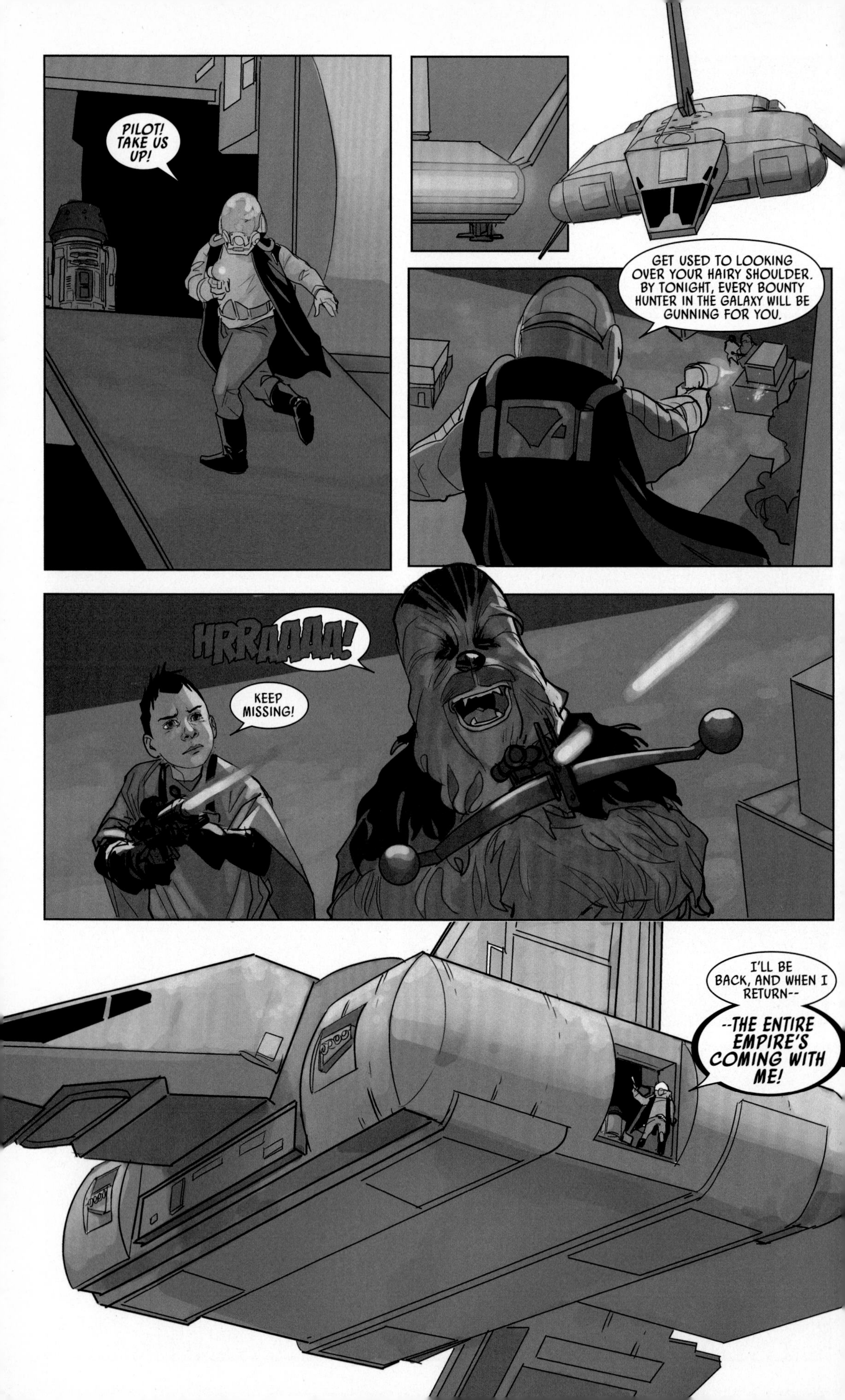
PILOT! TAKE US UP!
GET USED TO LOOKING OVER YOUR HAIRY SHOULDER. BY TONIGHT, EVERY BOUNTY HUNTER IN THE GALAXY WILL BE GUNNING FOR YOU.
HRRAAAA!
KEEP MISSING!
I'LL BE BACK, AND WHEN I RETURN--
--THE ENTIRE EMPIRE'S COMING WITH ME!

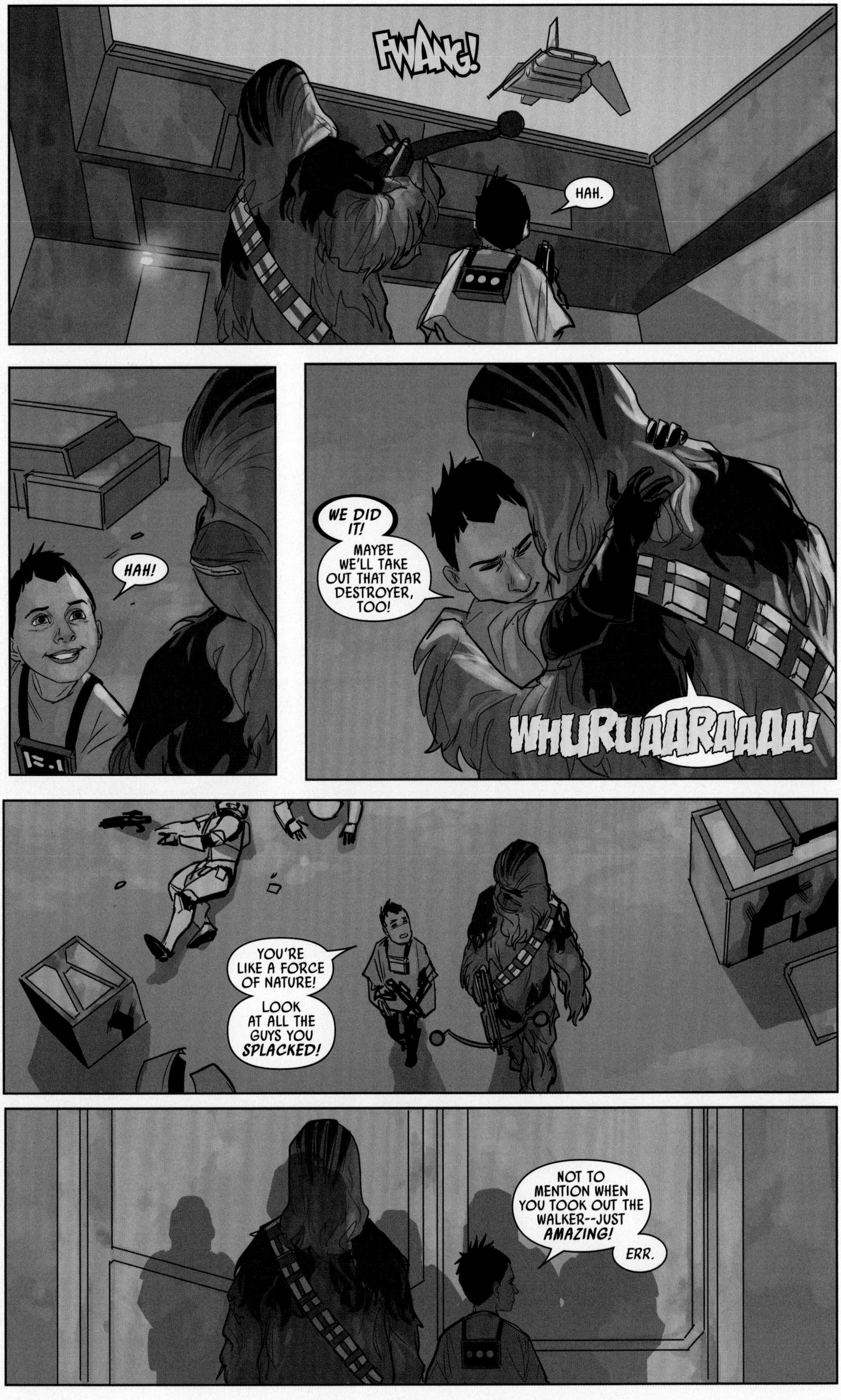
FWANG!
HAH.
HAH!
WE DID IT!
MAYBE WE'LL TAKE OUT THAT STAR DESTROYER, TOO!
WHURUAARAAAA!
YOU'RE LIKE A FORCE OF NATURE!
LOOK AT ALL THE GUYS YOU SPLACKED!
NOT TO MENTION WHEN YOU TOOK OUT THE WALKER--JUST AMAZING!
ERR.

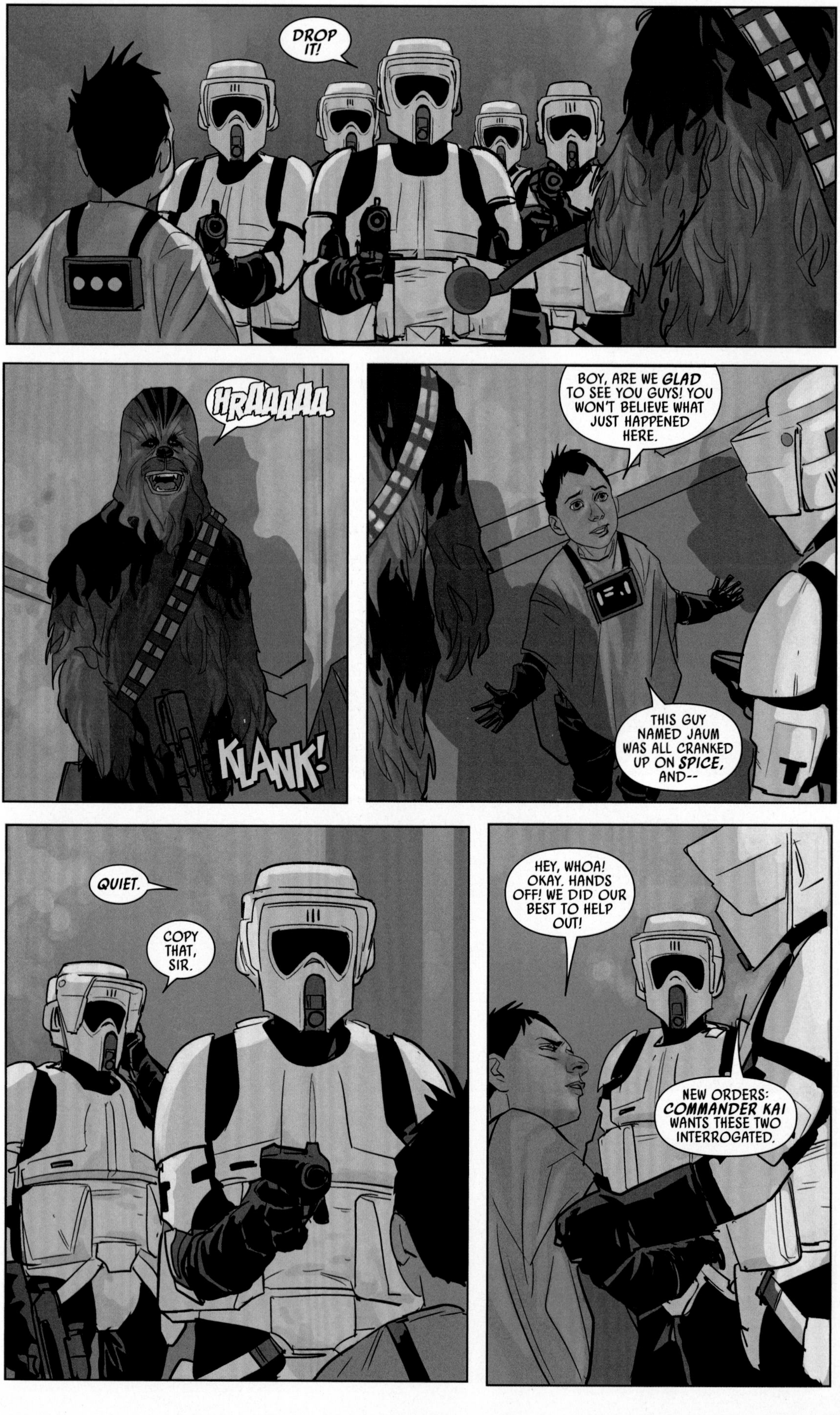
DROP IT!
HRAAAAA
KLANK!
BOY, ARE WE GLAD TO SEE YOU GUYS! YOU WON'T BELIEVE WHAT JUST HAPPENED HERE.
THIS GUY NAMED JAUM WAS ALL CRANKED UP ON SPICE, AND--
QUIET.
COPY THAT, SIR.
HEY, WHOA! OKAY. HANDS OFF! WE DID OUR BEST TO HELP OUT!
NEW ORDERS: COMMANDER KAI WANTS THESE TWO INTERROGATED.

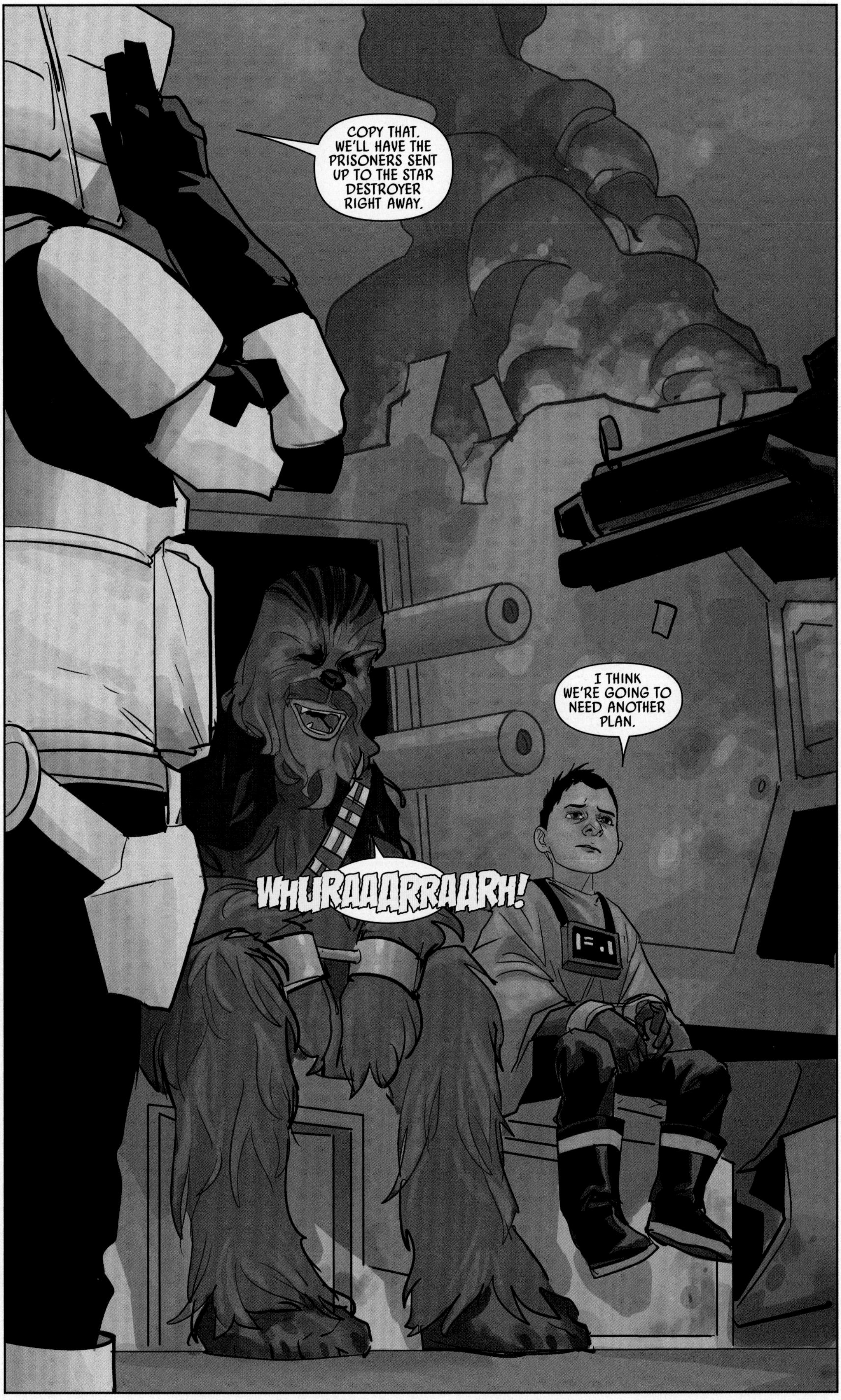
COPY THAT. WE'LL HAVE THE PRISONERS SENT UP TO THE STAR DESTROYER RIGHT AWAY.
I THINK WE'RE GOING TO NEED ANOTHER PLAN.
WHURAAARRAARH!

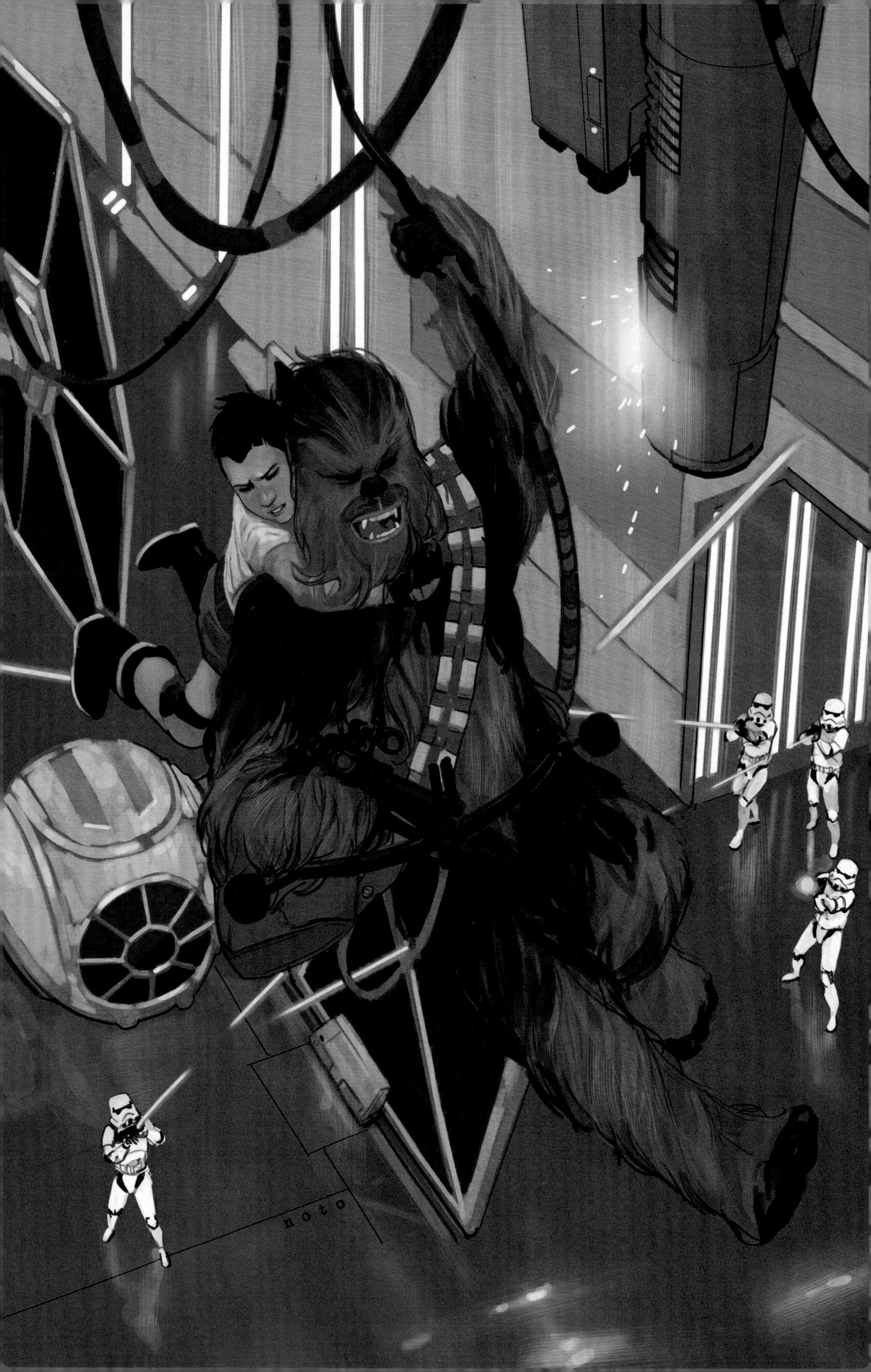
noto

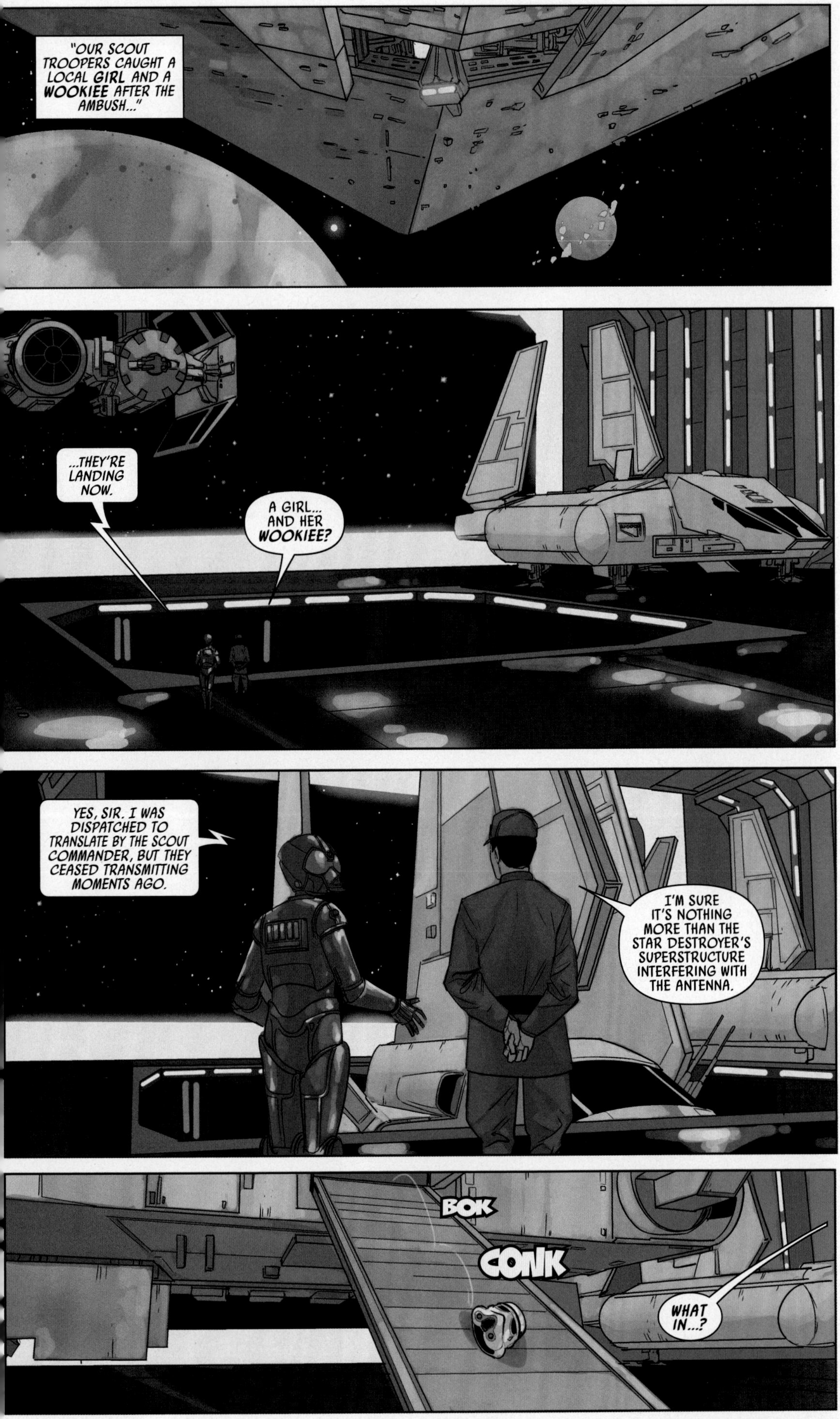
"OUR SCOUT TROOPERS CAUGHT A LOCAL GIRL AND A WOOKIEE AFTER THE AMBUSH..."
...THEY'RE LANDING NOW.
A GIRL... AND HER WOOKIEE?
YES, SIR. I WAS DISPATCHED TO TRANSLATE BY THE SCOUT COMMANDER, BUT THEY CEASED TRANSMITTING MOMENTS AGO.
I'M SURE IT'S NOTHING MORE THAN THE STAR DESTROYER'S SUPERSTRUCTURE INTERFERING WITH THE ANTENNA.
BOK
CONK
WHAT IN...?

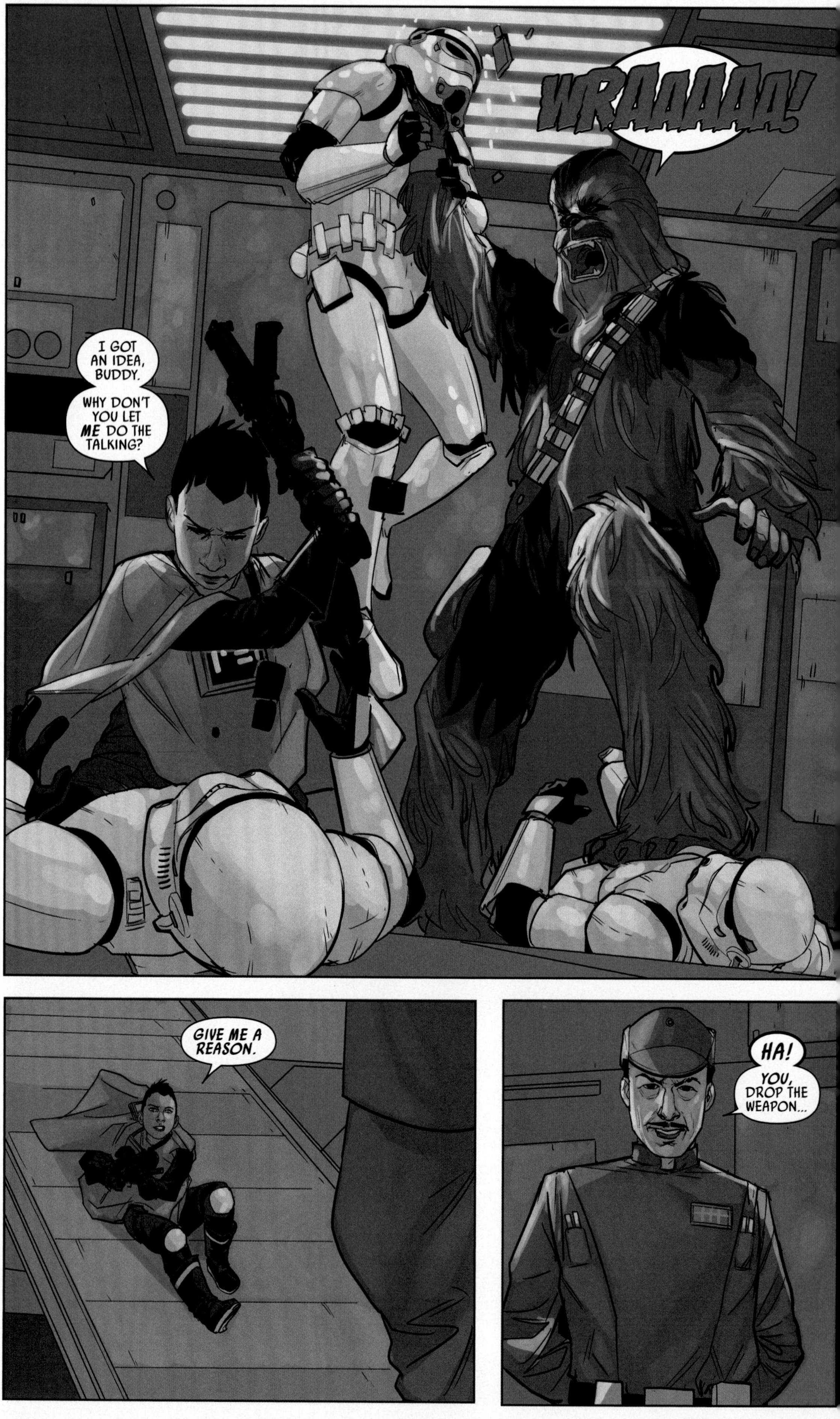
WRAAAAA!
I GOT AN IDEA, BUDDY.
WHY DON'T YOU LET ME DO THE TALKING?
GIVE ME A REASON.
HA!
YOU, DROP THE WEAPON...

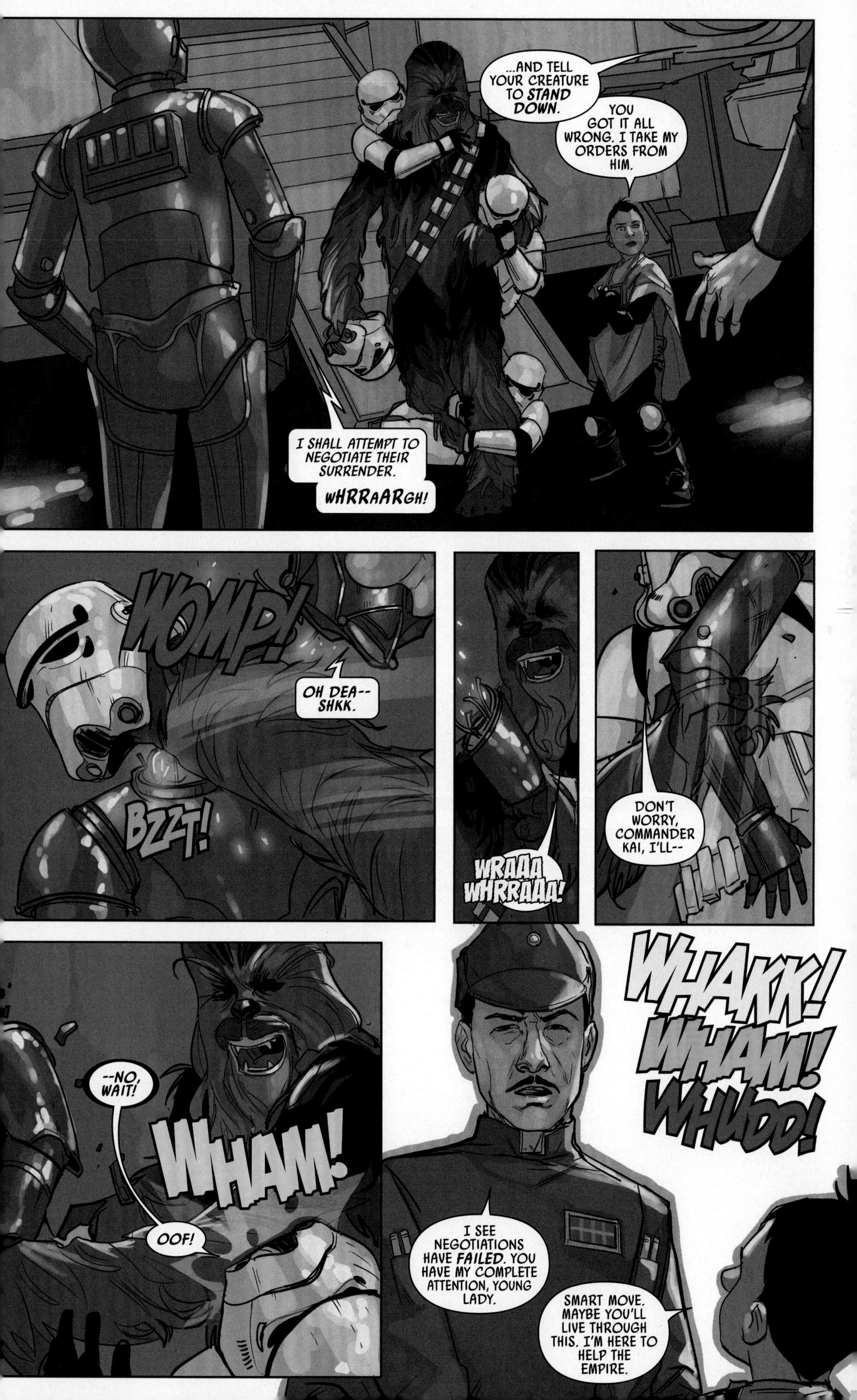
...AND TELL YOUR CREATURE TO STAND DOWN.
YOU GOT IT ALL WRONG. I TAKE MY ORDERS FROM HIM.
I SHALL ATTEMPT TO NEGOTIATE THEIR SURRENDER.
WHRRAARGH!
WOMP!
OH DEA-- SHKK.
BZZT!
WRAAA WHRRAAA!
DON'T WORRY, COMMANDER KAI, I'LL--
--NO, WAIT!
WHAM!
OOF!
WHAKK! WHAM! WHUDD!
I SEE NEGOTIATIONS HAVE FAILED. YOU HAVE MY COMPLETE ATTENTION, YOUNG LADY.
SMART MOVE. MAYBE YOU'LL LIVE THROUGH THIS. I'M HERE TO HELP THE EMPIRE.

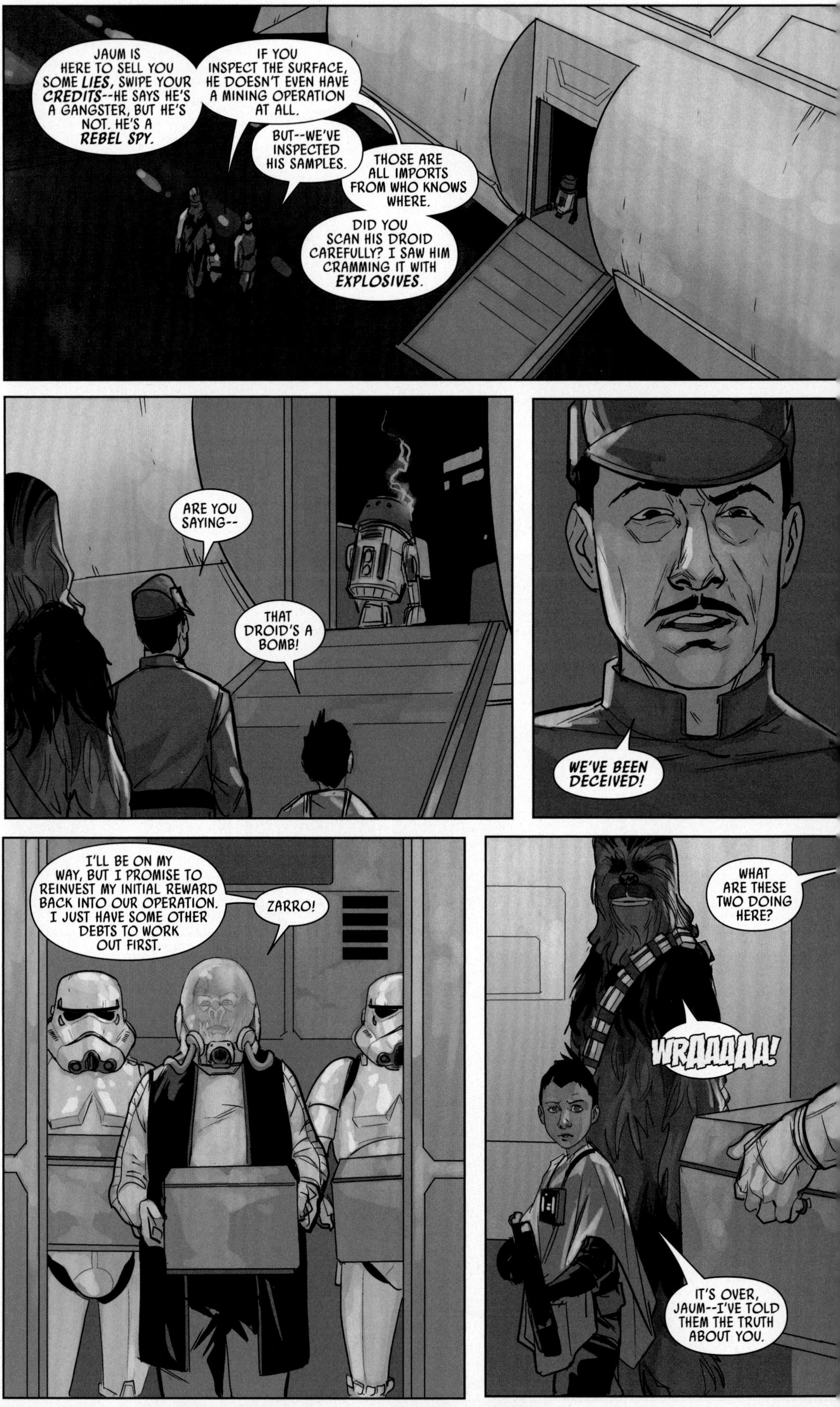

JAUM IS HERE TO SELL YOU SOME LIES, SWIPE YOUR CREDITS--HE SAYS HE'S A GANGSTER, BUT HE'S NOT. HE'S A REBEL SPY.
IF YOU INSPECT THE SURFACE, HE DOESN'T EVEN HAVE A MINING OPERATION AT ALL.
BUT--WE'VE INSPECTED HIS SAMPLES.
THOSE ARE ALL IMPORTS FROM WHO KNOWS WHERE.
DID YOU SCAN HIS DROID CAREFULLY? I SAW HIM CRAMMING IT WITH EXPLOSIVES.
ARE YOU SAYING--
THAT DROID'S A BOMB!
WE'VE BEEN DECEIVED!
I'LL BE ON MY WAY, BUT I PROMISE TO REINVEST MY INITIAL REWARD BACK INTO OUR OPERATION. I JUST HAVE SOME OTHER DEBTS TO WORK OUT FIRST.
ZARRO!
WHAT ARE THESE TWO DOING HERE?
WRAAAAA!
IT'S OVER, JAUM--I'VE TOLD THEM THE TRUTH ABOUT YOU.

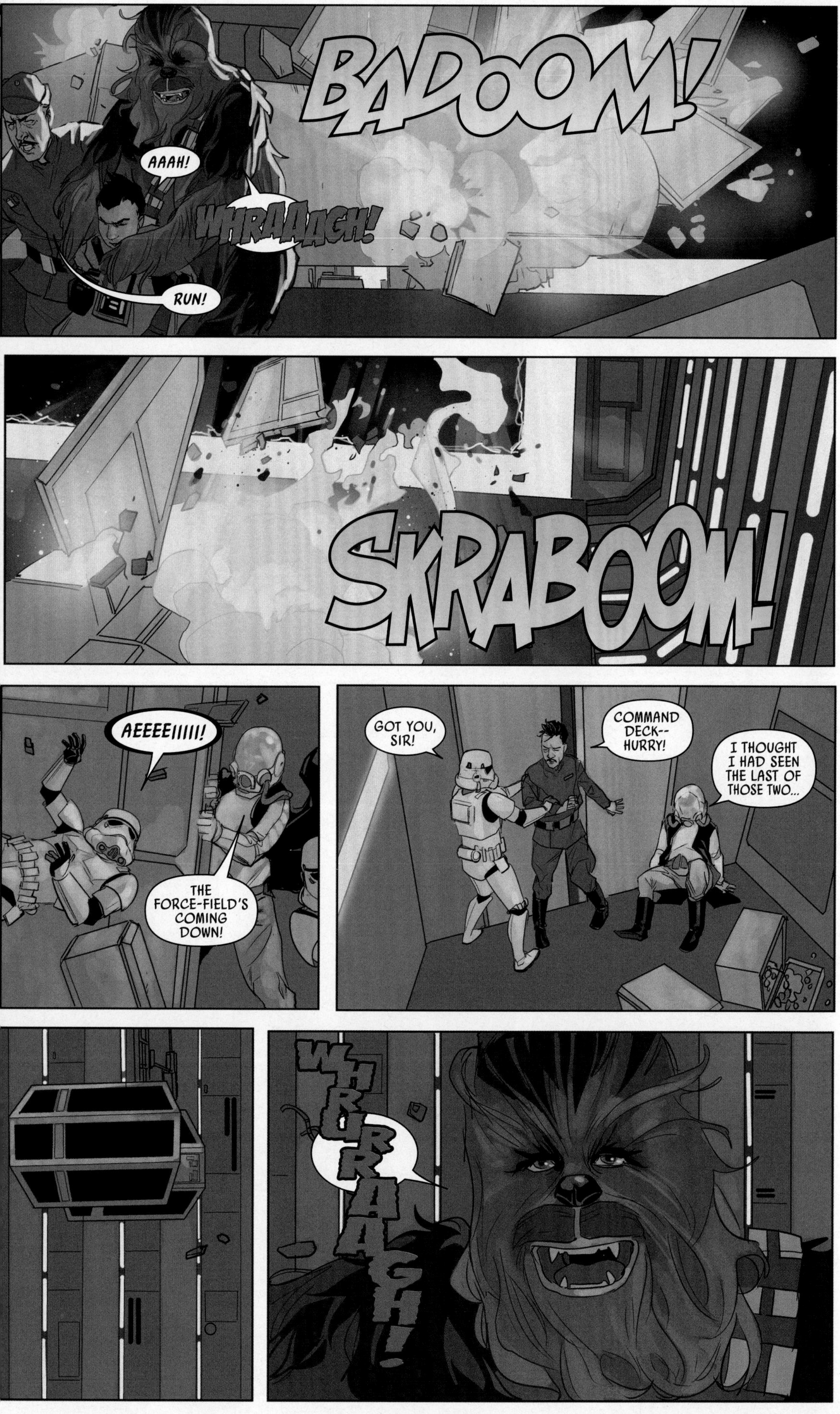

BADOOM!
AAAH!
WHRAAAGH!
RUN!
SKRABOOM!
AEEEEIIIII!
THE FORCE-FIELD'S COMING DOWN!
GOT YOU, SIR!
COMMAND DECK-- HURRY!
I THOUGHT I HAD SEEN THE LAST OF THOSE TWO...
WHRURRAAGH!

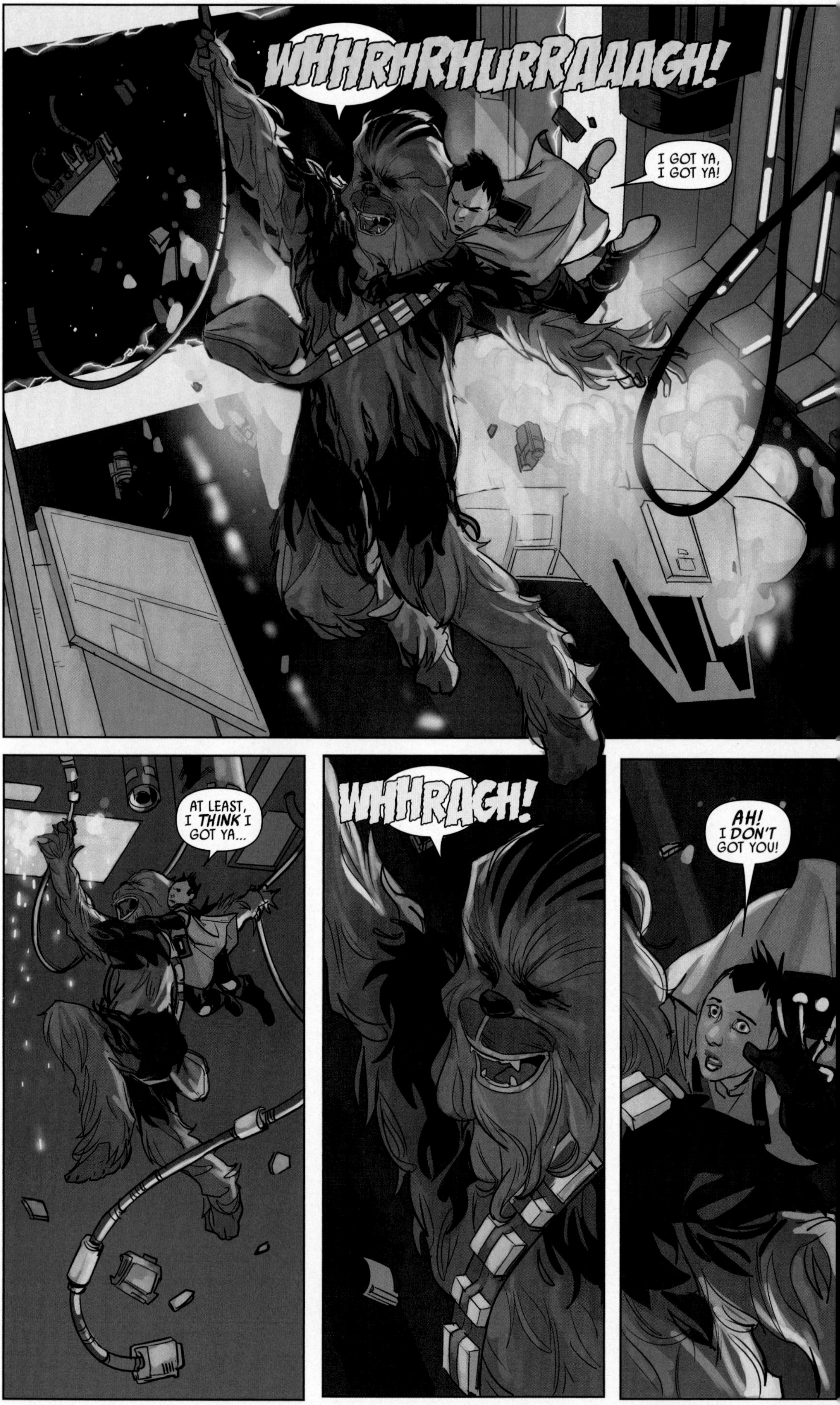
WHHRHRHURRAAAGH!
I GOT YA, I GOT YA!
AT LEAST, I THINK I GOT YA...
WHHRAGH!
AH! I DON'T GOT YOU!

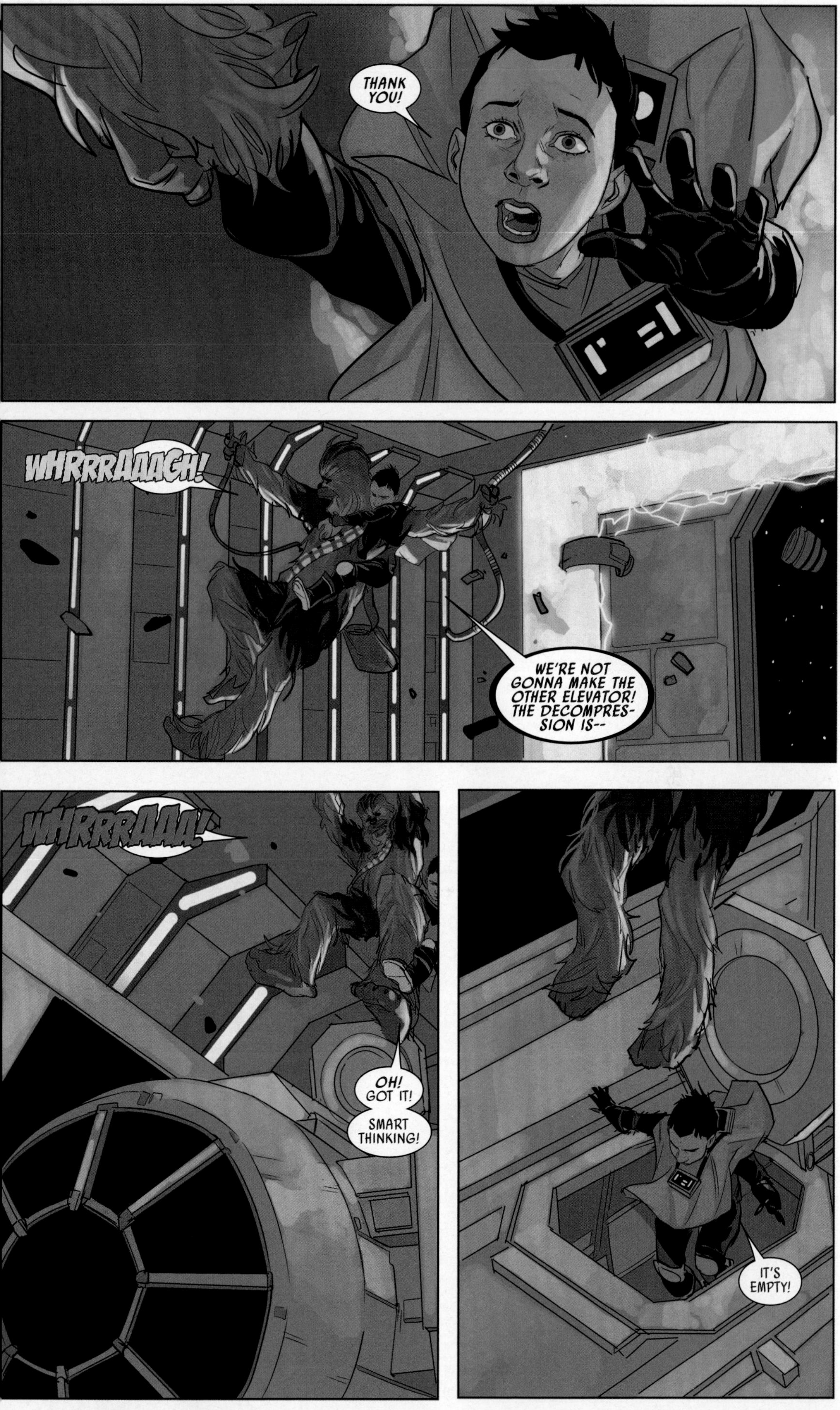
THANK YOU!
WHRRRAAAGH!
WE'RE NOT GONNA MAKE THE OTHER ELEVATOR! THE DECOMPRES- SION IS--
WHRRRAAA!
OH! GOT IT!
SMART THINKING!
IT'S EMPTY!

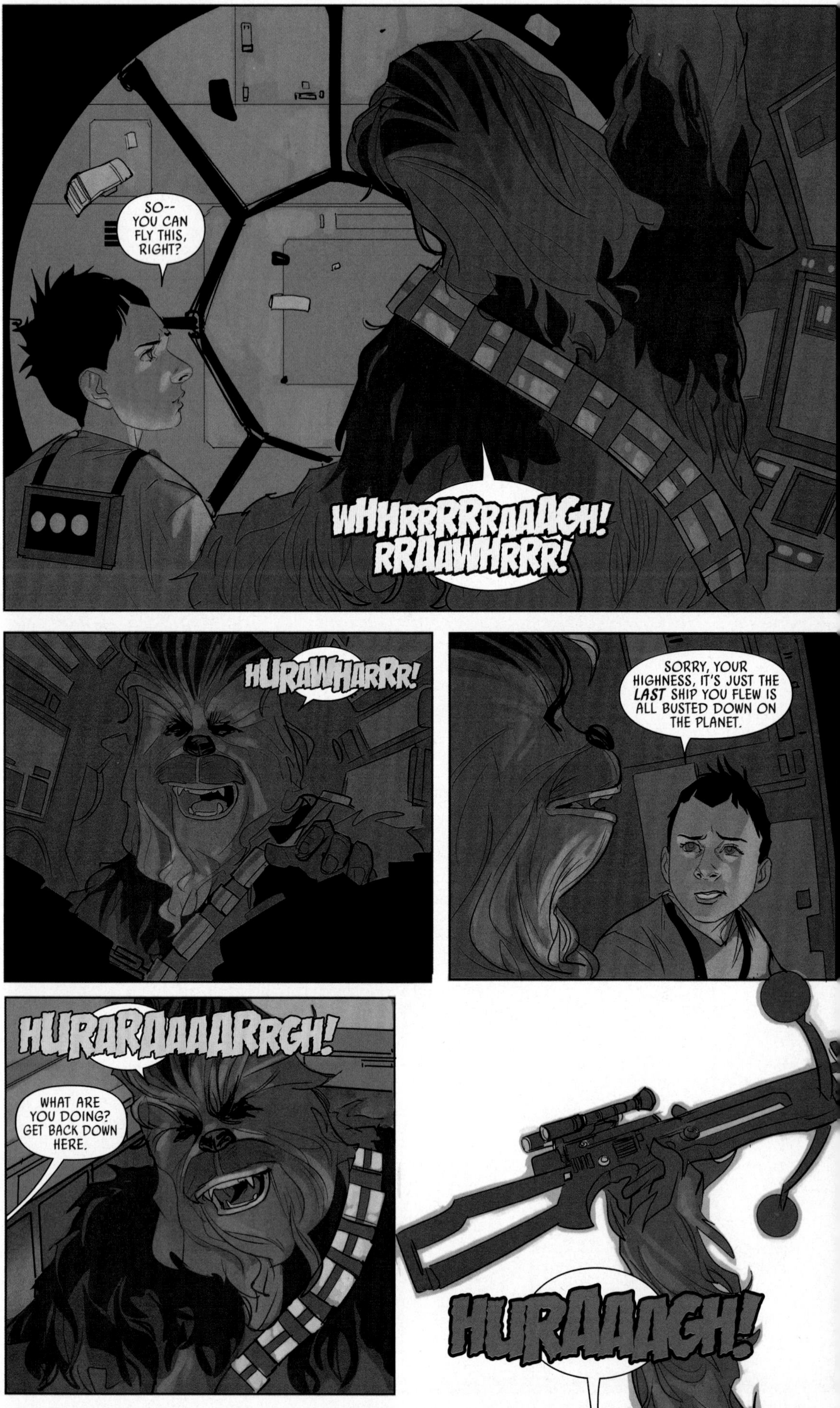
SO-- YOU CAN FLY THIS, RIGHT?
WHHRRRRRAAAGH! RRAAWHRRR!
HURAWHARRR!
SORRY, YOUR HIGHNESS, IT'S JUST THE LAST SHIP YOU FLEW IS ALL BUSTED DOWN ON THE PLANET.
HURARAAAARRGH!
WHAT ARE YOU DOING? GET BACK DOWN HERE.
HURAAAGH!

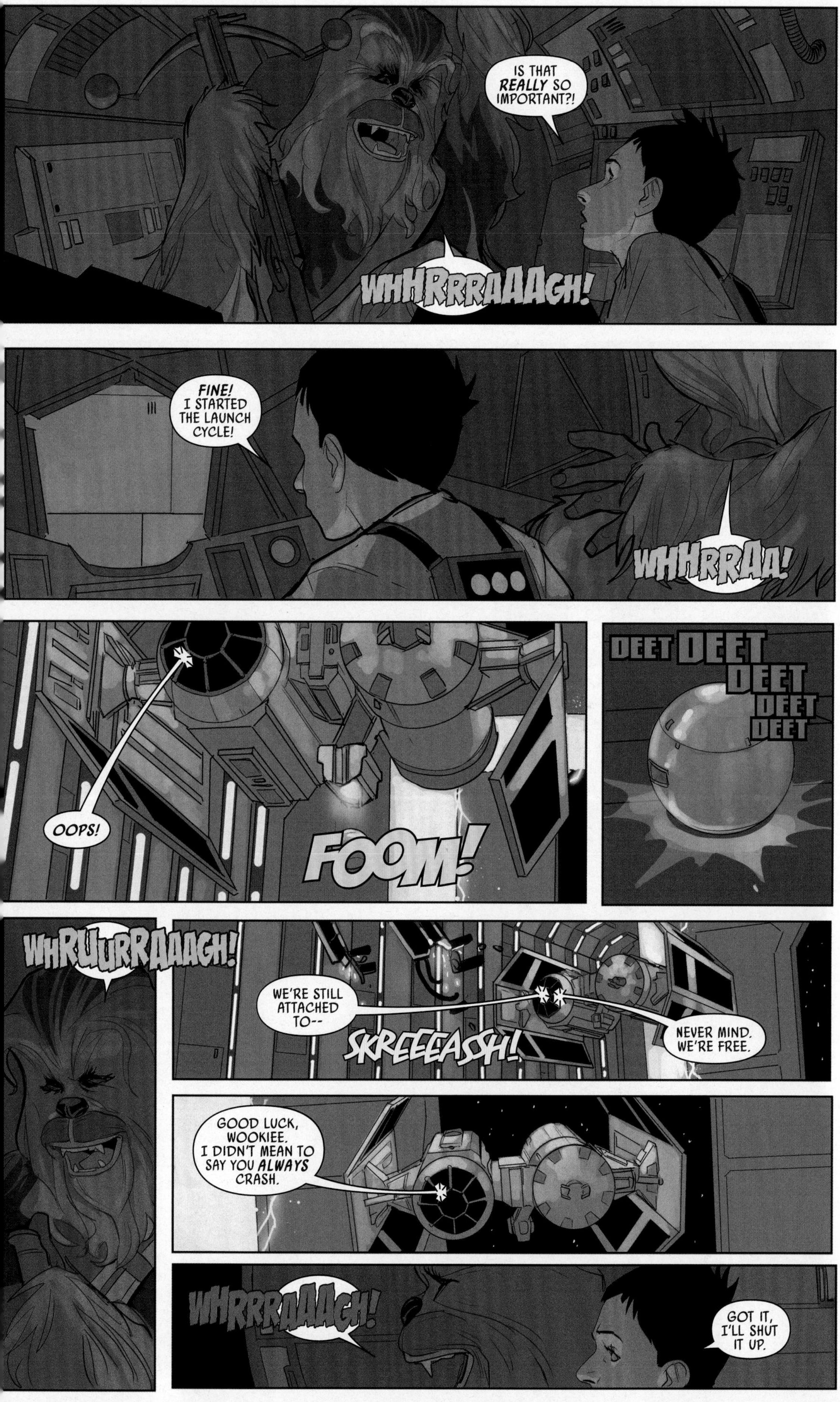
IS THAT *REALLY* SO IMPORTANT?!
WHHRRRRAAAGH!
FINE! I STARTED THE LAUNCH CYCLE!
WHHRRAA!
OOPS!
FOOM!
DEET DEET DEET DEET DEET
WHRUURRAAAGH!
WE'RE STILL ATTACHED TO--
SKREEEASSH!
NEVER MIND. WE'RE FREE.
GOOD LUCK, WOOKIEE. I DIDN'T MEAN TO SAY YOU *ALWAYS* CRASH.
WHRRRAAAGH!
GOT IT, I'LL SHUT IT UP.

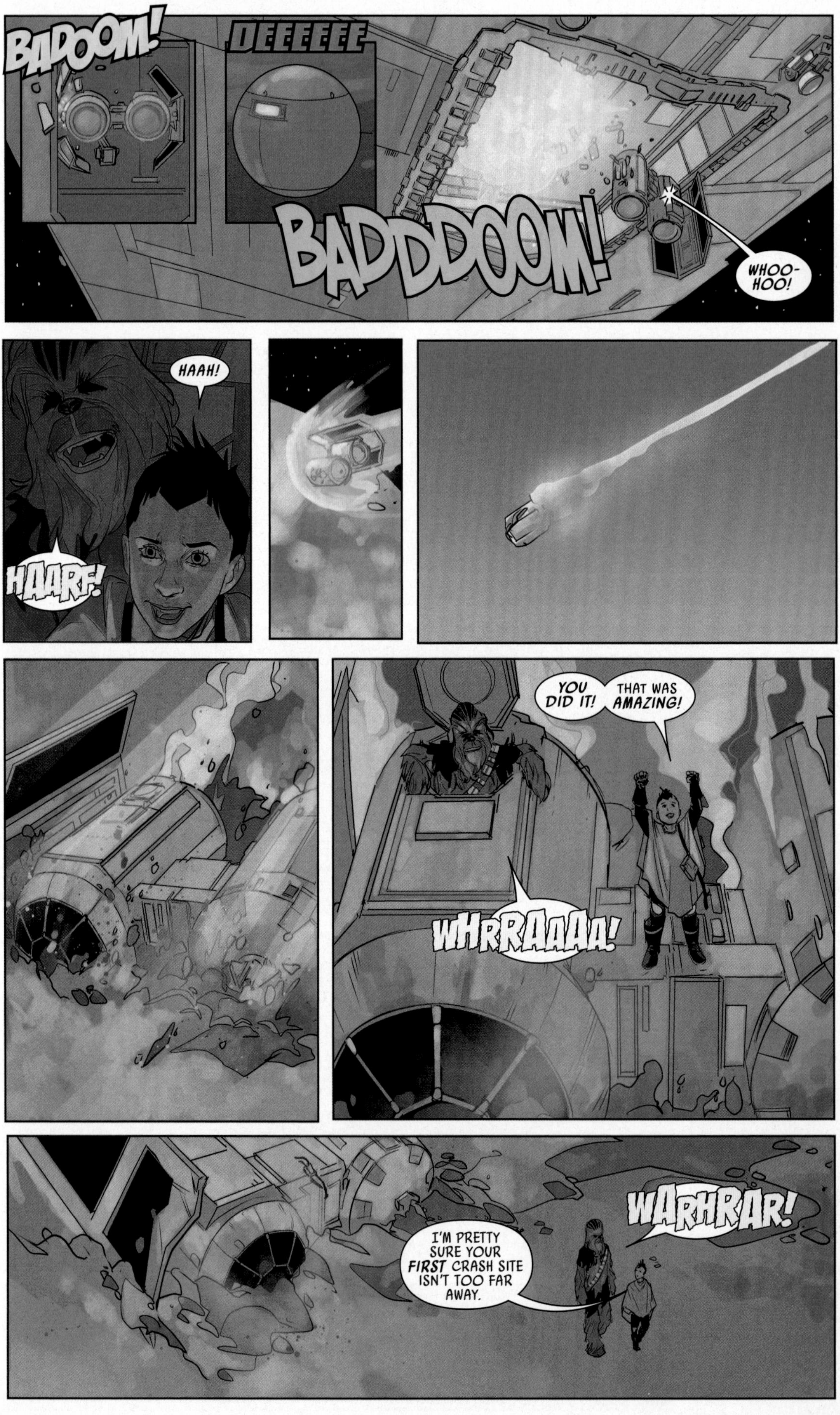
BADOOM!
DEEEEEE
BADDDOOM!
WHOO-HOO!
HAAH!
HAARF!
YOU DID IT!
THAT WAS AMAZING!
WHRRAAAA!
WARHRAR!
I'M PRETTY SURE YOUR FIRST CRASH SITE ISN'T TOO FAR AWAY.

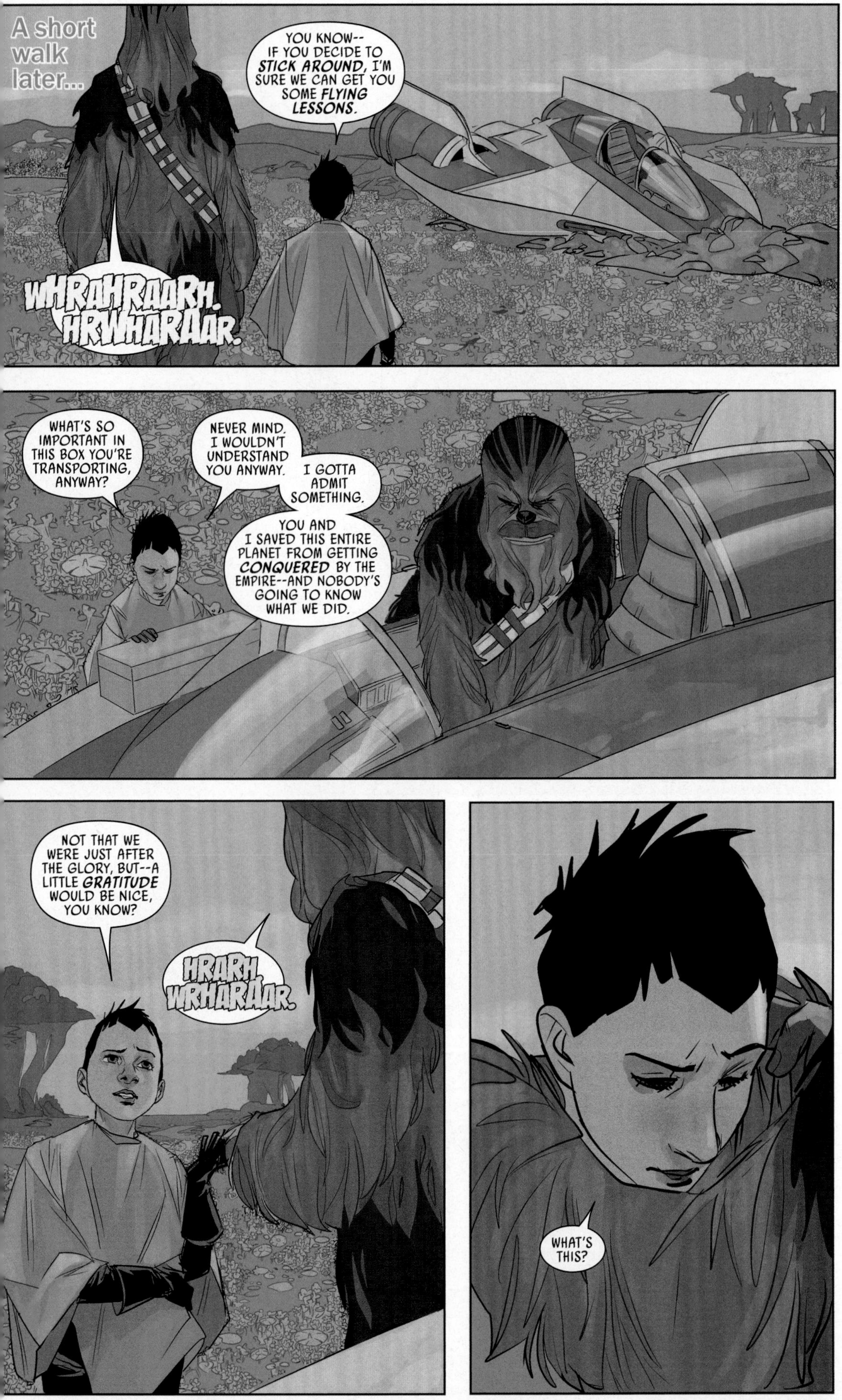
A short walk later...
YOU KNOW-- IF YOU DECIDE TO STICK AROUND, I'M SURE WE CAN GET YOU SOME FLYING LESSONS.
WHRAHRAARH. HRWHARAAR.
WHAT'S SO IMPORTANT IN THIS BOX YOU'RE TRANSPORTING, ANYWAY?
NEVER MIND. I WOULDN'T UNDERSTAND YOU ANYWAY.
I GOTTA ADMIT SOMETHING.
YOU AND I SAVED THIS ENTIRE PLANET FROM GETTING CONQUERED BY THE EMPIRE--AND NOBODY'S GOING TO KNOW WHAT WE DID.
NOT THAT WE WERE JUST AFTER THE GLORY, BUT--A LITTLE GRATITUDE WOULD BE NICE, YOU KNOW?
HRARH WRHARAAR.
WHAT'S THIS?

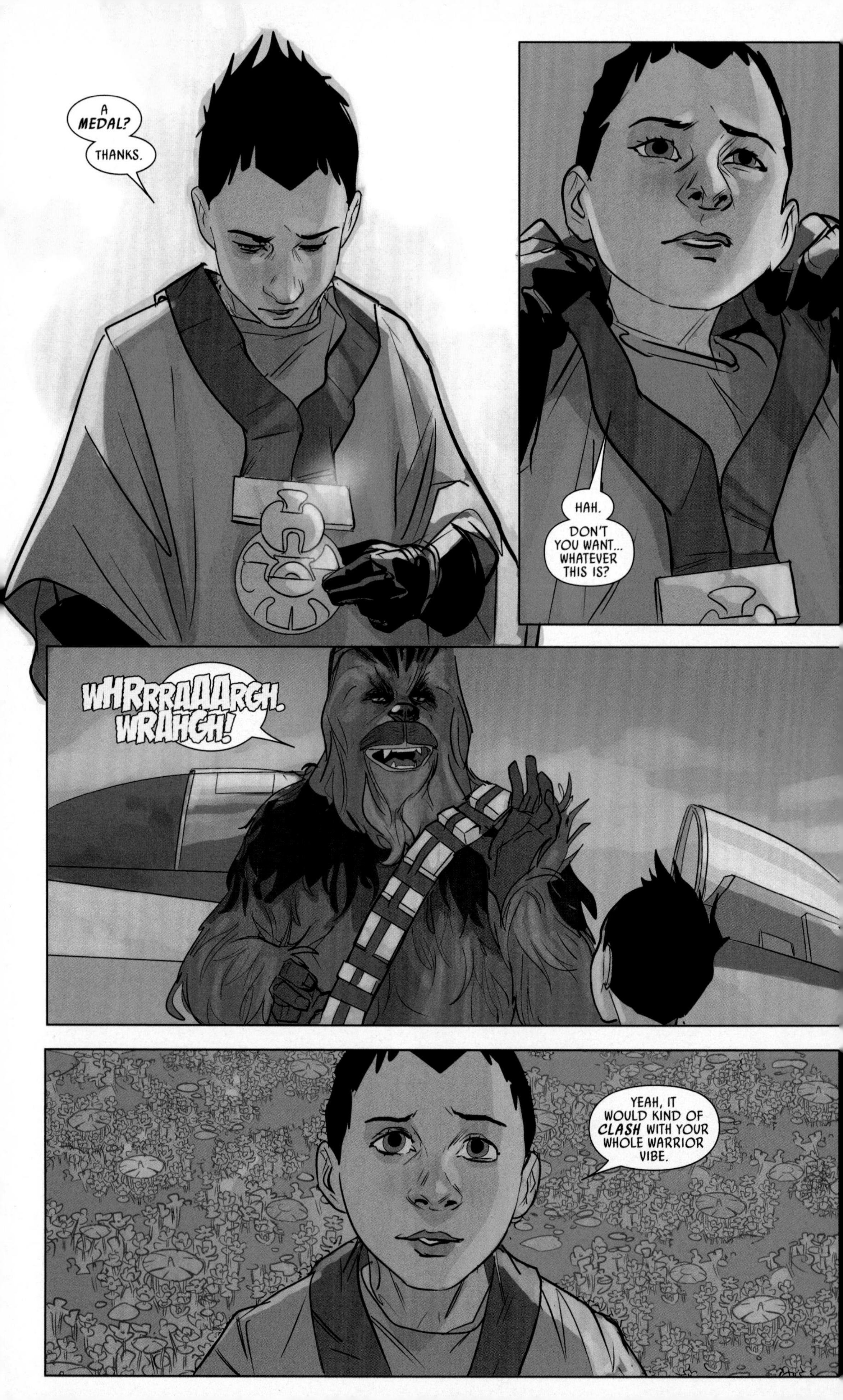
A MEDAL?
THANKS.
HAH.
DON'T YOU WANT... WHATEVER THIS IS?
WHRRRAAARGH. WRAHGH!
YEAH, IT WOULD KIND OF CLASH WITH YOUR WHOLE WARRIOR VIBE.

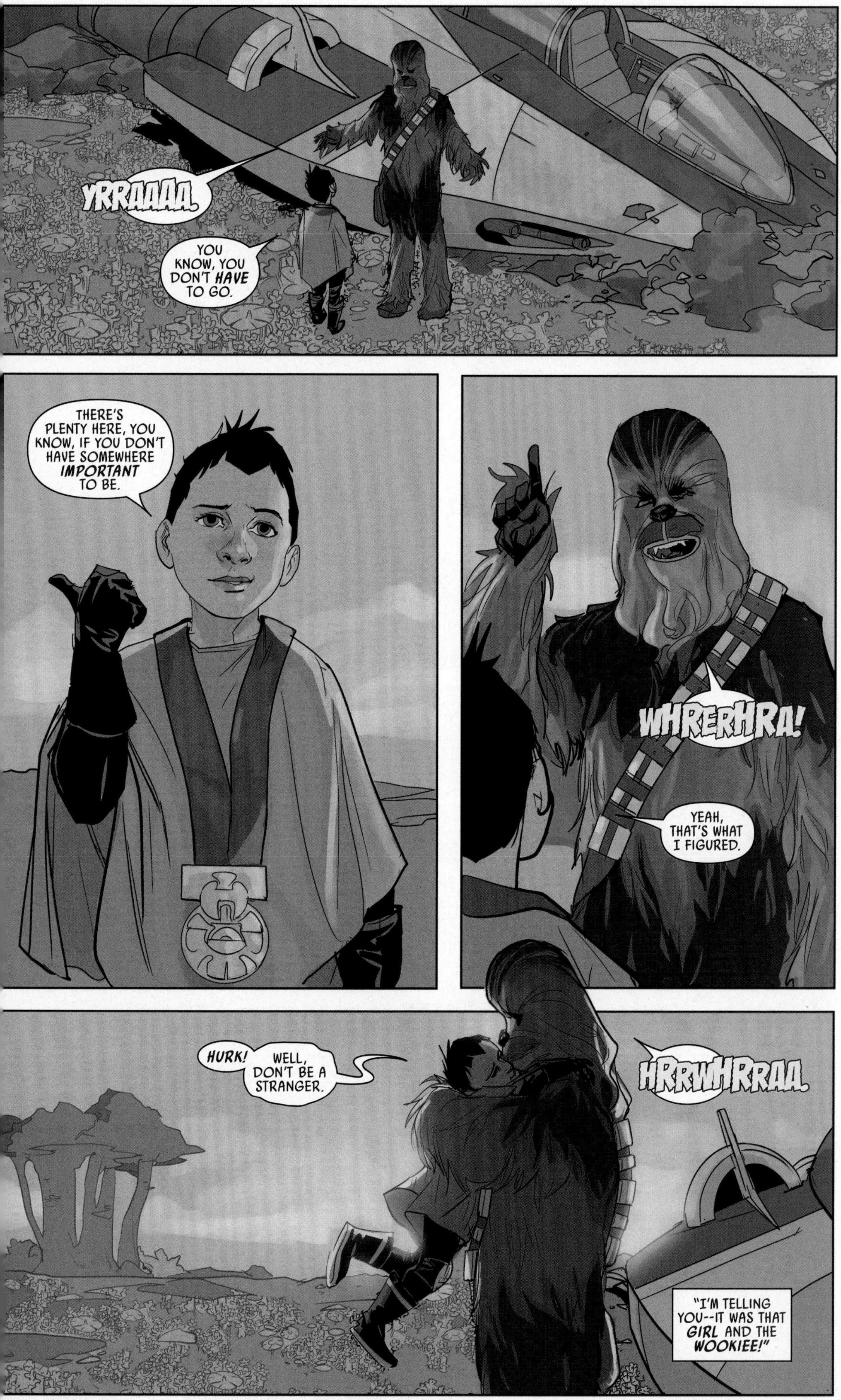
YRRAAAA
YOU KNOW, YOU DON'T HAVE TO GO.
THERE'S PLENTY HERE, YOU KNOW, IF YOU DON'T HAVE SOMEWHERE IMPORTANT TO BE.
WHRERHRA!
YEAH, THAT'S WHAT I FIGURED.
HURK!
WELL, DON'T BE A STRANGER.
HRRWHRRAA
"I'M TELLING YOU--IT WAS THAT GIRL AND THE WOOKIEE!"

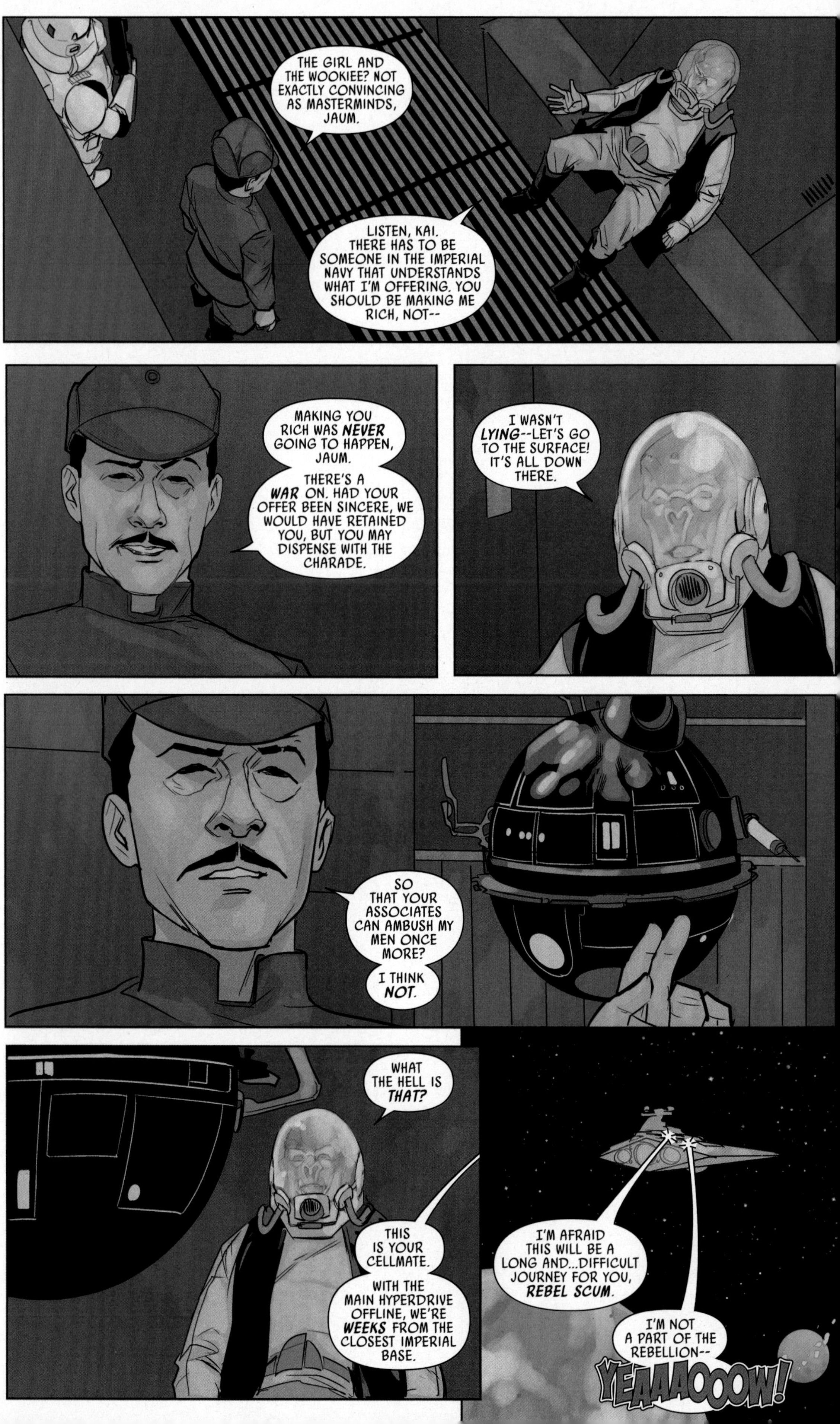

THE GIRL AND THE WOOKIEE? NOT EXACTLY CONVINCING AS MASTERMINDS, JAUM.
LISTEN, KAI. THERE HAS TO BE SOMEONE IN THE IMPERIAL NAVY THAT UNDERSTANDS WHAT I'M OFFERING. YOU SHOULD BE MAKING ME RICH, NOT--
MAKING YOU RICH WAS NEVER GOING TO HAPPEN, JAUM.
THERE'S A WAR ON. HAD YOUR OFFER BEEN SINCERE, WE WOULD HAVE RETAINED YOU, BUT YOU MAY DISPENSE WITH THE CHARADE.
I WASN'T LYING--LET'S GO TO THE SURFACE! IT'S ALL DOWN THERE.
SO THAT YOUR ASSOCIATES CAN AMBUSH MY MEN ONCE MORE?
I THINK NOT.
WHAT THE HELL IS THAT?
THIS IS YOUR CELLMATE.
WITH THE MAIN HYPERDRIVE OFFLINE, WE'RE WEEKS FROM THE CLOSEST IMPERIAL BASE.
I'M AFRAID THIS WILL BE A LONG AND...DIFFICULT JOURNEY FOR YOU, REBEL SCUM.
I'M NOT A PART OF THE REBELLION--
YEAAAOOOW!

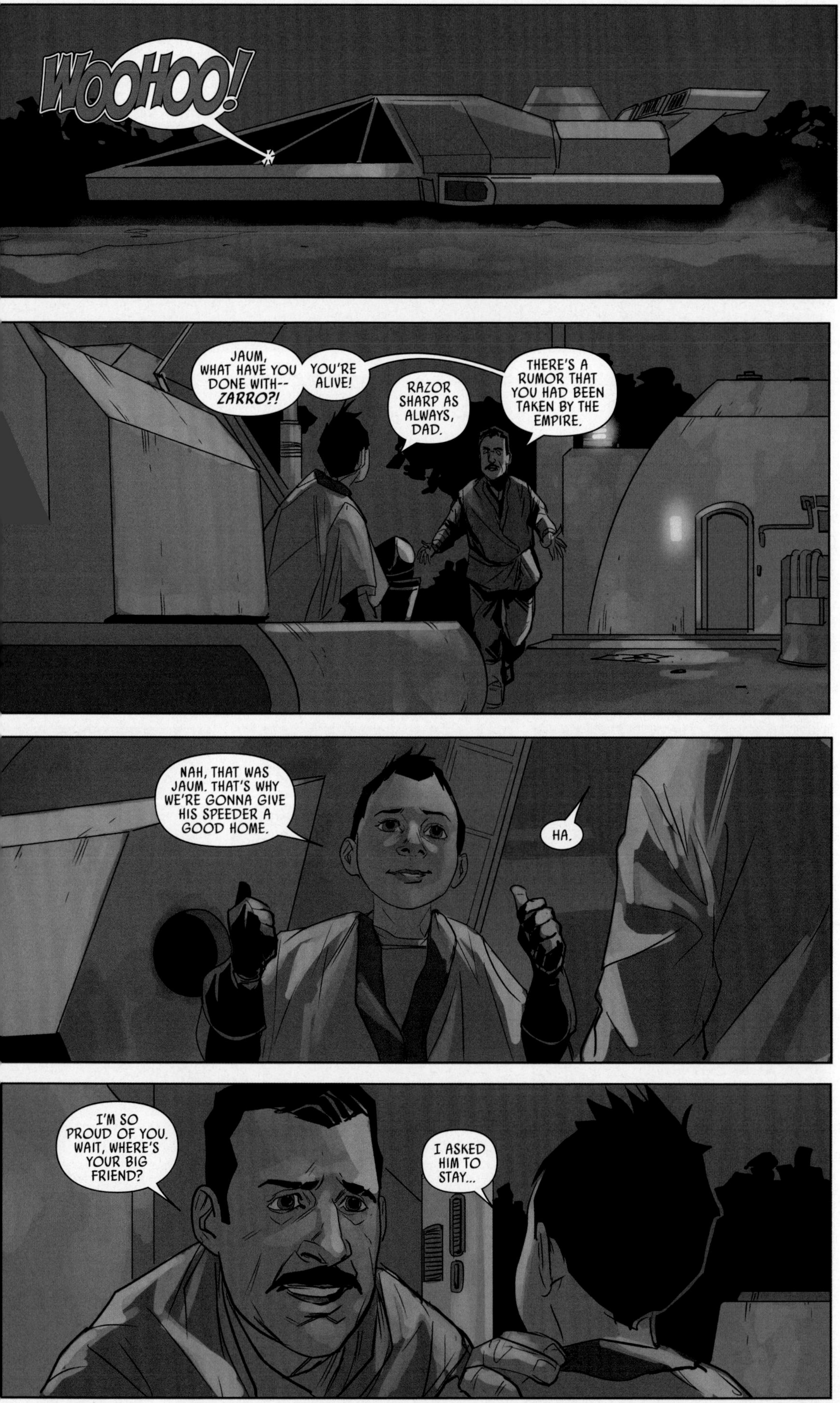
WOOHOO!
JAUM, WHAT HAVE YOU DONE WITH-- ZARRO?!
YOU'RE ALIVE!
THERE'S A RUMOR THAT YOU HAD BEEN TAKEN BY THE EMPIRE.
RAZOR SHARP AS ALWAYS, DAD.
NAH, THAT WAS JAUM. THAT'S WHY WE'RE GONNA GIVE HIS SPEEDER A GOOD HOME.
HA.
I'M SO PROUD OF YOU. WAIT, WHERE'S YOUR BIG FRIEND?
I ASKED HIM TO STAY...

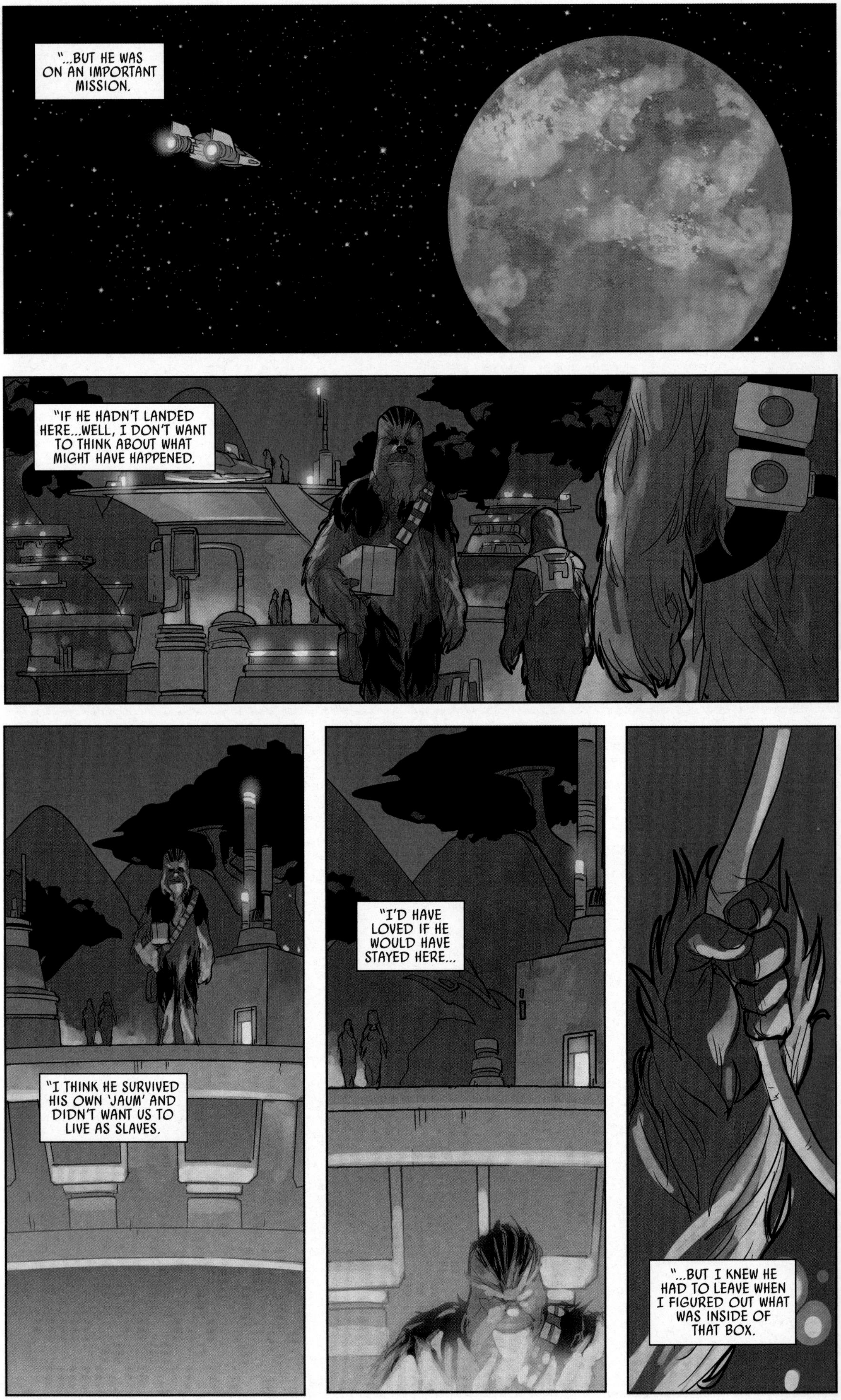
"...BUT HE WAS ON AN IMPORTANT MISSION.
"IF HE HADN'T LANDED HERE...WELL, I DON'T WANT TO THINK ABOUT WHAT MIGHT HAVE HAPPENED.
"I THINK HE SURVIVED HIS OWN 'JAUM' AND DIDN'T WANT US TO LIVE AS SLAVES.
"I'D HAVE LOVED IF HE WOULD HAVE STAYED HERE...
"...BUT I KNEW HE HAD TO LEAVE WHEN I FIGURED OUT WHAT WAS INSIDE OF THAT BOX.

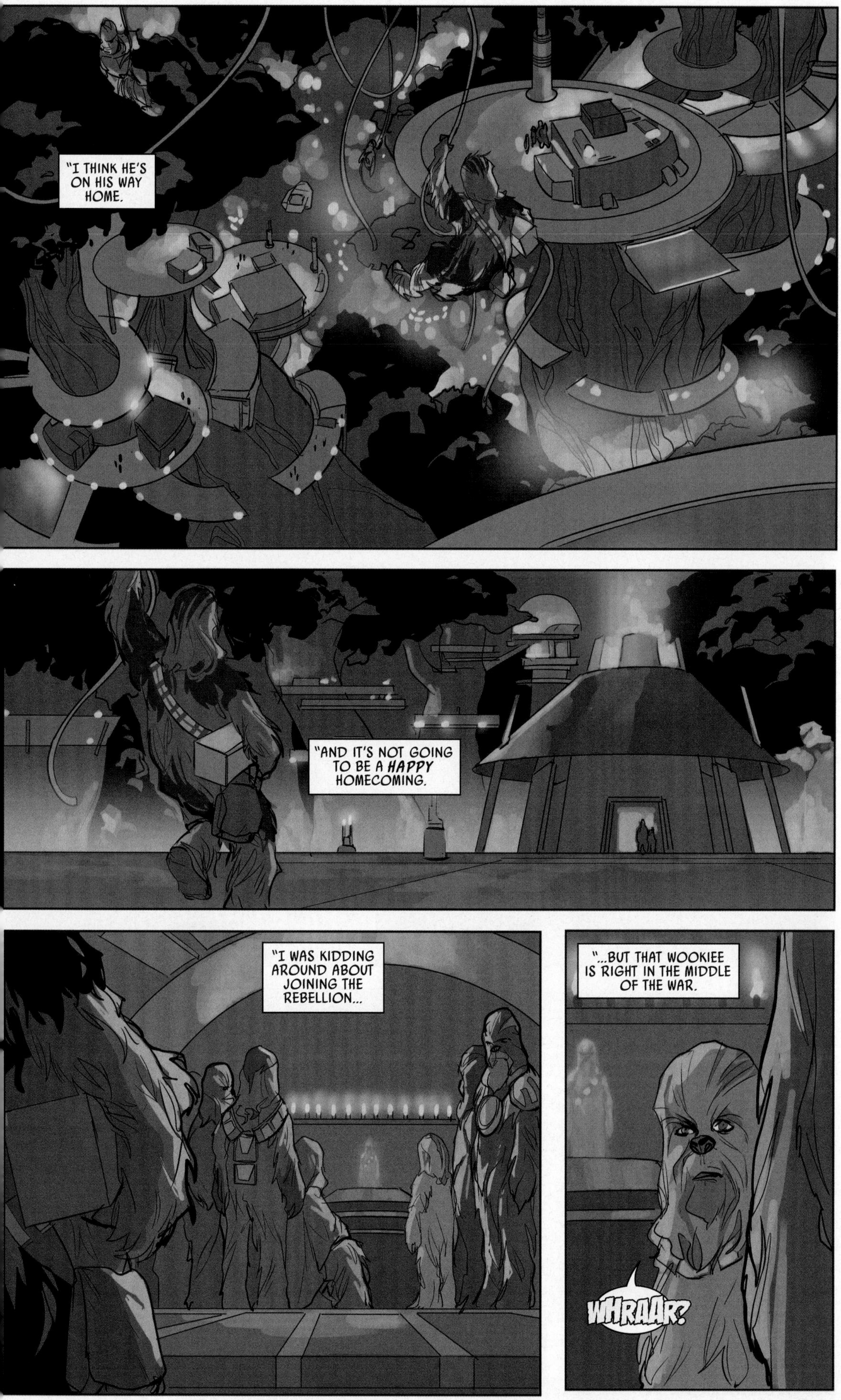
"I THINK HE'S ON HIS WAY HOME.
"AND IT'S NOT GOING TO BE A *HAPPY* HOMECOMING.
"I WAS KIDDING AROUND ABOUT JOINING THE REBELLION...
"...BUT THAT WOOKIEE IS RIGHT IN THE MIDDLE OF THE WAR.
WHRAAR?

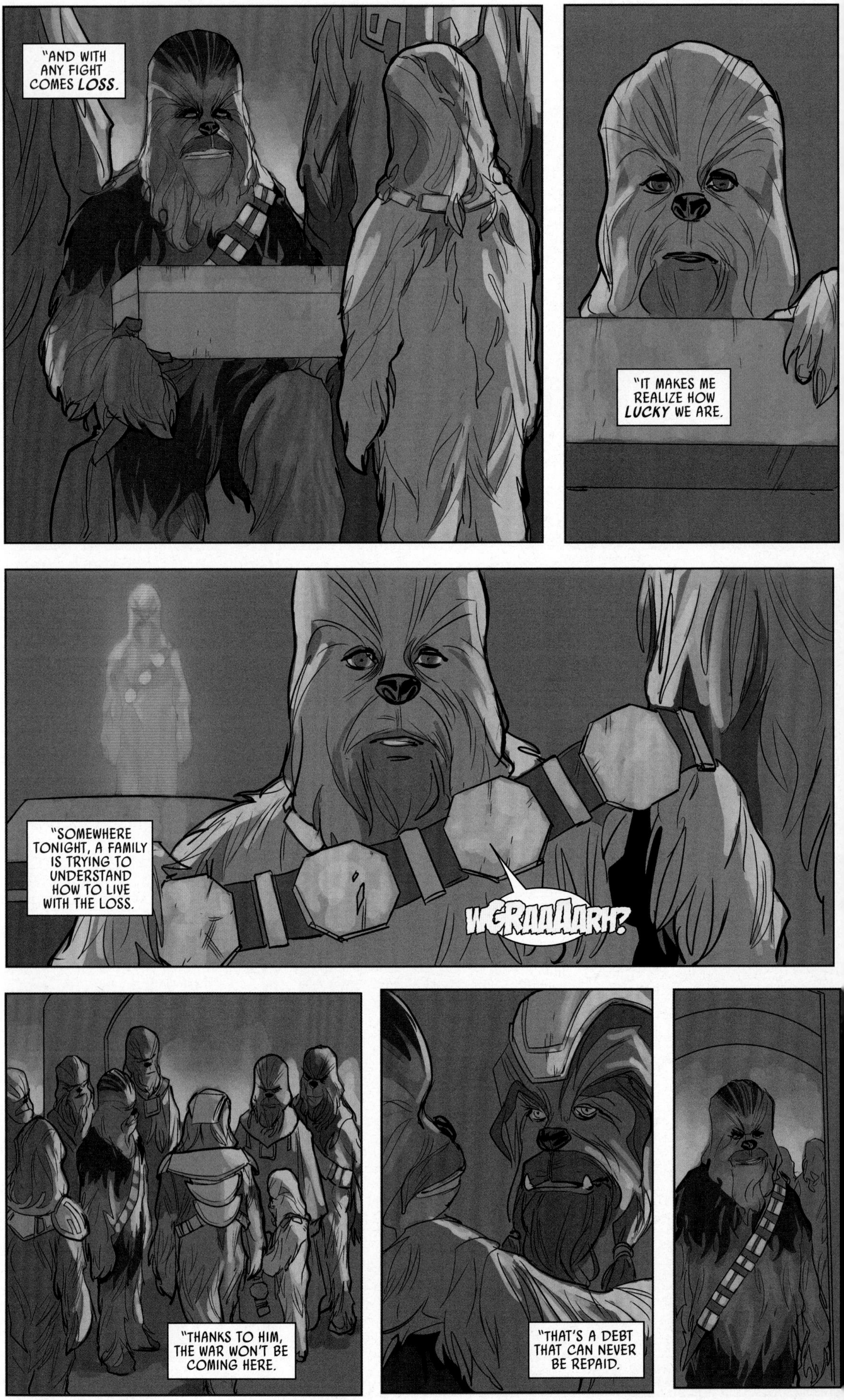
"AND WITH ANY FIGHT COMES LOSS.
"IT MAKES ME REALIZE HOW LUCKY WE ARE.
"SOMEWHERE TONIGHT, A FAMILY IS TRYING TO UNDERSTAND HOW TO LIVE WITH THE LOSS.
WGRAAAARH?
"THANKS TO HIM, THE WAR WON'T BE COMING HERE.
"THAT'S A DEBT THAT CAN NEVER BE REPAID.

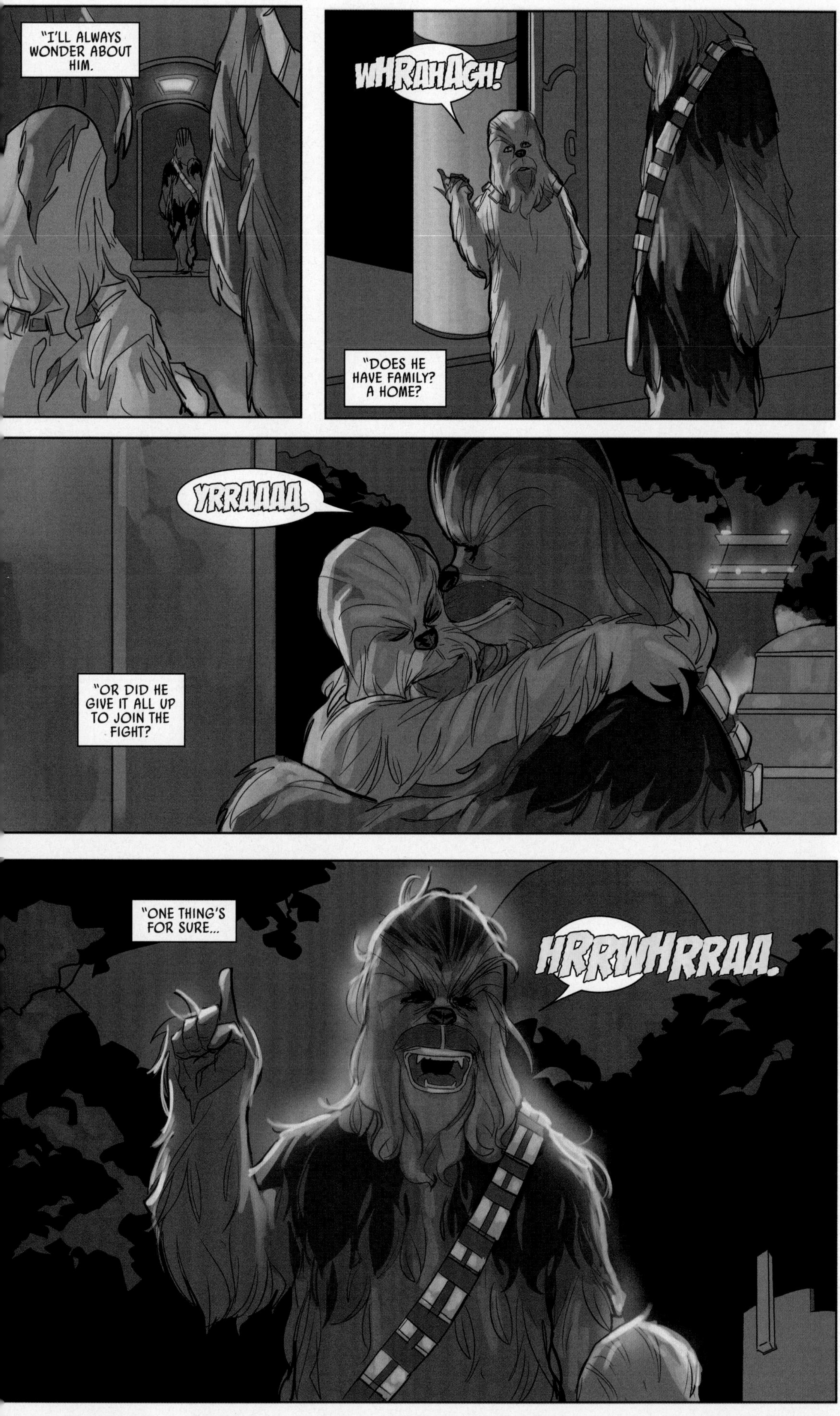
"I'LL ALWAYS WONDER ABOUT HIM.
WHRAHAGH!
"DOES HE HAVE FAMILY? A HOME?
YRRAAAA.
"OR DID HE GIVE IT ALL UP TO JOIN THE FIGHT?
"ONE THING'S FOR SURE...
HRRWHRRAA.

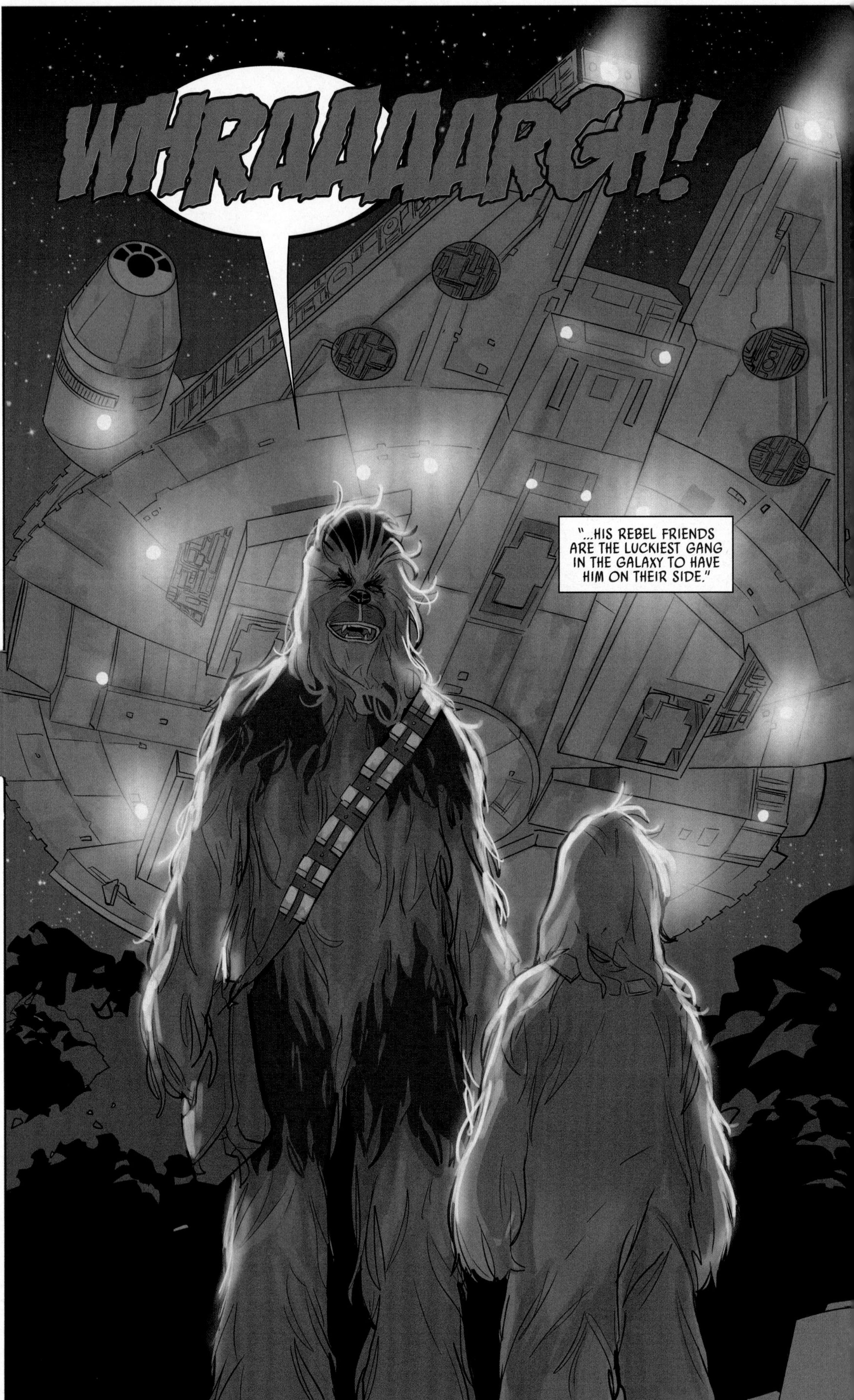
WHRAAAARGH!
"...HIS REBEL FRIENDS ARE THE LUCKIEST GANG IN THE GALAXY TO HAVE HIM ON THEIR SIDE."

WHAT IS A PRINCESS WITHOUT A WO

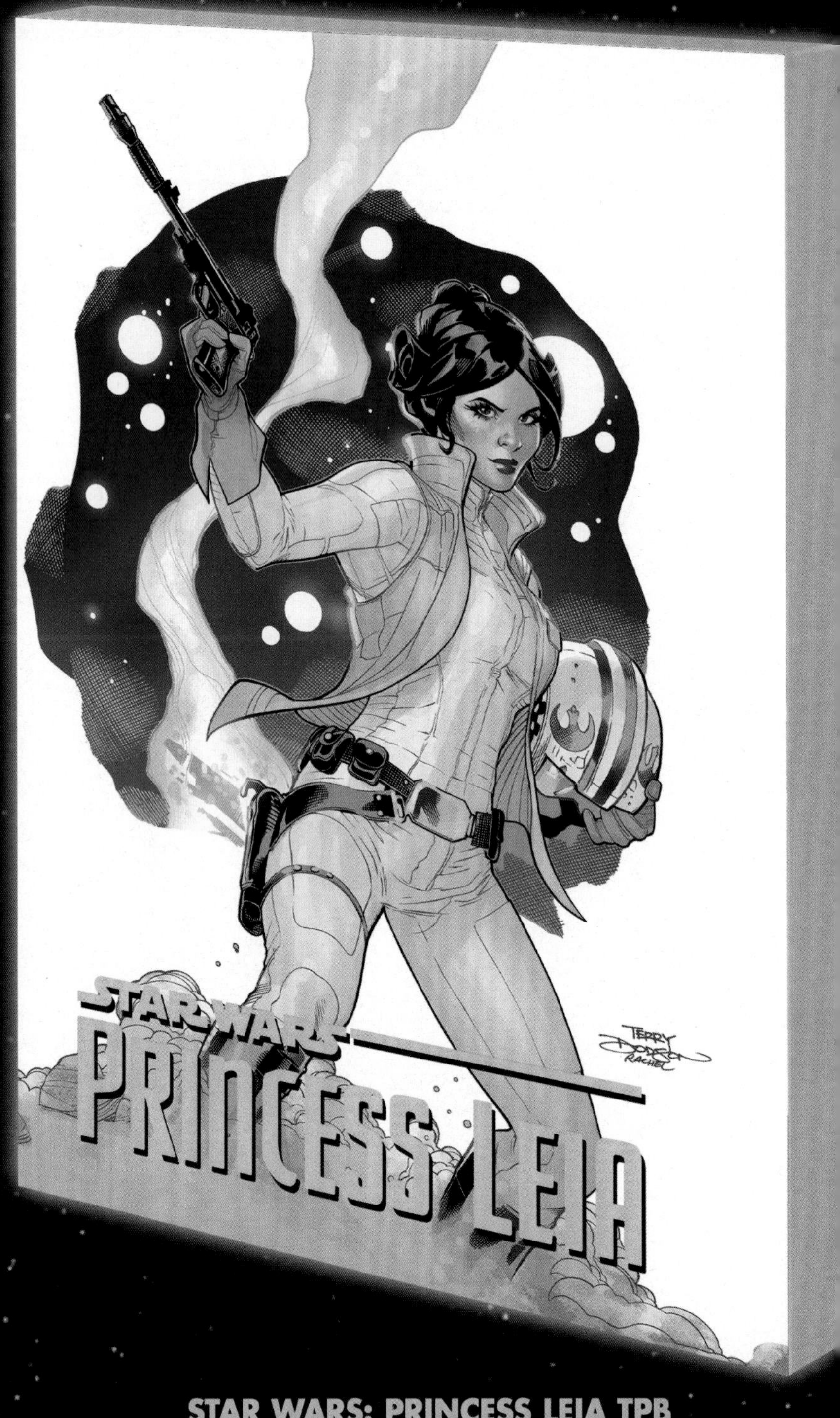

STAR WARS: PRINCESS LEIA TPB

978-0-7851-9317-3

ON SALE NOW
WHEREVER BOOKS ARE SOLD

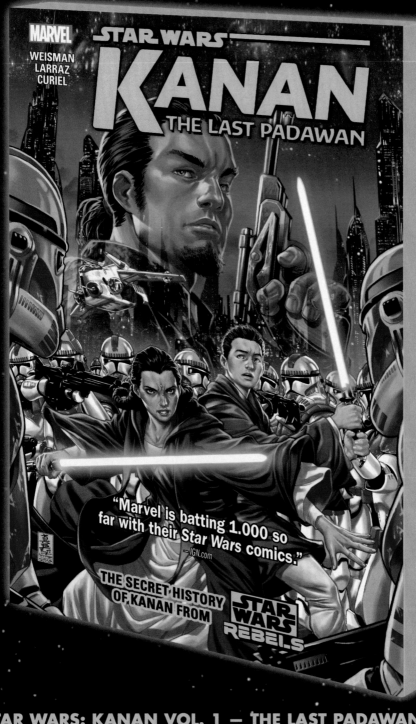

ONE BOOK YOU … Y ITS COVERS.

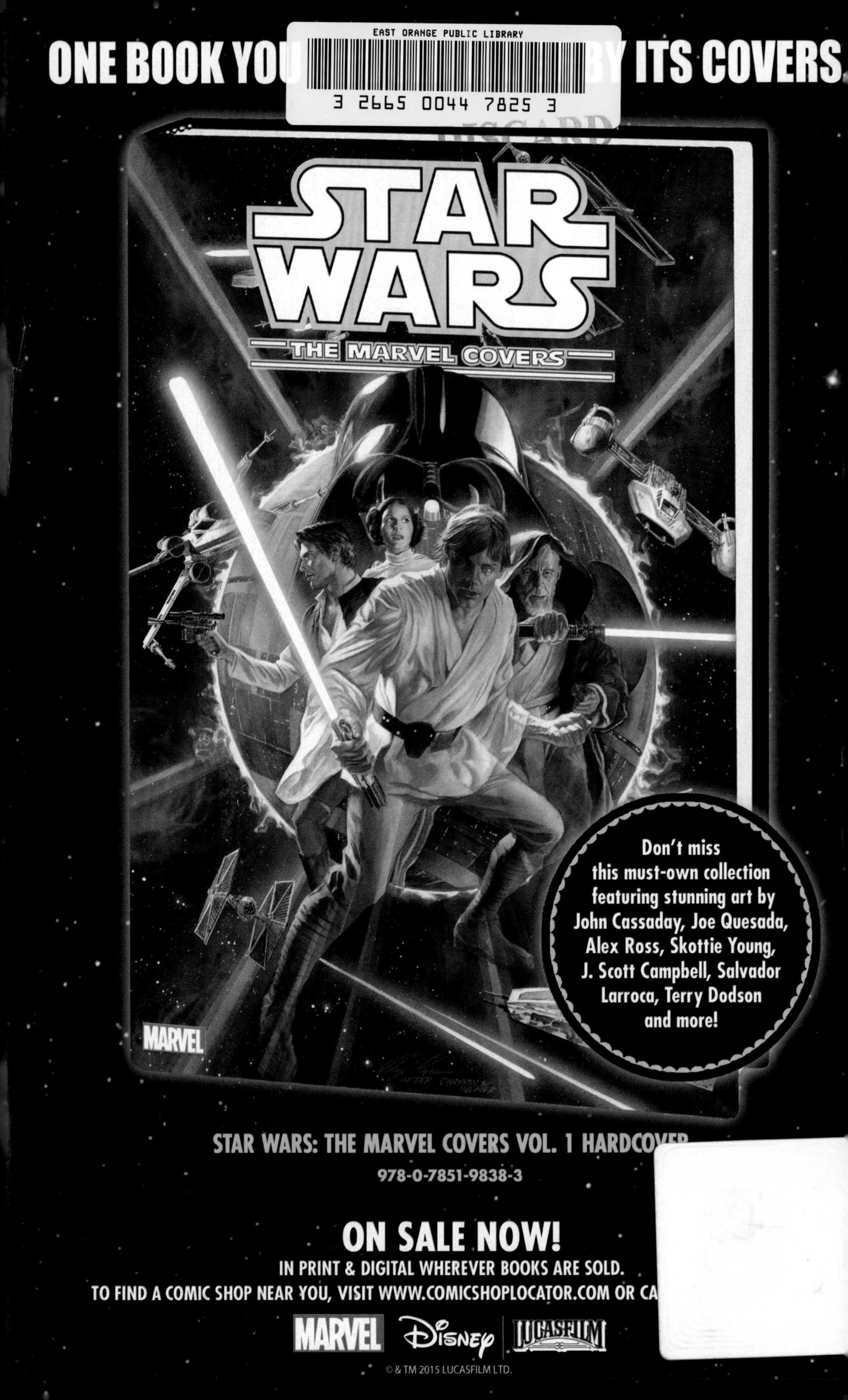
STAR WARS
THE MARVEL COVERS
MARVEL

Don't miss this must-own collection featuring stunning art by John Cassaday, Joe Quesada, Alex Ross, Skottie Young, J. Scott Campbell, Salvador Larroca, Terry Dodson and more!

STAR WARS: THE MARVEL COVERS VOL. 1 HARDCOVER

978-0-7851-9838-3

ON SALE NOW!

IN PRINT & DIGITAL WHEREVER BOOKS ARE SOLD.
TO FIND A COMIC SHOP NEAR YOU, VISIT WWW.COMICSHOPLOCATOR.COM OR CA

MARVEL Disney LUCASFILM